An Introduction to Writing for Electronic Media

An Introduction to Writing for Electronic Media
Scriptwriting Essentials
Across the Genres

Robert B. Musburger

Focal Press
Taylor & Francis Group
NEW YORK AND LONDON

First published 2007

This edition published 2013
by Focal Press
70 Blanchard Road, Suite 402, Burlington, MA 01803

Simultaneously published in the UK
by Focal Press
2 Park Square, Milton Park, Abingdon, Oxon OX14 4RN

Focal Press is an imprint of the Taylor & Francis Group, an informa business

Notices

Practitioners and researchers must always rely on their own experience and knowledge in evaluating and using any information, methods, compounds, or experiments described herein. In using such information or methods they should be mindful of their own safety and the safety of others, including parties for whom they have a professional responsibility.

To the fullest extent of the law, neither the Publisher nor the authors, contributors, or editors, assume any liability for any injury and/or damage to persons or property as a matter of products liability, negligence or otherwise, or from any use or operation of any methods, products, instructions, or ideas contained in the material herein.

Library of Congress Cataloging-in-Publication Data
Musburger, Robert B.
  An introduction to writing for electronic media : scriptwriting essentials across the genres / Robert B. Musburger.
       p.   cm.
  Includes bibliographical references and index.
  ISBN 0-240-80852-5
1.   Mass media–Authorship.   I. Title.
  P96.A86M87 2007
  808′.066302–dc22
                                                      2006102959

British Library Cataloguing-in-Publication Data
A catalogue record for this book is available from the British Library.

ISBN 13: 978-0-240-80852-9 (pbk)

To Pat — friend, companion, lover, wife, and editor.
For so many years of happy work, play, and living
life to its maximum.

Contents

Preface

Regardless of the technical level of a media production, analog or digital, electronic or motion picture, at an early point in time, the basic concept and plan for a production must be recorded in some form on a readable medium. The writer is responsible for that form by laying the groundwork, designing the blueprint, and providing the means for the production crew and staff to convert an idea to a completed production.

This text has been written as an introduction to the methods of creating scripts for eight different genres of media productions: spots, news, documentaries, informational, animation, games, dramatic, and Internet productions. It is not intended to provide the means for a first-time writer to reach the level of writing of an Academy-Award winning production, but it offers the opportunity to sample the eight genres and their various differences and similarities. This sampling intends to lead the reader to an understanding of the process of media writing and the realization of the importance of the relationships between the writer and the production crew and staff. The text offers brief explanations on the actual production processes to better help the writer accept the changes to his or her script that must occur during production and postproduction activities.

To help the writer reach an awareness of how both script formats and script writing for electronic media productions reached their present state, the background of each genre of media writing places the present writing routine in perspective. The reader of this text is offered basic grammar, sentence structure, and page formatting used in script writing to develop the basic skills of presenting professionally prepared scripts.

Since this is an introductory text, a final chapter offers suggestions on pursuing a career in media writing, preparing for interviews, and writing resumes. The author hopes this text will lead
the readers to further explore a career in writing by expanding their
educational options and continuing to write. The only way anyone
can reach a professional level of writing is to write, write, and keep
on writing.

R. Musburger
Seattle, WA

Acknowledgments

An author would have a difficult time completing any manuscript without some assistance. As a teacher and practitioner, my assistance has come from hundreds of students and co-workers, some for positive results, some for negative. I cannot recognize everyone, but a few that come to mind among students have been Gregory Gutenko, Charley and Nancy Welborn, Karen Foss, Joe Tankersly, David Garfield, Sarah Fife, and Dominic Sachse. A special thanks to Michael Carr and Dep-Wah Davis for their assistance with this text. Professionals include the Wormington twins and Murray Nolte from WDAF-TV days. Help from faculty came from Sam Scott, Gaylord Marr, Elizabeth Czech-Beckerman, Tom Hoffer, Norm Medoff, Jennings Bryant, Ray Fielding, and Ted Stanton. Larrie Gale warrants special thanks for his assistance on this text.

My relationship stretches for over 15 years with editors from Focal Press, during that time I have had the pleasure of working with Philip Sutherland, Mary Lee, and Lily Roberts. For Amy Jollymore, Doug Shults, and Elinor Actipis who guided me to the final paragraph of this book.

CHAPTER 1

Getting Started:
Loading the Application and Sharpening the Pencil

The wave of the future is coming, and there is no fighting it.
—Anne Morrow Lindbergh, 1940

Introduction

Before you sit down to start writing any form of script for any medium, genre, or method of distribution, you need to consider the common factors that exist among all media forms, despite their basic differences. This chapter will reveal as many common traits as possible to avoid repeating the same information throughout the text from chapter to chapter. Such topics include correct English that is written to be read out loud, writing for an audience, and understanding the laws and censorship affecting writers. At the same time, you may need to recognize that there will be duplication and repetition of some material when the redundancy is critical for that particular type of writing.

Topics included in this chapter cover the history and types of scripts, accurate and concise English, language discrimination, law and censorship, and the audience and distribution.

Background

The written forms used to instruct a production crew to carry out the writer's desires did not blossom forth overnight. Script formats evolved over many years through the development of a variety of entertainment venues. Even within a specific medium, variations of format style evolved as the technology of the medium changed to meet the combined needs of the production staff as well as the challenges of the latest technology.

Live theatrical performances presage all forms of modern media. You may learn much from the study of live theater in addition to recognizing the field of theatrical production as a predecessor of electronic media.

In the earliest time of live presentations by actors, the actor-director determined the story line, dialogue, and action. In many cases, nothing was written, but stories passed from one troupe to another or became simpler in the memory of the originator. When productions became more complex, notes were written and passed from one performing group to another. Finally, actors and directors wrote more detailed scripts to guarantee that a play would be performed as the writer had intended.

As the theater evolved, so did the scripts that the directors and actors followed. The format became relatively standardized so that whoever needed to read or follow the script would be able to understand what was expected of them as members of the cast or crew. The script was the bible for the director, listing all of the dialogue and who spoke the lines, as well as the basic settings and action. The director had the prerogative of making modifications as the rehearsal process moved forward. But, before rehearsals started, the actors needed the script to learn their lines and basic blocking movements, both of which could be modified by the director.

Before the end of the 19th century, motion pictures followed live theater in presenting dramatic productions, as well as documentaries and other genres as the field developed. The original filmscripts mimic the format layout of theatrical scripts once scripts became the rule in film. As with theater directors, early filmmakers shot film without recorded sync sound and so needed little in the way of a written script. The director/writer told the cinematographer where to place the camera, and the actors were told where to stand and move and what lines to mimic. As the camera rolled, the director yelled directions to the actors. Little postproduction was necessary since the early films often were shot in one or two long takes in the 10-minute-long scenes.

Figure 1.1. A typical Shakespearian era play script.

Mr. Morse angry and belligerent—Jamie takes a checker and throws it to the floor [beat]. Mr. Morse takes the candy stick from Jamie's mouth and throws it to the floor [beat]. Jamie takes a pencil from Mr. Morse's pocket, breaks it in his hands, throws it on the floor. Mr. Morse stands. Jamie stands. Mr. Morse takes up the board, spilling the checkers, and with difficulty tears it in two along the spine and throws it on the floor. Jamie glares. Takes up the checker box, tears it in two, and throws it to the floor [beat]. Mr. Morse overturns Jamie's chair. Now they grapple, slapping weakly at each other and making incoherent noises and grunts, two very weak individuals trying to do injury to each other. Injury would be impossible. When they struggle, Millie stands to get away.)

MR. KATZ. *(As Jamie tears the box.)* Here, that doesn't belong to you; stop it. Both of you; sit down and act right or you can't stay down here. Come on! Both of you!

GIRL. *(Overlapping.)* Jamie. Shame on you. Come on, stop that, what are you doing; you two babies. Shame on you. Stop fighting. What are you doing? *(Girl reaches them as they separate. Mr. Morse, from humiliation, shuffles directly to the only door in sight.)*

KATZ. *(Also coming from behind the office.)* Where are you going? Here, you can't go in there—

GIRL. Mr. Morse, come back and apologize; don't go in— *(To Katz.)* Oh, he isn't going to hurt anything. My God! *(Morse closes door as she reaches him.)*

KATZ. —Get him out of there.

GIRL. Mr. Morse, you can't go in there, that's the broom closet. *(Knocks.)* Mr. Morse? You're sitting in there on the slop sink, aren't you? With all those smelly mops. Mr. Morse, Jamie's sorry.

JAMIE. *(To her, joining her as Katz picks up checkers.)* I am not!

GIRL. *(Grabbing him, putting her hand over his mouth. The contact of a girl confuses and amazes him as much as the situation.)* He's sorry.

MORSE. *(Offstage.)* No, he isn't.

GIRL. *(As Jamie struggles to talk.)* What?

MORSE. *(Offstage.)* He isn't sorry!

GIRL. You hurt him very badly. *(Jamie struggles to protest.)*

MORSE. *(Offstage. After a beat.)* Where?

GIRL. You blacked his eye. *(Jamie gasps at the scope of the lie.)* *(To Jamie.)* Come here. I want to show you something. *(As she gets her purse.)*

37

Figure 1.2. A script from a 20th-century play.

FADE IN:
1.   INT CLUB CAR OF MOVING TRAIN   DAY   1

The desert landscape of central Arizona flashes by outside the window.
A drunken MAN staggers up the aisle holding a cocktail glass. He notices
ROBIN BALLARD, a delicate, 30-year-old woman, who stares blankly
out the window. He holds the glass out to her.

                         MAN
                       (slurred)
               Buy you a drink pretty lady?

Robin continues to stare out the window.

                        ROBIN
                       (coldly)
                         No.

The Man pulls back the drink.

                         MAN
                   Well, pardon me.

He turns and walks away. Robin's reflection in the window returns her gaze.

                                                       (DISS)

2.   EXT UNION STATION, LOS ANGELES   DAY   2

Robin, surrounded by other disembarking passengers, frantically searches the
crowded platform. She brightens as she recognized LAUREN CHANDLER,
a beautiful, 50-year-old, self-possessed woman, walking through the crowd and
waves at her.

                        ROBIN
                         Mom!
                   (calling louder)
                         Mom!

Lauren spots Robin, waves and hurries toward her. The women embrace.
Robin starts to cry.

                        LAUREN
                      (concerned)
               Baby, baby…What's the matter?

                        ROBIN
                   I. . .I left Tom.

                                                       (CONT.)

Figure 1.3. A modern film scene script.

RADIO DRAMA FORMAT

1.	SFX:	CAR TRYING TO START, FINALLY KICKS OVER
2.	BARBARA:	If I can just keep this thing
3.		going...wait...there's lights ahead, thank God for
4.		ghost towns. I hope it isn't a film set.
5.	SFX:	ENGINE DIES, CAR ROLLING ON GRAVEL AS IT
6.		COMES TO A STOP. CAR DOOR OPENS AND
7.		CLOSES -- FOOTSTEPS ON GRAVEL.
8.	BARB:	(HESITANTLY) Anyone home -- hello...hello there.
9.		(TO HERSELF) Why is it when you need a service
10.		station it's always closed? They weren't kidding when
11.		they said it gets dark fast once the sun goes down.
12.		(OUT LOUD) Hey, hello, anyone around.
13.	SFX:	RATTLING OF LOCKED DOOR, HEAVY
14.		FOOTSTEPS GETTING LOUDER
15.	BARB:	(STARTLED) Oh, hello, I'm sorry...you scared me,
16.		(NERVOUSLY) My car quit on me, it just stopped. I
17.		mean, the engine quit. I don't think I'm out of gas, and
18.		it's only a couple months old, I don't know what's
19.		wrong with it.
20.	SFX:	DESERT NIGHT SOUNDS, FOOT STEPS IN
21.		GRAVEL SLOWLY APPROACHING
22:	CAL:	What're you doin' out here? Your ole man in the car ?

Figure 1.4. A typical radio drama script.

When sound arrived, filmscripts became reasonably standardized in a single-column format. In individual portions of the script, scene description, action, movement, dialogue, and the name of the actor were set, each with variations in margins. That made it easy for actors and crew to concentrate on the their parts of the script.

Shortly after the turn of the 20th century, radio became a reality for drama, news, and, of course, commercials. The first radio scripts resembled theater scripts, except instead of describing scenes and action, instructions for sound effects and music cues completed the script. Dialogue was much more detailed since radio drama is, in essence, a series of dialogues with music and sound effects helping to build the imagination factor. Radio's advantage lies in requiring the audience to use its imaginations to fill in the visual gaps. This allows radio drama to achieve complicated effects that, until digital media arrived, were impossible to create in either film or video.

It became obvious early in the days of television that motion picture and radio script formats did not work well for live multiple-camera productions. A type of script developed for audio-video production at about the same time. The two-column format placed both sound and picture elements of the script on their own spaces in the script. This made it easier and more accurate for the cast, crew, and director to isolate the portion of the script critical to each. The left-hand column (at one time the networks NBC and CBS disagreed on the arrangement) now lists all visuals, with camera instructions, camera framing, shot selection, and transitions all entered in capital letters. The right-hand column lists all of the audio, including music, sound effects, and narration or dialogue. All copy to be read by the talent is entered in uppercase and lowercase letters, and all other instructions are in caps. This system developed to make it easier for talent to pick out their copy from all other instructions.

Some newscasters prefer to have their copy entered in all caps under the false belief that caps are easier to read on a prompting device. Readability studies indicate uppercase and lowercase copy on prompters prevents reading errors and helps readers add meaning to their delivery.

Most dramatic video productions are shot single-camera style, and some commercials and documentaries adapted the single-column

DUAL-COLUMN SCRIPT FORMAT

TITLE: PAGE:
WRITER: LENGTH:
CLIENT: DATE:

VIDEO	AUDIO
1. SINGLE-SPACE VIDEO INSTRUCTIONS	1. ANNCR: Audio copy is lined up directly across the page from its matching video.
2. TRIPLE SPACE BETWEEN EACH SHOT	2. Double-space between each line of copy.
3. EACH SHOT MUST BE NUMBERED ON THE SCRIPT	3. The audio column's number must match that of its video.
4. EVERYTHING THE VIEWER IS TO SEE; ALL VISUALS, VIDEO TAPES, CG, CAMERA SHOTS, ARE INCLUDED IN THE LEFT-HAND COLUMN.	4. Everything the viewer hears; narration, music, voices, sound effects, all audio cues are in this column.
5. EVERYTHING ON THE VIDEO SIDE IS TYPED IN UPPERCASE.	5. Everything spoken by the talent is typed in upper and lowercase letters. All instructions in the audio column are typed in UPPERCASE. (FADE UP NAT SOUND)
6. THE TALENT'S NAME STARTS EACH NEW LINE, BUT DOES NOT HAVE TO BE REPEATED IF THE SAME PERSON OR SOUND SOURCE CONTINUES.	6. SAM: Note—the name is in caps, what Sam says is in upper and lowercase.
7. DO NOT SPLIT SHOTS AT BOTTOM OF THE PAGE.	7. Don't split words or thoughts at the end of the line or page. If the story continues to the next page, let the talent know by writing— (MORE)

Figure 1.5. A dual-column video script.

FADE IN:
1.   EXT DARK WINDSWEPT KANSAS PRAIRIE BACK ROAD HIWAY   NITE 1

        A small compact car swirls through the darkness of a moonless Kansas
        night, semi-ominous music mix with sound of the purring motor

                            SALLY
                          (To herself)
            I'm free, finally free, I'm me, I can be what
            I want to be, who I want to be, where I
                       Want to be, and when...
        Sally glances out the window.

                            SALLY
                       (A little hesitantly)
            But it sure is dark out here, what happened
               to stars are bright out west and where
                         did that moon go.
        SFX: Car motor cuts in and out, sputters a couple times

                            SALLY
                       Well, pardon me.
                    What's wrong with this car
        SFX: The car motor dies completely, only sound of wind and tires rolling on pavement

                            SALLY
                       What's happening
                    What's wrong with this car.
        SFX: car starter grinding, music sting, motor finally kicks over and begins running

                            SALLY
               If I can just keep this thing going,
               Wait, there's a light ahead, thank God
               For ghost town, with or without ghosts.
                                                                    (DISS)

2.   EXT ABANDONED SERVICE STATION IN EMPTY TOWN   NITE 2
        Sally gets out of the car, SFX rattling of locked door and heavy footsteps on gravel

                            SALLY
                          (Nervously)
                    Hello, anyone around   (CONT)

Figure 1.6. A single-column video script.

Ideas about Interactive Script Elements & Format

1. Conventional Script Elements – Same and Similar Elements
   a. Description of scenes and visual elements; acting direction
   b. Transitions – timing
   c. Actor's lines – direction to actors
   d. Description of music, description of sound effects

2. Additional Script Elements – In Support of Interactivity
   a. Representation of the graphics and source
   b. Representation of the text and source
   c. Representation of the links, or branching logic
      i.   where linking or branching to and from
      ii.   which answers/choices/actions are "right"
      iii. answer processing, scoring & conditional branching
   d. Representation of the presentation type
      i.   what the video does, and when
      ii.   when the text appears
      iii. when the graphics appear
      iv.   which sound track when
      v.   nature and location of any feedback
   e. Filename, or DVD chapter/timecode

A Format Used with Interactive CDs and Laserdiscs

```
TITLE:   Checking Passports                                      IMI:01

FROM  : JAL01, JAL05, INT07, ORIENT14                            REV:03

VISUAL:  INT - DAY  INTERIOR OF AIPORT IMMIGRATION COUNTERS: POV KUROKAWA, WHO IS IN
THE RED LINE. HE MOVES FORWARD AS THE NEXT POSITION OPENS-HIS HAND PLACES THE PASSPORT ON
THE COUNTER WHEN THE IMMIGRATION OFFICER ASKS FOR IT.

AUDIO : SFX-HOLLOW, ECHOING SOUNDS OF AIRPORT CROWDS, PAGING, JETS TAXING IN THE DISTANCE.

                           IMIGRATION OFFICIAL
                   (DIRECTLY INTO CAMERA LENS; IN ENGLISH)
                        May I see your passport, please?

     POV KUROKAWA: KUROKAWA'S HAND PLACES PASSPORT ON COUNTER WITHIN VIEW, OFFICER
     PICKS IT UP-OPENS IT.

                           IMIGRATION OFFICIAL
                 * Why are you visiting the United states, Mr. . .
                      (PAUSES - LOOKS AT PASSPORT) Kurokawa?

COMPUTER SCREEN                          BRANCH TO:

@TEXT:
     I'm here on business.                IMI:02
     I'm attending a convention.          IMI:03
     I beg your pardon?                   *IMI:01

@GRAPHIC: USER-01 (standard user interface and logo)

@JUDGE:  none
@MOTION DVD:  21000-36872
             *36780-36872
@FILE: (left blank means "not applicable")
```

Figure 1.7. An interactive script.

script format. Since many of the writers and directors moved back and forth between shooting film and video productions, it became comfortable to use the same single-column format. The physical appearance of the format followed the same pattern as the film single-column format.

Multimedia, Internet, and Web page scripts have not been formalized in the same way as scripts for other electronic media. Digital scripts take a variety of forms, some borrowing from both motion pictures and video as well as from audio-video script formats. The problem of indicating branching, choices for interaction, and the variety of different media used in one digital production requires a specialized script tailored to the specific production. The script must contain enough information for the producer/director to understand what is required to assemble the segments. The editor must also be instructed on the specifics of chapter assignments, transitions, linking, and other specialized techniques in a digital interactive production.

Script Variations

Today, television writers use both dual-column and single-column script formats, depending on whether the script will be produced as a live multi-camera production or as a single-camera video production. Each studio, station, or production operation may require a specific script format for its own operation. A writer should determine from the client how to format the script. Even with the two basic standard formats, there are many variations. Such variations depend on the size of the production, the budget, the production methods used, and the personal preferences of producers. Such variations also exist in film and audio scripts, but as modifications of the basic format. Interactive script formats have not yet reached a standard format, leaving a great deal of variations in the scripts used today.

Media Differences

Each of the electronic media requires that scripts provide information in different formats to best serve the people using the scripts.

Radio scripts primarily serve the voices, secondarily served the director and, in some cases, a production operator. Therefore, a radio or sound script must accurately and precisely indicate the copy to be read, the music, the effects (if used), and timing factors. The writer must find a way to motivate the listeners so that the listeners visualize what they cannot see; the writer must prod their imaginations to feel what the writer is trying to convey using only sounds. For a writer, it is a daunting challenge, but at the same time, it is an opportunity to control the listeners by engaging their ears.

Filmscripts, like theatrical scripts, provide the basic blueprint of the production. The actors need to know their specific dialogue, and the director needs to have a written form of the overall concept that the writer's vision provided in the script. Highly detailed and specific shots and framing are not necessarily required in a filmscript. Each key member of the production crew gains an understanding of the part his or her work will play in the production, but the final decision of specifics rests with the director.

Television and video scripts must balance serving both the aural and visual needs to be met by the script. The script must give the director all of the necessary information, including accurate narration, detailed (depending on the type of script) visuals, and timing information. Whether the script is single-column or dual-column, the same information must be easily read and obvious to the director. Talent will be most interested in the lines they need to memorize or read. The crew, in addition to their specific instructions from the director, will need to find their technical needs answered in the script. A writer is less responsible for technical matters in video scripts, providing instead general shot and transition descriptions and minimal audio instructions. But the video writer must concentrate on the visual without ignoring sound. A balance must be reached between using the tremendous power of visuals and, at the same time, stimulating the viewer's hearing senses to match, contrast, or supplement the visual experience. The challenge for the visual writer demands that the balance between sight and sound make sense for the production and maximize the power of the medium.

Multimedia scripts must cover the same areas as a video script. If the script is interactive or branched, then additional instruction needs to be included to meet those needs. The writer working in multimedia must be aware of the technical aspects of the digital medium and must learn to use the wide variety of means to communicate to the audience without overwhelming the audience or misusing those same techniques. The world of digital production offers so many new and yet unexplored shapes, images, and combinations of the electronic media; much will come from writers exploring those avenues yet unexplored.

Basic Writing Skills

Audiences listening to radio, watching television, or viewing a film under normal conditions cannot go back and review what they have just been exposed to if they did not understand the message or were confused by plot changes. Obviously, with modern recording equipment and techniques, a replay is possible with any medium, but the goal of an audience absorbing a story as it unfolds requires that the story be told in as clearly a manner as possible. You should not write in such a muddled manner that the audience must review each section to reach an understanding of the presentation. This is not writing down to the audience, but more importantly, writing at the comprehension level of the audience within the time the audience has to grasp the material presented to it.

In order to write for the audience's comprehension level, you must know your audience. You should not write for yourself or, necessarily, for your own amusement; rather you should target a specific audience. To accomplish this, you must be aware of audience demographic analysis methods, broadcast ratings, market studies, ticket sales analysis, and Internet response analysis.

Reading to Be Heard

Media writing must be written to be read out loud by narrators, actors, and newscasters. Written material that is intended only for the eyes of a reader may be much more complicated than material to be read by a performer. You must write copy to sound as if the person reading the copy is speaking directly to one or two people, not the possible millions that a single media performance may reach at any one moment. Most media audiences (except for motion picture audiences) are small groups of people gathering in a home, restaurant, or club. Therefore, the copy must be as natural as possible. It is as important to make the copy natural as it is to avoid slang, poor English (even though we too often do not speak our language properly), and sloppy construction.

You may use slang only to develop a character's personality or to depict a specific incident or scene, but not to make the speech appealing to only one segment of the market. As our population becomes more diverse, the tendency to use colloquial speech to appeal to a segment of the population may, at the same time, turn off or annoy a major portion of the rest of the population. Using slang is particularly tempting when the targeted market includes young people who may be using the latest fashionable speech pattern.

The Passive Voice

One major danger of using what appears to be natural speech is the overuse of the passive voice. A verb may be either active—that is, indicating an action of some sort—or passive, using any of the forms of the verb "to be." The verb forms of "to be," including *is, are, was,* and *were,* describe nothing. They simply exist. Any sentence with a passive verb may be improved and carry the story forward if an action verb is substituted for the passive verb.

> "Attitude is a breath of fresh air." This sentence sounds better if an action verb replaces *is,* as in "Attitude provides a breath of fresh air."

Often, a sentence becomes passive because the position of the subject of the sentence and the object of the verb are reversed. Simply writing the sentence as a description of *who does what to whom* automatically changes the sentence from passive to active.

> "Joe was shot in the back by Sam" makes better sense if written "Sam shot Joe in the back."

The subject of the sentence is *Sam,* and the object of the action was *Joe;* therefore, if the sentence is written in a logical order, a listener will understand immediately what the writer says.

If you use a gerund form of a verb (i.e., a verb ending in -*ing*) with a passive verb, or if you attach *have, has,* or *had* unnecessarily to the sentence, that also makes the sentence passive.

> "Sara is graduating from Rice University" is strengthened by changing the gerund *graduating* to *graduates*, so that the sentence reads "Sara graduates from Rice University."
> "The family has arrived for dinner" sounds better without the *has*, reading "The family arrived for dinner."

Matching Subject and Verb

A tricky problem with writing involves matching subject and verb in number (i.e., singular or plural). Matching number in news writing can be tricky because of the number of sentences that include quantities of items and measurements. The verb must match the subject of the sentence, regardless of the position of the subject in relation to the verb. Units of measurements are generally considered as singular. In complex sentences, the subject may be hidden by phrases or clauses. You may prevent this error by writing simpler sentences.

> The *cause* of the multiple wrecks on Highway 10 *has* [not *have*] yet to be determined
> Three thousand tons *is* [not *are*] a lot of coal. [Although *tons* seems to be plural, as a measurement, it is treated as a singular subject.]
> The new telephone company, along with its two subsidiaries, *is* [not *are*] moving to town.

Adjectives and Adverbs

Adjectives and adverbs provide the spice to interesting writing. They modify either nouns or verbs, adding color, definition, and specificity. The problem in media writing is overuse of modifiers to the point of confusing the audience by hiding the important parts of the sentence, the subject, the verb, and the object. Well-placed modifiers add much to the meaning of a sentence, but too many can muddy the meaning. You may misuse modifiers by not being accurate, by overstating facts, or by misleading the listener with an inaccurate degree of intensity.

The *high* mountain
The *higher* mountain
The *highest* mountain
The river rising *fast*
The river rising *faster*
The river rising *fastest*

Pronouns

Pronouns take the place of nouns to avoid repetition and to add some flexibility to a sentence. There are three cases of pronouns: subjective, objective, and possessive. The subjective case (also called the nominative case) is used for the subject of a sentence.

Subjective

I, you, we, he, she, it

The objective case is used for the object of a verb or the object of a preposition.

Objective

Me, you, him, her, it, us, them, whom

Possessive pronouns indicate a relationship between at least two objects.

Possessive

My, our, your, his, hers, its, their, mine, ours, yours, theirs

A pronoun must have an antecedent. The antecedent is the noun that the pronoun refers to or replaces. Mismatching the pronoun with its antecedent contributes to most misuse of pronouns. If the antecedent is a subject, then the pronoun must be a subjective pronoun, and if the noun is an object, then the pronoun must be an objective pronoun. The same holds true with possessive pronouns and their matching antecedents. Limiting the use of pronouns avoids mismatched antecedents. Remember, the audience cannot go back and check to see to what or whom the pronoun refers, so repeating the noun avoids confusing the audience.

In another quirk of the English language, *who* generally is subjective and *whom* generally is objective, but there are acceptable violations of that rule.

Like-Sounding Words

When more than one meaning is attached to a word that sounds like another, the sentence must make clear which meaning is intended in that particular sentence.

To, too, two
Their, there, they're
Your, you're

The number *two* seldom causes confusion since the sentence will obviously refer to a quantity of some sort. (e.g., "*Two* horses raced to a close finish in the final race.")

The word *to* serves as a preposition. (e.g., "The house belongs *to* you and me.") *To* also is half of a verb infinitive. (e.g., "*to* run")

Too is an adverb modifying a verb. (e.g., "The coffee was *too* hot to drink.")

Their is a possessive plural pronoun referring to a plural noun and an object. (e.g., "Sue and Sam purchased *their* new home yesterday.")

There has two meanings and uses: an indication of location (e.g., "The book is over *there*.") or an expletive used to start a sentence (e.g., "*There* are twelve stores open late tonight.")

They're is a contraction of *they* and *are*. (e.g., "*They're* going to miss class this afternoon.")

Your is another possessive pronoun. It may be either singular or plural. (e.g., "*Your* iPod is in the knapsack.")

You're is a contraction of *you* and *are*. (e.g., "*You're* going to miss the bus if you don't hurry.")

Prepositions

Prepositions, although small, carry important meaning and accuracy to a sentence. There are many of them, and their close meanings create confusion if not properly used.

To, for, of, on, above, from, under, at, by, with, until, after, over

---

Each preposition carries a specific meaning. *Of* is different than *for*, although these are often used incorrectly, as if they offered the same meaning.

The more difficult prepositions to use properly are defined similarly but yet are not precisely the same. A writer needs to know the correct meaning so as to use each word properly.

> Among and between
> Beside and besides
> Beneath and below
> Because of and due to

In general, many prepositions indicate the location of the object. If the exact location is critical to the story, then the accurate preposition must be used.

Among refers to sharing by more than two people or objects. *Between* specifically refers to one-to-one relationships.

Beside indicates two objects close to each other. *Besides* indicates that an object is in addition to the original object.

Beneath indicates two objects in direct contact, one on top of the other. *Below* simply means one or more objects are in a position lower than the others or are lower in rank than the others.

Because of always refers to one object acting in a manner to cause a change in another. There must be a direct cause-and-effect relationship.

Due to simply explains a change in the condition of an object.

Pronouns used with prepositions always are in the objective case, even if the sentence structure makes it difficult to determine the antecedent's relationship to the preposition.

Punctuation

Punctuation marks help readers deliver the meaning of copy as is intended by you. You use punctuation to tell the reader when to pause; whether a pause is long, short, or medium; when to separate individual thoughts; when to shout; when to ask a question; and when to stop. Writers may find it easy to overuse punctuation. Just as with overused special effects, overused punctuation loses its value and may distort the intended meaning.

Basic rules exist for punctuation, but they need to be modified in media writing to help communicate meaning and correct interpretation for a listening audience, not a reading audience.

The Period

The period simply means stop. Nothing complicated. It is the end of the thought; start a new thought with the next sentence. A period ends an abbreviation and indicates a decimal point in numerals.

> A complete sentence contains a subject, a verb, and a period.
> The president spoke about his $100.5 million budget.

The Comma

Commas indicate a slight pause or a change of ideas, or they may connect a series of items or thoughts. It is the most commonly overused punctuation mark, but the comma serves to clarify meaning by separating long clauses or phrases. Of course, both long clauses and phrases should be avoided in media writing because they are too complicated to comprehend without seeing the sentence in writing. Commas may be used if more than one adjective modifies a noun, but the comma is not necessary if the comma may be substituted for a conjunction (e.g., *and* or *but*).

The Semicolon

The semicolon indicates a slightly longer pause than the comma, but not a full stop. Semicolons are most commonly used to connect

> The truck contained five hogs, two cows, and a sheep.
> When the cloudburst dumped 4 inches of rain on the county, the
>   citizens felt they had to evacuate.
> The snowstorm brought a shower of fluffy, white flakes.

independent clauses without a conjunction. Again, except for dialogue, you should rewrite copy to simplify the sentence into two sentences. You may also use semicolons to separate a complex series of items to clarify related information.

Sam drove the truck into the river; he drove without stopping to
  think of the consequences.
The vacation family consisted of the father, Sam; his wife, Sue; her
  sister, Olga; and her brother, George.

The Colon

The colon separates two related sentences as if the first introduces the second. The first word following the colon should be capitalized. You may also use the colon to introduce a direct quote or to separate numerals in time or citations.

The Incredible family came to a sudden conclusion: They had to
  take the battle to the enemy.
The mayor said: "No more taxes!"
5:15 PM
Section 5: paragraph 22.

The Hyphen

The hyphen connects compound modifiers when the first modifier modifies the second modifier but not the following noun or verb. Again, you often may misuse the hyphen when you want a pause longer than delivered by a comma, semicolon, or dash.

Bertha shows she is a some-time supporter.

The Dash

The dash indicates a longer pause than given by a comma or semi-colon. It is used to connect two thoughts for an effect—probably a comma or semicolon would have accomplished the needed pause.

Parentheses

You should best avoid parentheses in media writing, especially news writing. They do serve the purpose of allowing additional information or a side comment, but parentheses can confuse both the reader and the listener.

> The airliner landed at Miami. (The Atlanta airport was closed.)

Question and Exclamation Marks

Both marks need to signal the reader of a change in delivery. Unfortunately, in English, these marks come at the end of the sentence. A question mark ends a direct question but not an indirect question. Exclamation marks should be used sparingly to avoid losing the impact of the mark. Both marks are enclosed within the final quotation mark if either is part of a direct quote.

> How does the weathercaster know when it will rain?
> The volcano has erupted!

Ellipses

Ellipses indicate the longest pause without a full stop or indicate that something in a quotation has been omitted. You should carefully consider omitting sections of quotations, being careful to avoid misleading the audience by changing the meaning of the quote.

> The senator said, "I stand on my beliefs…you may accept that or not."

Quotation Marks

Quotation marks enclose a direct translation of a recording of dialogue or statement. Any punctuation that follows a quote is placed within the final mark. Quotation marks indicate works of art, television show episodes, and chapter titles. Titles of individual television film and radio programs, newspapers, movies, book titles, theatrical performances, magazine titles, and some reference book titles should be italicized or underlined.

> The county clerk concluded, "No more licenses today."
> *Toy Story*
> <u>Saturday Night Live</u>
> *Time* magazine
> *The Dictionary*
> *Courage, Justice*

For much more detail and for help with specific problems regarding grammar and other writing-construction problems, consult your personal writer's guide. One of the best has been prepared specifically for media writers and the individual problems faced in writing for the electronic media.[1]

Spelling

The comprehension, ease of reading, and accuracy of the meaning of media scripts, whether news, instructional, documentary, or dramatic, depends partially on precise and correct spelling of each individual word.

---

[1] Kessler, Lauren, and Duncan McDonald. *When Words Collide: A Media Writer's Guide to Grammar and Style.* 6th ed. Belmont, CA: Wadsworth Publishing, 2004.

The English language causes enough confusion to the audience's ears with words with more than one meaning, similar words carrying totally different meanings, and a variety of words misused in common speaking conversation.

To avoid these pitfalls, you must present the reader of the script accurately spelled and precisely chosen words. A script presented for professional consideration will be rejected immediately if misspelled and improperly chosen words appear. Various societies and editors compound the problem by attempting to simplify some spellings of words. The matter is worsened by the confusion when their suggested modifications have not been universally accepted. Also, the original spelling of some words still used by the British only adds to the confusion.

United States	British
Honor	Honour
Color	Colour
Defense	Defence

You may gain the basics of maintaining and improving correct spelling by reading, listening, and studying word construction and usage. Reading well-written copy from quality newspapers, magazines, and novels will furnish excellent and accurate examples of proper spelling. Again, listening to well-spoken individuals who enunciate the English language properly also provides excellent models for you as a writer.

If you concentrate on finding the correct spelling when in doubt, you will build the final bridge to accurate spelling in your writing. Computer spelling and grammar checkers offer a limited measure of accepted spelling, but they are not reliable all of the time. In addition, most spelling tools offer selections of spelling choices depending on usage and sentence structure, leaving the final choice to you. One of the most useful tools for you, along with an up-to-date comprehensive dictionary, is an *Instant Spelling Dictionary*.[2]

---

[2] Dougherty, Margaret M., Julia H. Fitzgerald, and Donald O. Bolander, eds. *Instant Spelling Dictionary*. 3rd ed. New York: Warner Books, 1990.

Clear, Concise, and Nontechnical Language

You must remember that the reader of the script, whether it is the talent, a producer, or a possible fund provider, may not have knowledge of the technical language used in media production or of any of the subjects covered within the script. Remember, the audience will have one opportunity to hear and see the production. If the language and terminology is foreign or confusing, the message will be lost. Simple, straightforward wording that makes sense to anyone with a minimal level of understanding of the English language will suffice. You must constantly remember to write to communicate to the audience, not to yourself. Mentally choose someone who has at the minimum an interest in the subject, but little knowledge, and then create language and descriptions that the person will easily understand upon hearing and seeing the production the first time.

Style Comes after Information

First-time writers may feel they must develop a style that will make their writing stand out from all the rest of the new writers. There is nothing wrong with striving to be an individualist, but a well-developed style will come with experience and much writing. Few successful writers look back after they have achieved a level of satisfactory success and can say they originally had any concept of what their style would finally become. Style is the frosting on the cake of an accomplished career and comes only after expending a great deal of effort and writing many, many scripts that never see the light of a studio or the eyes and ears of an audience. If your writing is effective and satisfactory to you and your audience, then your style will develop.

Language of Discrimination

A writer must deal with the "isms"—racism, sexism, ageism, and, if you will, disabilitism.

A difference exists between political correctness and depictions based on fairness and accuracy. Political correctness follows the law and the fashion of the moment, but you need to treat all individuals and groups of people with the same care and consideration you would expect to receive. We all are individuals, so we all must be respected for our individual characteristics.

Often the "isms" fall prey to the use of stereotypes and stereotypical depictions. Using stereotypes in a positive manner often is a necessity in media writing. Within productions of short time frames, especially commercials and animation, you may use stereotypes to quickly establish mood, location, and, often, descriptions of specific characters. A police officer may be depicted as a short, stocky, red-haired Caucasian male in a blue uniform. That quickly tells the audience this is a officer of the law without narration, labels, or other indication of the character because this has been the stereotype of a New York Irish policeman. It is not accurate, but virtually all audiences will accept and recognize the depiction without further explanation, saving time. If the depiction is not negative, it is neither racist and is only mildly sexist.

The danger in using stereotypes is inadvertently choosing negative characteristics or consistently creating a character in a negative role specifically because of gender, sexual orientation, ethnic background, religion, or national origin. The tragedy of 9/11/01 and the following unrest in much of the rest of the world should teach us all to carefully consider how we depict and think of people of other beliefs and backgrounds. You must be even more careful of considering the depictions and treatment of people with individual differences. This extends to remembering woman are not included in the term *mankind* and that a fireman actually is a firefighter. If you use a person's physical condition, religious beliefs, age, or sexual persuasion in a news story, it must be germane to the story, not used to categorize the subject of the story. In other formats, depictions may need to include descriptions of a character's race, gender, and even ethnic or religious beliefs, but only for the accuracy of the story, not as a shorthand escape from an honest description of the character. Obviously, the use of slang expressions to describe groups of people is not acceptable except as a part of dialogue to establish the personality of a character using the slang.

The tremendous power of the electronic media must never be forgotten as you place descriptions and develop characters in your stories and reporting. That power can cause far more harm than can be imagined until an incident reveals that power in a negative manner.

The Law and Censorship

Depending upon whether the media production is broadcast on radio or television or is distributed by cable, satellite, motion picture theater, recordings, or printed forms, certain laws specifically apply to the written word.

The First Amendment

The First Amendment offers a certain level of protection for anything spoken or produced electronically or in print. But the right of protection comes with a heavy dose of responsibility. The work (specifically, the words) must be original, defendable, truthful, and created within the laws, rules, and regulations of communication, and they must not be plagiarized.

Copyright laws protect your work from unfair or uncompensated duplication; at the same time, you must respect all other creators' ownership of their works. Copyright covers print, film, photographs, video, audio recordings, and reproduction of any media, whether they are analog or digital. Copyright is in a state of flux, caused partially by rapid changes in digital duplication technology.

Before publishing or producing any work, it will pay you to request qualified legal advice on both the originality of the work and the protection of the work once it is made public. As a guide, you may refer to a recently published guide on copyright and clearance.[3]

Defamation

Defamation law includes both libel and slander. Traditionally, libel suits were based on printed negative comments—slander, if spoken. Over the years, the two have come to be considered the same, and in fact, except in California, there is no legal difference between the two. Care must be taken to make certain your printed words

---

[3] Donaldson, Michael C. *Clearance and Copyright: Everything A Filmmaker Needs to Know.* 2nd ed. Los Angeles, CA: Silman-James Press, 2003.

are truthful. Anyone described in a negative manner (in the eyes of the subject) may file a libel suit demanding retraction and financial compensation for the damage caused by the written words. Anyone may sue for libel; the plaintiff then has to prove innocence—a reversal of the usual bromide of "innocent until proved guilty." Even if your published words prove to be truthful, if it can be proved that you intended to harm someone's reputation or personal privacy, you may lose the libel suit.

The second part of the laws of defamation, slander, parallels that of libel but is based on the spoken word, not printed information. With the confusion of whether electronic material, radio, television, and cable fall under either libel or slander, the two terms have converged.

To prevent a defamation suit, it is your responsibility to make certain your work is well within the law by fully understanding the end result of your written and creative works.

Broadcast Laws

The Federal Communication Commission's (FCC) responsibilities include setting rules and regulations passed by Congress for the broadcast, cable, satellite, and telecommunication industries. Theoretically, the FCC cannot censor broadcast content or programming. But, because broadcasters must apply for and periodically renew their licenses to operate on the air with the FCC, any action the FCC feels goes beyond the station's operating in the "public's convenience, interest, or necessity" may bring punishment. This statement gives the FCC the right to levy fines (set by Congress) and the right to cancel the broadcaster's license, putting them out of business.

The FCC operates within a process regulated by raised eyebrow. A broadcaster must determine if a program or its content falls outside of the inexact expectations of the FCC. If such a content offends the FCC, the station may receive a fine, or a threat may be placed on their license when renewal time arrives.

A second increasingly worrisome area of criticism for broadcasters now comes from parental and religious organizations who monitor broadcasts and file complaints with the FCC if they feel the broadcaster has stepped beyond the bounds of local standards. The FCC is more likely to respond to such complaints.

To you, these rules, regulations, and laws present a challenge to be true to your creative vision and yet to stay within the bounds of imprecise and inconsistent borders. Again, legal advice may be helpful, but these regulations change with each session of Congress and each time a station broadcasts something that annoys and displeases a large enough group of protesters.

Indecency, Pornography, and Obscenity

Two of the thorniest problems of broadcast content originated with the indefinite statement that the FCC was charged uphold the law stating that indecent and pornographic material cannot be broadcast. The original statement does not in any manner define what is or is not indecent or pornographic, except that broadcasts should be based on local standards. This concept was born from the idea that all broadcasting was intended for a local audience. Networks and cable and satellite operations changed the local status of broadcasters. What is a local standard of indecency in New York City varies considerably from that of Springfield, Missouri, yet both cities will receive the same television program and some of the same radio programs.

Court cases have periodically attempted to set standards, but generally these have been overturned by later court decisions or are simply ignored as the sophistication of America's audience has changed. The three levels of concern are defined as follows:

Indecent: (based on a 1975 FCC decision) Any material patently offensive, measured by contemporary community standards

Pornographic: Sexually explicit and intended for the purpose of sexual arousal

Obscene: A class of sexual material so offensive, because it is without any redeeming value, that it is not protected under the First Amendment

With the increased coverage of cable and satellite for distribution of video programs, which are not licensed under the FCC's mandate, broadcast television has to try to compete within the tighter standards impressed by the FCC. As a result, all electronic media continue to push the envelope in programming that 10 years ago would never have been allowed.

Writers forced by the undefined, yet flexible, standards on sexual programming are left to fulfill their creative stories with the hope that, with some guidance from the standards and practices departments of the networks, their work will be produced and broadcast. This chapter does not offer professional legal advice; it is only an introduction to the legal areas of which you need to be aware while pursuing your career. An up-to-date book on communication law may provide guidance during the writing stages.[4]

The Audience and Distribution

To you, the audience presents a dual target. First, the audience "buys" the product you produce (i.e., your show, article, game, or Web site), or not. Secondarily, the audience attracted by your work is sold to the advertisers. This dichotomy is true in broadcasting, cable, print, the Internet, and, with product placement, in motion pictures and television dramas.

Regardless of your creative motivation, you must write for an audience. To write for an audience, you must connect with the audience, stimulating its senses, appealing to their imaginations, and triggering mental pictures, either to support the presented work or to supplement the work if only audio or print appears.

A formidable isolation exists between the creator and the audience when communication is distributed by mass media, whether by electronic means or print. Despite creating for a maximum-sized audience, the communication actually is interpersonal, from you to each individual reader, listener, or viewer. You must write for

---

[4] Donaldson, Michael C. *Clearance and Copyright: Everything A Filmmaker Needs to Know.* 2nd ed. Los Angeles, CA: Silman-James Press, 2003.

that one individual, despite the fact that the audience consists of millions of other individuals.

The term *audience* is misleading. Programmers and editors compress all the members of the audience into a single mass with one set of characteristics. Such a mass does not actually exist as a single package of demographic descriptions. It is unlikely that any one member of the audience fits the demographic description. No one is average, and every single audience member exists as an unique individual. How do you then sell a film, radio program, TV program, game, or Web site that appeals to a maximum audience and the most sponsors? You must understand the differences and similarities within the audience and choose the topic and the plot to appeal to a specific targeted audience.

Differences exist among the media, but to succeed at distributing any created work, you must first choose the most likely audience and target the creation to that group. One of the problems to be solved depends on analyzing the fragmented nature of today's audience. Individual audience members have a high number of options to select among to suit their specific interests. Today's population is highly diversified, not only from new immigrants, but also from a general sense of independence of individuals within their own isolated personal world; people have begun to choose whatever interests them instead of following what once was the most commonly accepted fashionable activity or program.

For you to expect distribution of your work, a portion of research effort should be spent analyzing the potential and actual audience and the specifics of the media choice, as well as the practicality of the produced work. You should be as conversational as possible, using short words and short sentences. Print can be more detailed and authoritarian, electronic media can be more personal and exciting, and the Internet and games carry the advantage of interactivity.

With these general guidelines, each of the following chapters offers greater detail for writing within the specific genres and formats. Most of this chapter may be applied directly to the information within the following chapters, but a number of comments will need some adaptation, depending on the requirements of the genre.

Summary

Throughout the history of public performances, whether on the theatrical stage or on film, radio, television, or a digital format, the means of communicating to the production staff and crew from the writer have evolved. Some of the traditions have migrated from one medium to another; in other cases, totally new means of communicating were created. Each succeeding medium borrowed from previous media to suit the new demands of the new medium.

A script must be written to maximize communication. In some cases, it is written in order to most clearly communicate with the audience; in others, so that all members of the production staff and crew understand what the writer had envisioned. In all cases, sentences constructed using correct, straightforward language and proper punctuation are a necessity. The formats must be programmed for the purposes of the specific medium.

You are responsible for matters of avoiding discrimination and violations of the law, and if writing for broadcasting, for understanding the rules and regulations of the broadcast industry. It is necessary to understand the audience to accurately target the message and to avoid annoying or displeasing members of the audience.

Be Sure To...

1. Research your intended audience.
2. Understand the power of your words—especially to individuals in the audience.
3. Write simple sentences structures using well-known and understood vocabulary.
4. Create scripts that your director and crew will understand easily.
5. Avoid plagiarism and protect your own work.

Exercises

1. Write a brief (30–60 second) script on any subject of your choice. Create one copy of the script in radio format and a second in

film format, *or* create one script in single-column video format and a second in dual-column video format.
2.   Listen for someone speaking a passive sentence. Look for one example on radio, one on TV, and another on a film or even in a newspaper story. Rewrite each as an active sentence.
3.   Describe a scene in a film or TV program that uses a stereotype to describe a character or a character's actions. Explain whether you felt the stereotype was used legitimately (as a positive stereotype, not negative). If it is negative, how should the description have been written?
4.   Research the question of defamation of a person in the public eye, including who would fit that description and how the laws of defamation would affect such a person.
5.   Carefully watch your favorite TV program. From the content of the program and the type of commercials offered within the program, describe the targeted demographics of the audience.

Additional Sources

Print

Brockett, Oscar G., and Franklin J. Hildy. *History of Theatre*. 9th ed. Boston: Allyn & Bacon, 1998.

Head, Sydney W., Thomas Spann, and Michael A. McGregor. *Broadcasting in America: A Survey of Electronic Media*. 9th ed. Boston: Houghton Mifflin, 2000.

Macgowan, Kenneth. *Living Stage: A History of World Theater*. New York: Prentice-Hall, 1955.

Mamer, Bruce. *Film Production Technique: Creating the Accomplished Image*. 4th ed. Belmont, CA: Wadsworth Publishing, 2006.

Marx, Christy. *Writing for Animation, Comics, Games*. Boston: Focal Press, 2007.

Miller, Carolyn Handler. *Digital Storytelling: A Creator's Guide to Interactive Entertainment*. Boston: Focal Press, 2004.

Miller, Philip. *Media Law for Producers*. Boston: Focal Press, 2003.

Straus, Jane. *The Blue Book of Grammar and Punctuation: The Mysteries of Grammar and Punctuation Revealed*. 8th ed. Mill Valley, CA: Jane Straus, 2005.

Strumpf, Michael, and Auriel Douglas. *The Grammar Bible: Everything You Always Wanted to Know About Grammar but Didn't Know Whom to Ask*. New York: Henry Holt, 2004.

Thurman, Susan, and Larry Shea. *The Only Grammar Book You'll Ever Need: A One-Stop Source for Every Writing Assignment*. Avon, MA: F + W Publications, 2003.

Wexman, Virginia Wright. *A History of Film*. 6th ed. Boston: Allyn & Bacon, 2005.

Web

a4esl.org/q/h/mc006-ck.html
www.dailygrammar.com/
www.edufind.com/english/grammar/
owl.english.purdue.edu/handouts/grammar/

CHAPTER 2

Media Production for Writers

Aesthetics, then, means for us a study of certain sense perceptions and how these perceptions can be most effectively clarified, intensified, and interpreted through a medium, such as television or film, for a specific recipient.

—Dr. Herbert Zettl, Professor of Broadcast and Electronic Communication, San Francisco State University

Media is the manipulation of audio, video, and digital signals in order to create images and sound that develop the representation of events in the telling of a story or the clarification of information.

Introduction

Before your hard work as a writer can reach the audience, which is the primary reason for writing, the work must be converted from a piece of paper or a computer file to actual acted, performed, drawn, or physically created material and recorded onto some form of reproducible media. The creative production staff and crew must take your written ideas and convert them to a viable, entertaining, informative program for the audience to hear, watch, or interact with.

The relationship between you and the production process and your attitude as a writer toward the production process and the people who do the work is critical for your work to reach its best possible form for presentation to an audience.

Writer's Relationship with Production

The professional operation and eventual quality of a project may rely on the relationship that develops between you and the staff and crew of the production.

How you view your feelings, as well as your knowledge about the production process, may range from fear and loathing to total involvement, based on your previous experience with how your scripts have been produced. Traditionally, a mild form of a conflict exists between writers and the production crew. Writers long have felt their ideas were not well understood, and they often feel the end result of the production does not reflect what they envisioned when writing the script. On the other side of the conflict, the crew may feel the writer's concept and descriptions do not make sense. In addition, the demands of the script may exceed the capabilities of the budget, equipment, and crew. This means that compromises necessary to complete the production may lead the finished project away from the writer's vision.

This difference of opinion may never be completely resolved. What you created on paper may be impossible to convert to a finished media because of budget, time, or the capability of the available production process. One of the reasons many writers become producers and even directors is to protect their creative work, but this often does not solve the problem. Although the problems and solutions to the production conversion are now directly in the hands of the writer-director, he or she may or may not have the production knowledge and skill to carry out the original concept within the restraints of the production process.

A different attitude requires the writer to simply turn the script over to the producer and director and trust them to come close to the original concept. If the writer has written a script that falls within the availability of the production process and has convincingly explained the concept, characterizations, and plot lines, the production may very well accurately reflect the writer's desires.

Another attitude might find the writer maintaining a level of curiosity while watching from a distance as the production moves forward.

The distance might not be any greater than a phone call, a meeting, or a casual conference with the producer and director. This is the most comfortable position and leads to the least confrontational and most congenial creative relationship between writer and production staff. This position provides the availability to answer questions and to help in solving problems that may arise during the production process. This attitude finds that the writer's curiosity about the production techniques required to fill the demands of the script helps the writer understand how his or her concept or depictions must be dealt with to reach the vision within the confines of the production process.

At the extreme other end of the relationship, the writer becomes totally involved in the production process. A writer with professional knowledge of the production process may become an adjunct to the producer or director by applying production knowledge and experience to the solution of the production problems created by the script. The level of knowledge would come from actual production experience or from working on many productions while intentionally grasping and absorbing production techniques. This may offer a writer the opportunity to merge an interest and skill in writing with production knowledge, which could lead to the opportunity to produce or to direct the script. If taken to an extreme, this attitude also may become a problem for the producer or director if the "suggestions" reach beyond the responsibility of the writer and conflict with the needs of the producer or director.

What Is Production?

The production process consists of the operation of the physical and digital equipment combined to convert your written script to a completed program available to be distributed. The process incorporates three stages: preproduction, production, and postproduction.

As the writer, you have completed the majority of the preproduction stage. You prepared the original concept, proposal, treatment, preliminary budget, and various stages of writing and rewriting of the script to its final form. The production team then takes the written documents and organizes the equipment and personnel to operate the equipment needed to prepare for the actual production stage.

You and the producer share the responsibility for the preproduction stage. The director and the key members of the production staff and crew then plan and carry out the design, the set-up, rehearsals, and the recording of the production. During the postproduction stage, the editing staff assembles all of the material produced during the production stage and melds it into a completed package. The director or producer, or both, supervise the editing. Depending on the contract arrangement, you also may be asked to offer opinions on the final edited stage of the production.

Why Production for Writers?

In order for you to be able to communicate with the production personnel who will be interpreting your written text, you need to understand and be conversant with a minimal level of the unique language used by production staff and crews. A novelist describes the settings, action, and dialogue of the characters in his story, just as a screenwriter describes the setting, actions, and lists the dialogue expected to be heard from the actors. But the difference comes from the novelist relying on the imagination of the reader to fill in any gaps left in the descriptions, and, just as important, the novelist counts on the readers to use their imaginations to create a larger and more detailed scene, filled with action that is not necessarily described in detail.

In contrast to the novelist, the screenwriter must make certain that the descriptions in the script inform the director as to exactly what he or she, the screenwriter, visualized appearing on screen within the finished production. The simpler the script descriptions, the greater the leeway the director has to interpret the script in determining the action, blocking, and acting of the performers. You must write descriptions that clearly indicate your vision of the story.

If you understand the production process well enough to understand what it requires in time, energy, and money to complete the script, then the director and producer will work to create a finished production that is as close as possible to the written descriptions. The basic costs of completing a production may alter your more complex concepts to stay within a reasonable budget. This does not require specific budgeting and bookkeeping knowledge or experience on your part, but rather a level of applying common sense. To insist on a series of shots made from a helicopter when the same effect could be created with a crane or with alternate staging might make the difference between a script being rejected rather than accepted for production or completed as envisioned by you.

If you have acquired a sufficient level of production knowledge from experience working in production or from working on many different productions as a writer, then you may be able to offer your assistance to the director and producer when decisions need to be made that may affect your script. Use of prior knowledge of production should help you visualize and understand why and how changes must be made during the production process. No production ever has been produced exactly as it was scripted, with the possible exception of Alfred Hitchcock's later productions. As an artist, Hitchcock carefully visualized each scene and, just as carefully, drew storyboards for every shot. He expected the directors to shoot each shot exactly as he drew it, and they did.

To ensure the production process will follow your concept and script, a working knowledge of the unique language used in production should be acquired.

The Language of Production

The vocabulary of production may be broken into four areas, as follows:

- Descriptions of action (either personnel or equipment)
- Abbreviations and descriptions of transitions
- Abbreviations of object framing
- Abbreviations specific to audio

Action Descriptions

Pan   A camera movement that gives the viewer the feeling that the scene is moving past in an horizontal motion, either back and forth, left to right, or right to left.

Tilt	A camera movement that gives the viewer the feeling that the scene is moving past in a vertical motion, either up or down, top to bottom, or bottom to top.
Dolly	A camera movement that gives the viewers the feeling that they are moving closer or farther away from the subject. The movement displays a change in perspective.
Truck	A camera movement that gives the viewers the feeling they are moving past the subject on a path parallel to the subject, either from right to left or from left to right.
Crab or Arc	A camera movement that combines the view of a dolly and a truck. The viewer appears to move in an circle around the subject or else moves closer or away at an angle.
Pedestal	A camera movement that gives the viewers the feeling they are being raised or lowered in relationship to the subject. This movement usually is combined with a tilt to keep the subject properly framed.
Crane or Boom	A camera movement that combines one or more of pedestal, crab, dolly, and truck. It provides the viewer with an infinite number of continuous angles. Used most often for either extreme high- or low-angle shots.
Zoom	An optical movement created within the lens that duplicates a dolly, giving the viewer the feeling that the subject is moving closer or farther away, without changing perspective.

Abbreviations of Transitions

Fade in	The shot starts in black (i.e., no image), and an object gradually appears.
Fade out	The shot starts with a fully visible object, and it gradually disappears to a black screen (i.e., no image).
Take (Cut)	An instantaneous change of picture or sound. *Take* is the traditional television and video term; *cut* is the traditional film term. Both are used interchangeably.

Dissolve (DISS)	A slow change of picture, with one disappearing as another appears.
Wipe	A change of picture, with one replaced by another, with either a solid or soft edge between the pictures. The direction of the wipe may be from any part of the frame, and the wipe may be in any shape.
Special effects	Special effects are not transitions, but they may be used as such. They also may create a shot by combining two or more shots.
Super	One picture bleeds through the other, giving a ghost effect. Also used to list credits, titles, prices, or phones numbers over a plain, dark background.
Key	The same concept as a super, but instead of one shot bleeding through the other, the foreground shot is electronically "inserted" into the background shot. The foreground shot needs a plain, clear background.
Split screen	A wipe that remains in a fixed position.
Matte key	A shot requiring three sources: foreground, background, and a third to determine the shape of the separation between the two frames. A film and analog technique has been largely replaced by digital effects.
Chroma key	A specialized key, so that the foreground camera does not see a specific color (green or blue), which allows, for example, a weathercaster standing in front of a plain blue or green background to appear to be standing in front of a weather map, which is a separate frame from another camera or source.
Digital effects	An infinite number of transitions designed to replace dissolves, wipes, and keys, these are limited only by the complexity of the video switcher, film printing, or computer program. Examples include multiple images moving or placed in different positions in the frame, and a frame appearing to turn as if it were a page in a book.

Abbreviations of Object Framing (Shot Descriptions)

XCU or ECU	Extreme close-up: Used to show fine detail or to concentrate on a specific object.
CU	Close-up: Used to show detail missed in a wider shot.
MCU	Medium close-up: Used to show a relationship between objects. Often considered as a shot from the waist up on one or more human subjects in one frame.
MS	Medium shot: Used to show a larger area than a MCU. Often considered a head-to-toe shot of one or more subjects in one frame.
LS/WS	Long shot/wide shot: Used to establish location or environment of a scene or to include more than one person in a setting.
XLS/XWS	Extreme long shot/extreme wide shot: The widest shot in a sequence. Used only if a great expanse of space needs to be included in any one frame.
POV	Point of view: The viewer sees the perspective of an actor.
OS	Over the shoulder: A two-shot taken from behind the interviewer and facing the interviewee, or the opposite, with the interviewer facing the camera. It is the most common shot in interview sequences.
Two-shot	Two people or object in a single frame.
Three-shot	Three people or objects in a single frame.
Head shot	Framing a persons from the top of the head to either below the mouth or below the neck.
Bust shot	Framing a person from the top of the head to a line between the waist and chest.

Two notes on framing people and objects:

1. In all shots, especially of people, the shot should not be framed at a logical cut-off line.
2. All shot descriptions are relative. A CU in one sequence may be wider than that in another. The determination is the relationship between the widest and the tightest shots. The widest might be either an XLS or an LS, and the tightest is either an XCU or a CU.

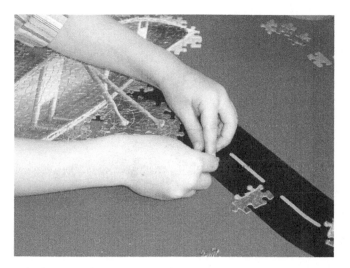

Figure 2.1. A close-up (CU) camera frame concentrates on one object, usually larger than life-size.

Figure 2.2. A medium close-up (MCU) camera frame shows more than one object or the relationship of an object to its environment.

Figure 2.3. A medium shot (MS) camera frames reveals more than a MCU and often includes more than one object and their relationships in the environment.

Figure 2.4. A long shot (LS) camera frame shows the entire setting or environment of a scene.

Figure 2.5. A two-shot camera frame includes two people or two objects and their relationship in the environment.

Video Production Techniques

The video portion of a program, whether it is film-, tape-, disc-, or Web-based, appears to be the most important of the media. The most attention and the greatest amount of financial investment applies to the technology, personnel, and effort in the creation of the visual of any production. An understanding of the basics of visual production is important only in that you must be aware of the limits or lack of limits imposed by budget and available facilities. Theoretically, with the advancement of digital techniques, there are no limits on what may be created in any visual or aural format. The limits come from budget, personnel, and facility availabilities. You should be aware of the differences between various shot framings only to understand what those shots say to the audience. Writing camera moves and complex shot sequences normally belongs to the director in his interpretation of the script. A well-written script will guide the director in the correct direction envisioned by you, without your specifying exact shot descriptions.

If you can visualize what a scene looks like in your mind's eye, then simply describe the scene as if you are viewing it through a window. If the description is complete and accurate, an experienced director will understand and will follow the vision on to the finished production. Your control of casting, scene design, and the overall mode of the production depends on accurate and complete descriptions in the *bible*. The bible contains a list of characters, character relationships, scenes, locations, and treatments of the production, which gives the producer and director the means to reach an understanding of your concept. It is a method used to match your concept of the script to the work they must accomplish.

The production skills and techniques listed earlier in this chapter should provide you with the necessary information to fulfill your production obligation as the writer of your script.

Audio Transitions

Cut	An instantaneous change from one audio to another.
Fade in	Audio changes from no sound to sound at a full level.
Fade out	Audio changes from a full sound level to no sound.
Segue	One audio fades out to silence while a second source fades in. At no time is there dead air between the two sources.
Cross fade	As one audio source begins to fade out, a second source begins to fade in. The sum total of the sound is a combination of the two sources, with a full audio level maintained throughout the transition.
Bridge	An audio link between two segments, either as a segue or a cross-fade.

Audio Abbreviations

SFX/EFX	Sound effects: These may originate from a live source or a recording, or they may be digitally manufactured.
ANNCR	Announcer: A voice generally not seen on camera.
VO	Voice over: Indicates narration with some other audio in the background. Also used in visual productions, indicating narration heard without viewing the source.
MUSIC	Music: Integrated from the same sources as sound effects.

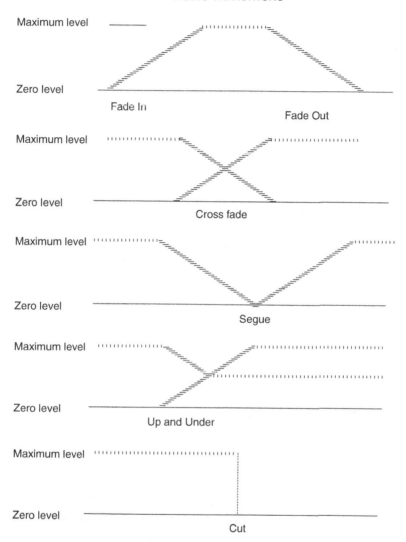

Figure 2.6. The lines on this diagram indicate the level of each of the two audio sources as transitions occur between the two sources, except for fades that involve only one source.

General Descriptive Terms

Audio   The sound source of a production, either sound or visual.
Video   The visual source of a production.
Dialogue   Speech delivered by a performer who is usually visible
             on camera.
Narration   Speech delivered by a performer who is usually not
             visible on camera.

See the glossary for more abbreviations, descriptions, and definitions.

Audio Production Techniques

The importance of the audio portion of media productions cannot be underrated. Audio carries a significant amount of information, regardless of the type of production. Obviously, for radio or another audio-only program, 100% of the information is carried to the listener by audio. But even for video productions, including Web-based programs, audio is critical to fully carry the message in the most accurate and complete form. Audio should be considered at the beginning of any production and not added as an afterthought once all visuals have been determined.

Audio immediately tells the viewer or listener the mode, time, and even location of the program if the music, sound effects, and voice casting are thoughtfully designed. The introductory music indicates the level of gaiety or darkness in the mode; the historical time, be it present day, last century, or even the past decade; and, if the location is important, the music will tell the audience if the location is the deep South, Ireland, or the Middle East. Other subtle characteristics of the production may be passed to the audience by the sounds of the environment, such as if the action is in a large auditorium, a small phone booth, outdoors, or in a raging snow storm. All of these factors of the production may be created easily, efficiently, and at much less cost with sound effects and music, rather than depicting the same characteristics using a visual technique.

The correct choice of music may be the most memorable aspect of the program that the audience retains. The vocal quality, style, and patterns of an actor immediately tell the audience critical aspects of that actor's character, background, personality, and, possibly, part of the story line.

You do not need to be an audio engineer or technician to write scripts that take advantage of the benefits of audio. Think about sound constantly while writing the script, along with the dialogue and the action. Think in terms of how sound can enhance the mood, support the action, and provide a background for the subtle aspects of the subplots or foreshadow coming twists in the plot. Listen carefully as the production moves forward and during postproduction to make certain the sound says what you want it to. Audio is the easiest part of the production process to correct or change during the final stages of the process.

Digital and Web Production Techniques

As with your writing scripts for video or audio distribution, scripts written for the Web, games, or other interactive distribution do not require you to be an expert in the production. But, because the process of distribution is more closely aligned with the actual scripts itself, as much knowledge as possible should be gained in the field before attempting Web-based and interactive scripts. Greater detail in the process is covered in Chapter 10.

Expertise in writing audio and video scripts makes writing for digital formats easier, but, in addition, some knowledge of project management and multi-level scene writing skills are needed, especially for interactive scripts. Although storyboarding an interactive script helps visualize the concept, the design of flowcharts is more important. Flowcharts visually show the direction and steps in movement of the project. Since most interactive productions are nonlinear, a flow chart illustrates the options of interaction. Flowcharting computer applications makes the process simpler for all of the people involved in the project. At the very least, a rough outline of the flow of information will be required to clarify the basic concepts and directions of flow.

Word processors, graphics applications, storyboards, script formatting, and HTML applications make up the basic tools of a writer of interactive or Web-based scripts. Using a data-based application such as FileMaker Pro also provides an alternate for organizing the material to be assembled into an interactive script.

The basic knowledge required for the production of interactive or Web-based scripts is the same as that for any media script: a knowledge of visualization, an appreciation for sounds, and a sense of composition.

Summary

This chapter introduces the writer to the basic concepts of media production and the relationship the writer needs to maintain with the production staff and crew. The writer's attitude should not be one of fear of the process; rather, the writer should maintain a curious cooperation as the process continues, accepting the reality that compromises will have to be made on the original script as the process moves forward.

Production simply is the physical process of translating the writer's original concept into a completed project that may be recorded, distributed, and archived. The language of production evolved from live theatre, motion pictures, radio, television, video, and, now, digital processes. It is at times an unique vocabulary that a writer needs to be acquainted with in order to communicate with the production personnel.

In production of audio, video, and digital, as used in Web-based and interactive productions, media, the writer must choose the best techniques to depict the concept the writer proposes in the script. A wide knowledge of production techniques is not necessary for a writer, but enough knowledge to provide a means of understanding how the production process operates is helpful.

Be Sure To...

1. Become acquainted with the organization and responsibilities of the crew and staff with whom you will work on your script.
2. Learn basic production techniques and alternate choices to fulfill your concept.

3. Think through clearly how you want your production to sound and look.
4. Be ready to accept some changes in your script that must be made to complete the program.
5. Be knowledgeable about how your production will be distributed.

Exercises

1. Record a television drama program that you do not usually watch. Play the recording without watching the screen. Take notes on what you think is happening, who is speaking, and what action occurs. Then play the recording again to check your observations.
2. Record a different program that you have not watched before. Turn the sound off and watch the program without the sound on. Take notes on all aspects of the program, as in Exercise 1. Replay the recording with the sound on and check your observations.
3. Observe a recording of a program produced on film and for television. Compare the differences between production techniques used in the two productions.
4. The novel *War of the Worlds* has been produced as a radio program, a television program, and a film feature. Compare the production techniques of the three, especially the differences in how audio was handled in the radio production from the visual productions. If possible, read a portion of the novel for another comparison.

Additional Sources

Print

Alten, Stanley R. *Audio in Media.* 7th ed. Belmont, CA: Wadsworth Publishing, 2005.

Benedetti, Robert. *From Concept to Screen: An Overview of Film and Television Production.* Boston: Allyn & Bacon, 2002.

Block, Bruce. *The Visual Story: Seeing the Structure of Film, TV, and New Media.* Boston: Focal Press, 2001.

Cederholm, Dan. *Bulletproof Web Design*. Berkeley, CA: Peachpit Press, 2006.

Elin, Larry. *Designing and Developing Multimedia: A Practical Guide for the Producer, Director, and Writer*. Boston: Allyn & Bacon, 2001.

Holman, Tomlinson. *Sound for Digital Audio*. Boston: Focal Press, 2005.

Honthaner, Eve. *The Complete Film Production Handbook*. 3rd ed. Boston: Focal Press, 2001.

Kellison, Cathrine. *Producing for TV and Video: A Real-World Approach*. Boston: Focal Press, 2006.

Kindem, Gorham, and Robert Musburger. *Introduction to Media Production: The Path to Digital Media*. 3rd ed. Boston: Focal Press, 2004.

Marich, Robert. *Marketing to Moviegoers*. Boston: Focal Press, 2006.

May, Pete. *The Essential Digital Video Handbook*. Boston: Focal Press, 2006.

McLeish, Robert. *Radio Production*. 5th ed. Boston: Focal Press, 2005.

Musburger, Robert. *Single-Camera Video Production*. 4th ed. Boston: Focal Press, 2005.

Rabiger, Michael. *Developing Story Ideas*. Boston: Focal Press, 2005.

Thompson, Roy. *The Grammar of the Shot*. Boston: Focal Press, 1998.

Wheeler, Paul. *Practical Cinematography*. Boston: Focal Press, 2005.

Zettl, Hebert. *Sight Sound Motion: Applied Media Aesthetics*. 4th ed. Belmont, CA: Wadsworth Publishing, 2005.

——. *Television Production Handbook*. 9th ed. Belmont, CA: Wadsworth Publishing, 2006.

Web

www.aes.org
www.art.net
www.computerhistory.org
www.eia.org
www.fcc.gov
www.howstuffworks.com/hdtv1
www.hollywood.com
www.itu.ch
www.smpte.org

CHAPTER 3

Spots:

Public Service Announcements, Program Promotions, and Commercials

Advertisers are the interpreters of our dreams....Their weapons are our weaknesses: fear, ambition, illness, pride, selfishness, desire, ignorance. And these weapons must be kept bright as a sword.

—E. B. White, author and editor

Introduction

Short bursts of information spaced between and within programs on radio and television earned the nickname *spots*. Spots include three specific type of announcements: public service announcements (PSAs), program promotional announcements (promos), and sales advertising (i.e., commercials, or commls). Each type fills a specific purpose in broadcast communication, but all have in common the required task of *selling* an item, a business, a concept, a philosophy, or a need to be filled in some way through an interchange of money, time, or effort.

Spots range from 10 seconds to 2 minutes. Longer announcements than 2 minutes fall into the category of mini- or full-length infomercial programming. This chapter will concentrate on broadcast announcements, motion picture theater trailers, and commercials, all of which use the same production and sales techniques, as well as a growing variety of sales tools used on the Web.

Background

Announcements, especially commercials, were not expected to contribute to radio when it first began at the start of the 20th century. By 1916, before radio was regulated or even heard much beyond a few miles from the transmitter, announcements were made in exchange for either a sample of the product or an exchange of service. By 1922, sponsors would lease a station's airtime for several hours for rates ranging from $35–50. There are no precise records of how much actual airtime was delivered for the recorded amount of money. Despite both audience and government disapproval of actual commercials aired on the early stations, there were neither laws nor guidelines setting limits of any kind. AT&T, the first company to operate a station (WEAF) on a professional level offered to sell airtime—just the airtime. The sponsor would be responsible for the program, as well as any commercial announcements within the program. They had little success in making any sales until August of 1922, when a New York Queens company paid $50 for a 15-minute block to talk about a new condominium type of development. The program was repeated several times and was credited with selling over $150,000 worth of properties within days of the announcements. This often has been called the first radio commercial, but there were many others not as well documented or purchased, and these probably aired as informal arrangements rather than formal commercials.

The AT&T station avoided "direct selling" and prohibited mentioning prices, locations, or offers of samples. They also maintained control over the type of announcement to prevent offense to the listeners. But in 1923, AT&T offered "soft infomercials," which were talks about folklore sponsored by such companies as Macy's department store and Gillette shaving products. At that time, companies would sponsor a program titled with the company name for identification. For example, the Browning-King Clothing Company sponsored the Browning-King Orchestra, with plugs throughout the program for the company by name. In 1924, WHB in Kansas City, Missouri sold tickets to the "Invisible Theater" to the audience to help support the production costs of the program. The first singing commercial was produced to promote the new Wheaties cereal on WCCO in Minneapolis in 1926. In that same year, NBC banned spots adjacent to network programs. NBC also limited commercials to 3.5 minutes per hour. Unfortunately, non-network stations ran commercials for at least 15 minutes of each hour.

In 1928, the newly formed National Association of Broadcasters (NAB) requested that stations avoid airing commercials between 7:00 PM and 11:00 PM, the 4-hour block considered family time, but by the next year sponsors pressed the new CBS network to mention prices.

By 1930, "direct advertising" commercials only avoided mention of prices. By then, advertising agencies, which sold and produced the bulk of the daily programs, demanded stations provide airtime in order to air promos to advertise their programs at no additional cost. By 1931, the advertisements were called *spots*, but they varied in standardization of length. Some spots were sold by word count, which ranged from 50–200 words. Other stations sold their spots by timed segments of 2 minutes or longer. Also at this time, the technique of "mentions" of sponsors' products were worked into plots and dialogue without extra charge. NBC felt this "interweaving" added force and credibility to the product without causing offense.

One of the earliest popular radio programs was *Amos and Andy*, produced in Chicago. The show was recorded on large discs coated in wax and was distributed by mail to other stations. This was the beginning of syndication. At that same time, sponsors discovered that recording their spots on these discs, called electrical transcriptions (ET), to be played to fill the space between programs, guaranteed quality and exact timing in the production and airing. By 1932, the shows produced by the advertising agencies, call "cooperative broadcasting," were completely controlled by the agency. The scripts, casts, and direction were all under the agency's control. The agency just purchased airtime and delivered to the stations the ET of the program they wanted aired.

The passage of the 1934 Communication Act, which created the Federal Communications Commission (FCC), motivated the stations to limit commercials to 10% of airtime at night and 15% during the daytime. No laxatives, patent medicines, or other personal products could be advertised.

Since that time, the rules and regulations controlling commercials have virtually disappeared. The only rule still remaining came from a congressional law stating that tobacco products could not be advertised on radio or television. There are some restrictions designed to protect children viewers and listeners from over-commercialization, but the restrictions are quite liberal, allowing advertisers much freedom in content and the number of commercials aired each hour.

Public Service Announcements

PSAs promote nonprofit organizations and their activities. PSAs generally run on radio and TV stations at no cost to the client. The spots may be produced by the station as a public service, but major national nonprofit organizations produce high-quality, high-budget spots to maximize their effectiveness. To qualify for PSA status and, therefore, to be able to ask stations to run their spots at no cost, an organization must be listed with the state as a nonprofit 501(c)(3) organization. The exceptions to this rule are civic units: cities, counties, states, and even divisions of the federal government qualify for PSA-announcement status.

During an election year, federal rules governing "electioneering communications" go into effect. Such an announcement may not be aired as a PSA if the spot clearly identifies a candidate for federal office or if the spot is schedule to run within 60 days before a general election or 30 days before a primary election. The spot may not be classified as a PSA if it refers to promoting, supporting, opposing, or attacking a federal candidate. Such spots must be paid for (and most stations request payment in advance).

The stations maintain the option to schedule and run any PSA at their convenience, which is why most PSAs run late at night, on weekends, or early in the morning, when demand for availabilities for commercial spots are at a minimum. On the other hand, if a nonprofit organization wishes their spots to run at a specific time, they may use the same spot as a commercial by simply paying full commercial rate to have the spot run on a specific schedule. The military services often want their recruiting spots scheduled to reach the maximum number of the young men and women, so they run their commercials during programs aimed at that target age group; these spots are paid commercials, not PSAs, so that they can specify scheduled times and days.

Writing PSAs requires a special skill because the audience is asked to donate money or useful items or to volunteer their services or labor for no material object in return. The writing must make a strong argument for the legitimacy and urgency of the appeal, and, at the same time, ask for a specific response. PSAs must *sell* the requests as effectively as a commercial by using the same writing and production techniques as those used in producing commercials.

The same sales techniques used in writing commercials and, to a lesser degree, promos are also favored for PSA writing. You will need to rely on gaining sympathy from the audience, and making it feel a little guilty and willing to send money or volunteer time to benefit those not able to help themselves. Empathy may also arouse feelings that will release the purse strings of the audience. Fear is a powerful motivator to drive people to respond to appeals or warnings broadcast as PSAs. Fear of catching a disease, of falling prey to criminals, or of being harmed by weather or other uncontrollable natural phenomena has proven successful in leading the audience to support the requester of assistance.

Promotional Announcements

Promos are spots written and produced to promote programs on the same station that is airing the spot. The concept is based on notifying viewers or listeners of another program broadcast on the same station that they are tuned to at that moment. Promos are considered very important in the highly competitive field of broadcasting. As a result, much time, effort, and consideration in the writing and scheduling of promos goes into a station's letting its audience know about its other programs. Since the income of a station depends on the maximum size of the audience, convincing people to tune into a show requires a special skill in writing and producing promos that will *sell* the audience to tune into a program it might not have planned to watch or listen to.

The key to writing promos depends on depicting the promoted program as important to the viewer or listener. The promo should warn the audience of the folly of missing key dramatic moments and plot twists, winners of talent contests, or the winners or survivors of dreadful competitions. The promo must make the upcoming program absolutely critical to the audience's viewing life. The audience must be teased into wanting to watch or listen to the indicated program. The promo must make an indelible impression on the mind of the audience so that they will remember to tune in to the promoted show. Your writing of a promo fails if it does not clearly impress upon the minds of the audience the station's channel or frequency, the day, and the time of airing of the program.

Some commercials may appear to be promos, but upon closer examination, the audience will find that the spot that looks like a promo actually promotes another station or network. Radio stations often run commercial or promos on television stations, and vice versa, especially if they are owned by the same company. Cross-promotions between cable channels appears to promote a competitor, but again, on closer examination, the viewer will find that both networks are owned by the same corporation.

Commercial Announcements

Advertising is considered one of the basics of American economic strength. Without advertising, consumers would not become aware of new products, the choice in products, how to modify their lives with different products, where to get the products, and how much the products may cost. At the same time, advertising is accused of selling consumers what they do not need and do not even know they want, and once they have it, these consumers do not know what to do with the product. The advertising has just one goal: *sell, sell, sell.*

Advertisements on radio and television are called commercials. This term originated from the first radio operation, AT&T. Originally a telephone and telegraph company, AT&T entered radio at broadcasting's beginning. They billed their regular residential telephone clients on a monthly basis, but the sponsors of programs, along with other irregular long-line clients, were billed as *commercial* operations.

As a commercial writer, you must be a master of persuasion, using all of the techniques of propaganda and emotional appeals to achieve your client's goals. Commercials may be produced in-house at the advertising agency, at an independent studio, or at a broadcast operation. As the writer, you must please at least four groups of people: you must win the approval of the sponsor, the agency, the producer and director, and the audience. Most importantly, you must prove that your sales techniques actually accomplished the goal by motivating the audience to buy the product or service.

Advertising agencies operate by analyzing the ratings of the television shows on which their spots are placed. The Nielsen rating service uses several different methods to determine who is watching which show and for how long. All ratings are based on statistical analysis. A small sample of a specific demographic group is monitored with phone calls, by having them keep diaries, or by electronic means. The results of the small sample are then expanded statistically to cover the entire group. Hopefully, the statistics will accurately reveal who is watching. Enough figures are gathered that, depending on who does the analysis, most anyone can come out a winner in one demographic category or another.

Radio determines its listeners differently. Arbitron traditionally used diaries but discovered that because most radio listening occurs while driving in a vehicle, diaries were not reliable. Arbitron experimented with a portable people meter (PPM) to increase reliability and accuracy in their sampling. The small meter, about the size of a cell phone, is carried by the listeners wherever they go. The meter automatically detects the stations that the listener hears and records that data in the meter. Periodically, the meter is placed in a special docking station, through which the data is transmitted back to Arbitron for analysis. These more accurate ratings could bring about major changes in program schedules and content.

Radio stations' sales departments also use other methods to determine who among the audience is listening, and how many. Contests, public service appearances, and direct responses to commercials present the client with some indication of the value of their advertising.

CALCULATIONS USED IN MEDIA RESEARCH

Ratings % (Average Audience)	Households Using TV (HUT)	Persons Using TV (PUT)
$Rating = \dfrac{Audience}{Estimated\ Universe}$	$HUT = \dfrac{HH\ TV\ sets\ in\ use}{Total\ HH\ Universe}$	$PUT = \dfrac{\#\ Persons\ watching\ TV}{Total\ person\ universe}$
Share of Audience (Share)	Ave. Audience Projection (Projection)	Viewers per Viewing Household (VPVH)
$Share = \dfrac{Rating}{HUT}$	Projection = Rating x Universe	$VPVH = \dfrac{Persons\ Projection}{Household\ Projection}$

Figure 3.1. Ratings charts list the statistical data that provide the sales department with the information they need to convince a possible sponsor to the value of advertising at a certain time block or within a specific program.

Audience Analysis

Demographic groupings are arranged by a person's age, income, education, gender, occupation, and home location. A different method of grouping audience members is called psychographics. Using psychographics, people are grouped by lifestyle, personal interests, hobbies, attitudes, beliefs, and political preferences. The groupings help target specific groups of people for specific products or services so that time and energy are not wasted on people who would not be interested in or capable of purchasing the product being sold. Both analysis methods also help manufacturers develop products for specific groupings and their responses to certain forms of advertising. Increasingly, the study of demographics and psychographics reveals gaps in targeting and provides for specific ethnic or minority groups that were not considered viable customers. As the diversity of the country increases, there are fewer true minorities, and all people, regardless of their background or origination, should be considered as part of the audience.

Audience Analysis Groupings

Demographic	Psychographic
Age	Lifestyle
Income	Personal interests
Education	Hobbies
Gender	Attitudes
Occupation	Beliefs
Home location	Political preferences

One of the most important classifications is age. Each category of age (e.g., children, teens, 18–35-year-olds, young adults, and older adults) responds to different products and to different stimuli. Therefore, every commercial must target the specific age group that will be interested in the product and, most importantly, can be convinced to part with their money. Children also have a major affect not only on products of direct interest to them, but also, as studies have shown, automobile, travel, and home purchases. Most advertisers, regardless of medium, like to target the 18–35-year-old group. This group, in theory, has disposable income and can be easily motivated to spend on impulse items. For that reason, much of radio programming, cable programming, and a high percentage of television programming is aimed at attracting the 18–35 bracket. This, in turn, attracts the high-spending sponsors of products that appeal to this age group.

Another difference among commercials depends on whether the spot is for a national product or a local product or service. Often, the two are combined in one commercial: a nationally produced automobile spot will be tagged with a message for a local dealer and that dealer's address. Local commercials generally cost less for production, are less complex, and tend to be local personality oriented. The emphasis is on the address, phone number, and Web site URL. Also, they focus on price, loan figures, and availability of specific models, with an emphasis on local fashions and traditions. The local seller will concentrate on his or her product or service.

National spots generally are better produced, require a larger budget, have more complex production techniques, and emphasize the product and its quality, characteristics, and value. If a personality is used, then that person must be of national notice—a star in the media—and not the owner or manufacturer. The concentration will be on the institution or company, not a specific product.

Obviously, most commercials, both local and national, will use characteristics from both lists as the client's needs occur, but exceptions do exist. Oreck vacuum cleaner and Orville Redenbacher Popcorn spots break the national rules and try to look as down-home and local as possible. If it works, they use it. Some local and regional advertisers may budget and produce commercials that appear to be national for added sophistication value.

Broadcasting survives through the support earned from income from commercials. That sum amounts to over $15 billion for television and a fraction of that amount for radio. But that amount began to decrease in 2004 as more advertisers spent their money on cable and the Internet. The development of digital technology has made it possible for viewers and listeners to be more selective in their use of media. Delayed recording and selective dubbing have made commercial placement less certain as the audience zips past or ignores commercials. The solutions include creating longer or shorter spots, more interesting commercials to hold the audience, and a technique developed years ago for motion pictures, product placement. A can of a specific band of soda is placed so that the camera shows the brand name clearly. Or a product's name or image may be digitally inserted into the picture at the will of the sponsor, as is done on baseball and football games. That image may vary in the same production depending on whether the distribution is by theatrical film, broadcast television, cable, or DVD release, or for a portable player or game. Such variations in placement require you to study carefully to become aware of the planned distribution of the spot.

In an effort to better understand the audience's reaction to commercials, studies concentrate on trend spotting to determine what the audience wants in both the announcements and the programs. Focus groups viewing samples have been used in the past, but some doubt has been raised regarding the value since the group knows they are expected to show a reaction; their true feelings might be different if they were not sitting in an auditorium for the specific purpose of making judgments. Instead, experiments have shown that watching people's reactions without their knowledge and polling specific groups of people at work may provide more accurate data if a large and systematic sampling is taken.

The length of commercials has now come under question. Over the past 50 years, television commercials were reduced from 2 minutes to 1 minute, and then they settled at 30 seconds. Now longer spots, from 90–120 seconds, that allow for greater development of a story within the spot show signs of better reception from the audience and less of a chance of being skipped or ignored. The longer spots have shown value especially for brand identification, rather than for an individual product. Longer spots provide the base for explaining in greater detail the value of the product or service and its superiority over competitors. The extra time also allows space to reveal specific points on the operation of the product, as well as the specifics of purchase price, sales, rebates, and long-term purchase plans.

Experiments include the production of shorter spots, lasting 5, 10, and 15 second in length, to help spread the sponsor's budget and still remain effective in reaching the audience. Shorter spots must accurately target the audience with one key sales point. The spot must make the point obvious and avoid confusing the audience with too many facts and figures. Short spots become a matter of a rifle shot straight on target rather than the shotgun scatter approach of longer spots.

Commercial-free programs with simple brand identification at the beginning and end of the program have shown increased audience interest since the program continues without breaking the rhythm of the story. This is considered "institutional" selling, relying on building goodwill by avoiding annoying the audience with commercial interruptions.

All of these changes mean you must become extraordinarily aware of the audience and the audience's control over its viewing and listening habits if your commercial is to first, reach an audience; second, be accepted by the audience; and third, make the audience understand and react in a positive manner to the commercial. If it does not sell anything, you have failed.

Ethics

A critical concern of all involved in sales is the ethical guidelines and legal laws and rules of the communication business. Any consideration of ethics becomes a slippery slope since an ethical action on the part of one person may be considered unethical by another. There are no hard-and-fast rules of ethics. Personal ethics should be the guiding force for professional ethical judgments. But more often, the threat of legal recourse or professional punishment provides greater motivation for responsible ethical actions.

Whenever a discussion of ethics is raised, the issue of morals also appears, sometimes as an equal to ethics, and other times as the basis for making ethical judgments. "Moral" comes from the Latin, meaning "way of life," and "conduct" and "ethics" from Greek, meaning "usage" and "character," respectively. There is a difference, but to a commercial writer and broadcast sales staff, the difference is unimportant. What needs to be impressed is that ethics or morals, whichever is acceptable, should help those involved in the complex world of media advertising to use the best of the theoretical background of both.

Ethics involves a method of making choices between good and bad, fair and unfair, true and false, and responsible and irresponsible. Personal ethics is a matter of a person's character; professionally, it is a matter of behavioral conduct when faced with critical decisions of choice. Because sales techniques use the best of communication persuasion techniques, care must be taken to avoid misusing those same techniques. A product or company may be described accurately with veracity, but it also may be described using half-truths, evasions, and untold truths, all of which are unethical. The disinformation disseminated by governments to pacify the press without telling all that is known falls into the same category of unethical communication.

Ethical decisions often fall well within a gray area between true and false, and the final decision, difficult as it will be to make, must be made on the side of truth. If commercials for a client consistently stretch the truth, the consumer will find out eventually, and the credibility of the product, the company, and the media operation will be severely damaged.

One major problem with maintaining ethical standards comes from the conflict between the news and programming departments against the sales department of a media operation. If a news story criticizes a client or even a type of client, that client has the right to withhold financial support from the media operation. The program or news story may well be of benefit to the audience, but, at the same time, may annoy or damage the client. Unfortunately, most of the decisions that must be made from such conflicts will be made on a financial basis. If the client represents major income to the operation, the story or program will be canceled. If the client does not represent a major sacrifice for the operation, the stories may be aired, and the operation will absorb the minor financial loss.

A second type of client control over programming comes from sales contracts that are written with riders containing cancellation clauses for conflicting programming. For example, airlines may have in their contract a clause that calls for cancellation of their commercial within a newscast if an airline crash is going to be covered as a news story in that newscast. This requires that the producer or news director decide whether the story is important enough for their audience that they are willing to lose the income from that commercial, or whether the story can be canceled, letting the newspaper cover it instead. At one time, sales departments were kept totally isolated from programming and news departments. In theory, the separation continues, but it is a very thin wall between sales and news today. News and documentary programs are expensive to produce, and the loss of any support from a major advertiser must be considered, regardless of the ethics of that decision.

In order to help maintain a minimal level of ethics, all media professional organizations publish and expect their members to follow the codes agreed upon by the membership of that organization. The National Association of Broadcasters (NAB), the Radio-Television News Directors Association (RTNDA), the Public Relations Society of America (PRSA), the Society of Professional Journalists (SPJ), the American Advertising Federation (AAF), and the American Association of Advertising Agencies (AAAA) all maintain such codes to provide guidelines for their members. The codes have limited powers to punish any company that violates any of the rules, but unfortunately, the worst offenders do not belong to any of the code organizations. (See Appendix A.)

The Law

Of the many laws that affect citizens and businesses, this text will discuss six areas of greatest concern for writers of spots:

Freedom of speech (The First Amendment)
Deceptive advertising
Obscenity
Defamation
Privacy
Copyrights and trademarks

Freedom of Speech (The First Amendment)

The laws affecting the publication of information, whether as spots, programs, speeches, or print material, are reasonably clear, but through the past years changes in the political structure of the country and attitudes toward communication have brought about changes in how the original laws have been applied, and those changes will continue to occur. When First Amendment issues arise, you should consult an attorney with a specialization in communication law.

The law specifically protects writers from preventing distribution of their works except under three conditions:

1. If the broadcast would hinder a war effort
2. If the material were obscene
3. If the communication would incite acts of violence

Obviously, each of these three exceptions could be interpreted in either very broad or very narrow terms. But these rules are rarely prosecuted. Instead, as a copywriter, you should be aware that there are some specific laws to be followed. Cigarettes may not be advertised; beer may, but without any reference to alcohol content; and hard liquor and wine are not prohibited, but the NAB policy advises against advertising those products. NAB policy suggests actors not be shown consuming alcohol beverages on camera during a spot. Lawyers and medical personnel now may place advertisements, but pharmacists may not list prices of drugs. Some states apply individual restricts on some forms and methods of advertising.

A special category of advertising involves spots for politicians and political issues. An "equal time" rule requires a station to offer the same type and placement of a spot to any legitimate candidate within 60 days of a general election and 30 days before a primary election. The commercial must be offered at the *lowest* unit charged for the same time and amount of time, even if a single spot's price is compared to the price for a large number of a bulk purchase of time. Any spot that identifies a candidate for federal office and any "attack" spots must run as commercials, not as PSAs.

Deceptive Advertising

Two systems of controlling deceptive advertising include self-regulation by the advertising industry and regulation by the Federal Trade Commission (FTC). The advertising industry, over the years, has been attempting to avoid specific federal control of advertising by invoking self-regulation rules to their members. The control can not extend to agencies or advertisers who are not members of the professional advertising field. The temptation to stretch the depiction of products and their value often places the producers in a battle with the sponsor or the agency attempting to create the maximum sales effort.

The FTC regulations are designed to prevent "unfair or deceptive acts or practices in or affecting commerce."[1] This means that any "material representation, omission, or practice that is likely to mislead a consumer acting reasonably under the circumstances"[2] is a violation, and the sponsor may be required to:

1. Stop running the commercial
2. Run a commercial explaining or correcting misleading information

---

[1] 15 U.S.C. sec. 45(a)(i)(1999)
[2] Amrep Corp v. FTC, 798 F 2.nd 1171 (10th Circ. 1985)

3.   Run a commercial contradicting the original spot, admitting
     fault, and at the same time, run a like number of spots in the
     same time frame and the same number of times as the original
     spot campaign

This third punishment was invoked against the Ford Motor
Company in reference to commercials selling the Pinto car in
the 1970s. And in the fall of 2006, the United States attorney of
the eastern district of Missouri reached an agreement with the
Sporting News Company. For 3 years, Sporting News had been
advertising illegal Internet and telephonic gambling enterprises
in print, on the Internet, and on the radio. The company was
fined $4.2 million dollars, and for the following 3 years, it must at
their own expense produce and air $1 million worth of PSAs each
year, informing the public of the illegality of commercial Internet
and telephonic gambling in the United States. Such heavy fines
and punishment should act as a deterrent for advertisers to try to
skirt the law on what can and cannot be sold on the air.

The golden rule for writers is to make certain that all claims are
accurate and independently substantiated for each advertised sales
point. Great care needs to be taken in accurate pricing, especially
for those commercials plugging high percentages of sales. The percentage must be based on the actual last retail price, not a price
increased just before the sale. Endorsements and testimonials from
famous people must be based on that person actually using the
product, and the personality must have a full understanding of the
qualities used in the sales pitch.

Obscenity

Copywriters must take care that the spots they create offend the
smallest portion of the audience possible. A critical measurement
of offense is material that might appear to be pornographic to any
segment of the audience. Good taste and thoughtful consideration should guide a writer to avoid problems in this realm, but
inadvertently, and possibly from an effort to appeal to a specific
segment of the audience, material may fall within the categories of

pornography. The term "pornography" refers to any material that is sexually explicit and is intended to arouse the audience sexually. That is a very broad category, but the two specific areas of pornography of concern to the media writer are spots containing material declared indecent or obscene.

Any material is obscene if is sexually explicit and offensive. Such material is not protected by the First Amendment and may be prosecuted and punished for distribution in any manner.

Material declared indecent is not necessarily obscene and may be distributed on some media, but not broadcasting. Broadcasters are regulated by the FCC, which sets a relatively high and continuously changing standard for what is indecent and cannot be broadcast without fines or threat of loss of the broadcaster's license. The same material may be distributed by cable or satellite without fear of retribution from the FCC.

In 2002, only 8 stations of 15,000 were cited by the FCC for airing indecent content. In 2003, 15 were cited, and in 2004, there were 208 citations (189 of those citations were from two programs). In 2005, there was not a single citation. Unfair rulings have thrown a cloud over broadcast programming, with owners being overly cautious to avoid high fines for material that had been acceptable in the past and is still acceptable on other media but might possibly not be accepted on broadcast media. Even though 80% of the households in this country receive their *broadcast* signals over either cable or satellites, few viewers know or make the distinction between locally originated or broadcast network programming and broadcasting from cable or satellite programming.

An 8-hour time block, from 10:00 PM until 6:00 AM, is considered a safe harbor from children viewing broadcasting. During that time, more relaxed rules allow broadcasting of material that might be considered indecent (but not obscene) at other times of the day.

The difference between indecent and obscene was set down by the Supreme Court in a 1973 case, *Miller v. California*, which defined *obscene* as any material fulfilling all three of the following characteristics:

1. The average person, applying contemporary community stan-
    dards, would find that the work, taken as a whole, appeals to
    the prurient interest.
2. The work depicts or describes in a patently offensive way sex-
    ual conduct specifically defined by the applicable state law.
3. The work, taken as a whole, lacks serious literary, artistic, polit-
    ical, or scientific value.

State laws also apply to the second rule and may add more restrictions.
Part of the problem for broadcasters is that their signal may cover a
broad area of different cities, states, and even national regions that,
when taken together, have a wide range of community standards. Such
a restriction means you must consider the lowest common denomina-
tor of standards when preparing copy for broadcast distribution. Your
awareness of the distribution of whatever you create is critical. Edgier
and more creative work may not be permissible on broadcast outlets;
yet, the same material could play to the same audience by cable or
satellite without the fear of punishment to the distributor.

Defamation

You must avoid attacking any person or company, especially in
terms of reputation. The laws of defamation include libel (referring
to written defamation) and slander (referring to spoken comments).
With the rise of electronic communication, the difference between
slander and libel has become so narrow that in most states the law
applies equally to both, especially since electronic communication
may be a combination of the two.

There are six aspects of a comment that attacks a person's reputation that, if present, may very well cause juries to award damages
in the millions of dollars.

1. There must be actual defamation content, meaning statements
    that cruelly attack the person's reputation.
2. The statement must be false, which is sometimes a very diffi-
    cult aspect to be proved or disproved.
3. The statement must be distributed or published to at least one
    other person.

4. The statement must be specifically identifiable as referring to a specific person, the plaintiff.
5. Malice or the intent to do harm must be proved.
6. There must be intangible or actual damage.

You must be extremely careful to avoid any and all of the aspects listed above, especially in spots comparing or attacking a competing client.

Privacy

The concern for respecting privacy relates to defamation as well. Some of the aspects to avoid include the following:

1. The use of the name or likeness of a person without consent
2. Embellishing or fictionalizing information and placing an individual in a false situation
3. Trespassing without permission by using a long lens or super-sensitive microphones
4. Publishing embarrassing private facts

Again, in the effort to maximize points in commercial copy, you may be tempted to use such information for the benefit of the product or against a competitor. You must avoid such temptation since the courts have had little sympathy for such transgressions, especially in commercials or print advertising.

Copyrights and Trademarks

The control over a writer's work is a two-edged sword. First, copyright laws protect intellectual property, that is, work created within a person's own brain. That, of course, includes whatever you create. It means no one may use your work without permission or payment. The law was passed and has been revised over the years to give creative people a reason to publish and show their work without fear of losing control over and income from their work. The work must be original and must be fixed in a tangible means of expression; in other words, in the case of written material, it must be published. *Published* also means performed on an electronic medium.

Copyright protects the following:

1.   Literature, including computer programs
2.   Music, including lyrics
3.   Dramatic scripts, including music if it is part of the original script
4.   Choreography and pantomime
5.   Photos, maps, graphics, sculpture, and animation
6.   Motion pictures and other media, whether analog or digital

Copyright does not protect an idea, a concept, or a story plot, even if written.

Nor does it protect the basic information used to create a work unless that information is absolutely unique. Works for hire, that is, a script written by a staff writer or a freelancer on contract, is owned by the employer unless a specific contractual agreement giving the ownership rights to the writer was drawn before the work was completed.

A variety of time limits have been modified over the years, generally to increase the time the author or the estate of the author maintains rights and income. Today, works created after 1978 remain in the control of the author for life plus 70 years. Before 1978, works were protected for approximately 50 years. Once works pass into public domain, that is, without any copyright, that work may not be recopyrighted, but the copyright may be transferred by licensing to a new copyright holder.

You must observe and respect music copyrights. A recording of any music may not be used without receiving permission from and paying fees to two sets of copyright holders: first, to the composer and lyricists, assuming they are two different people, and second, to the recording studio that made the recording.

To facilitate what may become a very complicated search to find copyright holders of music, three licensing companies were organized to represent musicians, to collect fees, and to pay the copyright owners. The American Society of Composers, Authors, and Publishers (ASCAP) originated the process, followed later by a competitor, Broadcast Music, Inc. (BMI), and the Society of European Stage Authors and Composers (SESAC), which originally represented European musicians but now also represents domestic performers. To use a recording, the writer or producer must contact the licensing society and negotiate the use and fee. Limits on the number of times the performance may be used with that fee partially depend on the potential audience of the final production or spot. The fee is separate from a performer's fee for live performances, which is set by the union representing the performer.

Limited use of a portion of a copyrighted piece comes under a portion of the law called "fair use." If a portion of the work is used to illustrate a comment, in a news story, as a criticism, in a classroom, or for research, the use may fall under fair use laws if the amount of the original work used is relatively small and is used for noncommercial purposes. That means commercials are not eligible for fair use, but, under some conditions, PSAs and promos may qualify.

With the advent of increased capabilities of digital modification programs, such as Photoshop and MIDI programs, it has not yet been determined by case law whether sampling of music and modifying photos, graphics, films, and video recordings falls under fair use. From an ethical point of view, nobody's work should be used as the basis for a new work without the permission of the original author. At this point, the amount of modification and how recognizable the new work compares to the original may determine the owner of the new work.

Trademarks

Any name, slogan, or symbol that clearly identifies a company or its product is a trademark. Trademarks provide the company with maximum protection for their use in marketing and identification by the consumer. A company is granted exclusive use of a trademark and the rights attached from its first use and publication. A trademark does not need to be registered. Trademarks include

titles of books, magazines, newspapers, film, and television programs, as well as slogans identifying a product or company.

A writer must be careful not to use a trademark as a generic term
for an object or type of product. The following is a list of some of the
common trademarks misused and their proper generic substitutes:

Trademark	Generic Term To Be Used
Frisbee	Miniature flying disc
Pyrex	Heat-resistant cookware
Teflon	Nonstick coating
Coke	Soft drink (except in Texas)
Fiberglass	Glass fiber material
Xerox	Copy machine
Univac	Electronic computer
Scrabble	Crossword game
MACE	Disabling spray
Band-aid	Antiseptic or adhesive bandage

For other possible substitutes, consult an up-to-date stylebook,
such as the *Associated Press Stylebook*.

Writing Spot Copy

Systems and Placement

The broadcast day is divided into time blocks: early, morning drive
time, midday, afternoon drive time, local origination, prime time,
late night, and overnight. The blocks' beginning and end times are
not precisely set; the times depend on whether the distribution is by
radio, television, or cable, and whether the station is non-network,
independent, or network affiliate. Each block offers a different value
to the sponsor, and the price varies accordingly.

The value is determined by the number of viewers or listeners
calculated during the time of the airing of the spot. That number is
determined by the use of the statistical calculations derived from the
ratings system. That figure is then used to determine how valuable
that time slot is in delivering an audience to the sponsor of the spot
at that time of day. At its best, ratings are an approximation, but

throughout the years of broadcasting, the sale staffs and sponsors have accepted and continue to accept those figures as accurately representing the value of their spot.

Programs are separated by a station break, generally running from 10–70 seconds. Programs plan on a specific number of breaks within the program, allowing for a specific time for breaks in a set length of time. Each of the holes planned within a program is designed to air a spot or series of spots. The spaces allowed for spots within a program and between programs are called *availabilities*, or *avails*. The avails must be scheduled and fixed in advance so that sales and promotion departments will know how much time is available for spots to be sold or scheduled. Generally, the sales department has first call for avails. If an avail is not filled with a commercial, than a promo may be inserted. As the value of promos has increased in building audience numbers, promotion departments may fill an avail rather than fill the spot with a commercial. If neither a commercial nor a promo is scheduled for an avail, then a PSA may fill that time slot. Every avail must be filled, with either a commercial, promo, or PSA, because the overall timing of the program has been predetermined to count on a certain amount of time to be filled with spots.

The value of an avail depends partially on whether the spot is placed within a program or within the break between programs. The spots between programs are called adjacencies. Ratings are counted by programs, so a spot within a highly rated program or one scheduled between two highly rated programs will be of greater value, and the sales department will charge more for that placement. For the past several years, the avail for a commercial sold to run within the football Super Bowl has cost approximately $2.5 million dollars for each 30 seconds.

Spot Timing

Generally, the break between network programs is 70 seconds long. That time allows for two 30-second spots and a 10-second spot to run within the 70 seconds. The 10-second spot may be only 8 seconds long if a 2-second station identification is required to run every hour on the hour. A typical local newscast will be scheduled to run for 28:50. That allows for a 70-second break following the newscast before the next program. Most newscasts offer 6 minutes of avails within the program. That leaves 22:50 for news, minus the opening, the closing, and section transitions, leaving, at the maximum, approximately 21–22 minutes for actual news reporting.

Other types of programs, depending the on time of day, offer approximately the same avails schedule. There are restrictions for programs produced for an audience consisting primarily of children, and there are more lenient times for late-night and weekend programming.

Avails for program interruption follow a fairly standard pattern of a break after the opening scene, which teases the audience and grabs it to stay with the program. The second break in a half-hour program will come near the mid-point, and the last break should be scheduled to follow the climax, but hopefully before the resolution so that the audience will stay through the break to find out how the story ends.

Timing of spots must be absolutely accurate. The completed spot will be aired in an avail that is computer controlled. If the spot is too long, it will be cut; if short, an anathema of broadcasting, dead air, will occur. In reality, no spot is aired until it has been viewed and time-checked before loading it in the playback system. Each word must count as a critical part of the spot.

The question of how much material may be squeezed into a specific spot determines the type of production and how much music and how many sound effects and other production techniques are used. General guidelines for you as a writer to follow are given in the chart below.

Copy Length, Determined by Time or Word Count

Length of Spot	Word Count
10 seconds	25
20 seconds	45
30 seconds	65
60 seconds	120
90 seconds	180
2 minutes	200–250

Accurate timing of copy is achieved by reading out load while including pauses for all effects and music that are critical to the copy.

Copywriting

The term *copywriting* belonged originally to the art and science of
creating the words and designs for print advertising. Since that time,
the term has been attached to any writing of advertising materials,
whether it is for print, electronic, or now digital advertising on the
Internet.

Writing copy for spots, whether the spot is a commercial, promotion, or public service announcement, is still copywriting and
shares most of the techniques and methods of communicating to
an audience. Certain differences exist among commercials, promos,
and PSAs, but those differences were pointed out earlier in this
chapter.

All spot writing may be compared to writing miniature dramas.
Each spot must capture the audience's attention, hold its interest,
and then convince them to take some kind of action. To control the
audience in that manner, you must introduce a conflict, characters,
and a story line; build to a climax; and then solve the problem at
the resolution. The solution, of course, is to motivate the audience
to take the action anticipated and preferred by the sponsor. All of
this may need to be accomplished in 30 seconds, or even sooner for
a 20-, 10-, or 5-second spot. A 1-minute, 90-second, or 2-minute-long
spot allows greater leeway in reaching the same goals, but those are
still very brief time spaces to develop the story needed to accomplish
the purpose of the spot.

The spot must grab the audience members, not letting them leave for
a snack or potty break, but rather making them want to stay to satisfy
their curiosity about the conflict laid out to them. The conflict is critical:
it may be based on exposing a problem in the world that needs assistance (a PSA), a gripping story to be broadcast later (a promo), or
a need aroused in the audience to purchase something (a comml).
To develop that perceived need, the writer may use music to arouse
emotion or as a reminder of good or bad times, humor to keep the

audience waiting for the punch line, or a clever gimmick to intrigue it. You must dazzle the audience with your creativity as you develop the drama. A drama needs characters, but more important than strong characters is a strong story line. The story must show the audience members that if they stay with the spot, they will learn to solve a problem in their life.

Some of the tools used in dramatic structure include emotion by creating a sense of fear in the audience of consequences if it does not purchase or use the product indicated. Other emotions evoked are happiness, fantasy, and of course, sexual arousal. The product may show the user how to achieve a state of happiness, to reach personal fantasies about travel, to acquire wealth or power, and of course, to reach their sexual goals through the use of the product. The characters used to achieve these effects may be authoritative figures such as a medical doctor, lawyer, or scientist, or else they may use the testimony of a famous person. Such testimonials of sports and entertainment stars or personalities who gained fame through politics or adventures add credibility to the claims of the commercial.

Next, the audience must be held through the sales pitch, which may be a hard sell or a more soft, subtle sell, which the audience might not even recognize as a sales message. Although hard sells used by cars dealers and furniture sales personnel appear to cross the line of maintaining reasonably good taste, the techniques work, or else there would not be so many spots produced in that mode. The most subtle type of spots are called *institutional*, produced to keep the company's name in the memories of the audience, without any specific sales goal in mind.

Other sales styles may be more sophisticated and appeal to a different audience. From blue-collar settings to fancy settings, the targeted buyers, such as homemakers, potential home purchasers, vacationers, hunters, sports fans, and travelers, all may react to a different appeal. Other audience segments chosen by a study of demographics (as covered earlier in this chapter) may indicate that the spot should be designed to appeal to a specific ethnic or nationalistic group. As the diversity of this country increases, minority groups once thought of as too small to be specific targets have gained significance. Spots appealing to Hispanic, African-American, Southeast Asian, and Eastern European populations have proven beneficial to both those populations and to the sponsors.

Young people, who make up a major portion of the population with disposable income and easy-to-affect spending habits, may respond to their music and to characters depicting their lifestyle, from new wave to punk rock to high tech. Too narrowly targeting a specific demographic group may turn off other groups who disapprove of others' lifestyles and habits. You cannot write a spot to appeal only to you or your immediate group; the spot must be written as a result of research that shows where the appeal must be aimed to accomplish the sales goal.

Once you have the audience interested, then you have to close the deal by showing the solution. For a commercial, the solution requires the audience to purchase a product, attend a event, or take a vacation. For a promo, you want the audience members to be certain to watch or listen to the program and to tell their friends about it also. For a PSA, you hope the audience members will send money, volunteer their services, or in some manner take part in activity to support the nonprofit organization. Without a response, you have failed as a copywriter.

Some of the techniques that work show (remember, television is a visual medium) how something works better than anything produced by a competitor; that the price offers an excellent value, beats the competitor, or cannot be matched by anyone else. The best commercials concentrate on the product (except for some local spots, which may concentrate on the dealer or local merchant) to build loyalty beyond the one spot. The name value is important; it is critical that a spot will leave the name of the sponsor imbedded in the minds of the audience. If a few minutes after the spot has aired the audience has no idea who or what it has just viewed, then the spot failed.

The solution must tell the audience where to get the product, where it can help a nonprofit, or where and when it is to watch the promoted program. The price also must be shown clearly, especially if price is a key sales item. Such sales pitches as percentage off, rebates, or other money matters should be obvious, with clear indication as to how such matters may affect the final price. When a sale occurs, it should be clear how long the sale lasts, when the item may be available, and location, location, location. The location includes the address, being specific in a large metro area where finding a merchant may be confusing and difficult for the consumer, who will not bother if it is a problem. The location also includes the phone number, including a 1–800 number if available, and the URL of the Web site for the company, which is becoming more important every day. You must make it easy and convenient for the consumers to find the product so that they may make a purchase. The specific times and dates of the promo must appear so boldly so as not to be missed and, in such a manner, to impress in the mind of the audience the time, date, and channel. If a program has its own URL, that should also be featured in the spot. PSAs also may be time- and date-critical, with such information clearly shown. URLs are very important for nonprofits.

Writing Traps to Avoid

Research will target precisely who the audience should be, and the copy should accurately reflect that target by appealing specifically to that audience. No time may be wasted with extra verbiage, and the choice of words must fit the audience without sounding pretentious. Slang expressions should be avoided unless those expressions are part of the targeted audience's normal method of communicating. Remember, even though you may be targeting a specific audience, broadcasting is a mass medium, and many in the audience will not be members of the targeted audience and may very well be turned off or away from a spot because of the language used.

Avoid passive verbs. They take space in a spot but say nothing. Always use action verbs that move the subject forward.

Avoid gender-specific terms unless the product is aimed at a specific gender. The person operating a camera is not a *cameraman*, but rather a *camera operator*. Use *firefighter* instead of *fireman*.

Avoid false claims, exaggerations (beyond reasonableness), false testimonials, false depictions, and language and scenes in poor taste. Taste is very difficult to determine because taste may be determined by cultural and age differences. Use common sense and the golden rule: do not write anything you would not do or say to your grandmother's face. Stereotypes are a necessity in spot writing due to the short time allowed to develop an environment, a story line, and characters. But negative stereotypes must be avoided. That means using a specific ethnicity, religion, age, gender, or cultural class as a negative character or example is not acceptable. Positive or neutral stereotypes help the audience quickly understand points made in a spot without lengthy establishing scenes or dialogue.

The temptation to use sexual or violent scenes or language to make a point must be avoided. Using attractive actors, if the product or scene requires such casting, is acceptable as long as the attraction is not based only on a sexual basis. The argument that sex sells cannot be denied, but quality copywriting avoids using sex and violence gratuitously as it turns people away from viewing rather than attracting them. Targeting the incorrect audience must be avoided. Specifically targeting young people for beer commercials when a portion of that audience would be underage and illegal for purchasing or consuming such a product is unethical. To use high-speed and dangerous driving depictions to sell cars that appeal to young people also is unethical.

Copy Formatting

The form that copy takes on the printed page signifies whether the writer is knowledgeable of professional writing techniques and standards or not. The standards vary among levels of media and even among individual studios and production operations, but there are basic tools used to place written material on a page so that everyone involved in the actual production of the spot understands what the writer had in mind and what concept the writer was trying to express.

Two basic formats dominate the industry: single-column, sometimes called *film style,* and double-column, called *television* or *AV format*. Spots produced on film and single-camera digital video tend to use single-column as most directors with a film background prefer that format. Directors with live television backgrounds tend to be more comfortable with double-column scripts. Double-column scripts also tend to include much more specific shot framing and movement detail than single-column scripts. Single-column scripts describe briefly scenes and general action but seldom specify shot framing or talent movements. The double-column format very often specifically indicates framing, movement of both camera and talent, and transitions. Graphics, audio, and special effects, along with storyboards, are more easily incorporated within double-column scripts than single-column ones.

Both single- and double-column scripts are viewed with the assumption that you have carefully written precise instructions after much thought of how you want the spot to look and what the audio should sound like. Indicate music type, tempo, and a possible example of the type of music you were hearing in your head. Special effects, either audio or video, need to be described in enough detail that the director will know what you envisioned. Be specific, but do not try to direct the spot. Let the producer, director, and producing crew understand what you are trying to say, and give them the tools to fulfill your vision. Use professional abbreviations and terminology. (See Chapter 2.)

Instructions for Dual-Column Format Using Microsoft Word

Header

Pull down VIEW → HEADER AND FOOTER.
Within the block, insert name, code, date, titles, and other pertinent information.
Tab to the right, and add copy on that side (it automatically formats flush right).
Double-space, and then add VIDEO at left margin, and AUDIO in the middle.
Double-space again.

Double-Check

Pull down PRINT PREVIEW. It will show the header in position on the page. Click off, and then click CLOSE in the header frame.

Setting Cells

Pull down TABLES. Select 2 columns and 4–6 rows.
Adjust the vertical border by pulling to approximately 2.5.

Setting Spacing

Wipe the AUDIO column.
Pull down FORMAT, click PARAGRAPH, and click DOUBLE-
    SPACE.

Removing Borders

Wipe the entire page.
Pull down FORMAT.
Click BORDERS AND SHADING.
Click NONE.

Entering Copy Within Cells

Video cells are *always in caps*.
Copy will automatically single-space and will expand the cell, if
    needed.
To move to the AUDIO cell, hit the TAB key.
Audio cells require *caps* for instructions, and uppercase and lower-
    case letters for all copy to be read.
Copy will automatically double-space.
At the end of the pair of cells, add an extra line at the bottom of the
    VIDEO column.

To Add Cells

At the bottom of the last AUDIO column, press TAB, and a new
    pair of cells will appear.

Modifying Cells

Pull down TABLE and follow the options.

LAW & ORDER PROMO CODE 2835 KPRC-TV	Prime time 30 seconds Fall 2/7/04—Spring 2005

VIDEO	**AUDIO**

1. XCU FLASHING POLICE
     CAR LIGHTS
	1. ANNCR: Tonight at 9 on
	             Law and Order

2. MS BRISCO AND ANXIOUS PACING
    BLACK FATHER
	2. FATHER: She's not the type of girl to run off.
	   You assume she's just out doing drugs or
	   Whatever because she's black ?

3. MS CRIME SCENE; TECHNICIANS, POLICE CARS, LOGAN AND BRISCO	3. ANNCR: A serial killer …
4. CU LOGAN AND BRISCO	4. LOGAN: It's the same m-o as the others. Twelve, thirteen, preteens…female and black.

5. WS CROWD OF BLACKS YELLING,
    WAVING FISTS AND SIGNS
    IN FRONT OF POLICE
    HEADQUARTERS
	5. ANNCR: With an explosive motive !!

6. MS CROWD WITH MIDDLE-AGED BLACK WOMAN, CRYING IN FRONT.	6. She was my baby !!!

7. STILLS OF LAW AND ORDER CAST,
    KEY LOGO OVER
	7. Tonight at nine on K-P-R-C,
	   Channel two.

8. FADE BLACK	

Figure 3.2. Spot dual-column script format is the same for other media productions, including specific details of shot framing, transitions, and audio.

Every shot must have some audio indicated, even if it is a continuation from a previous shot. Each shot should be described in the following order:

Transition (A zoom is a camera movement, not a transition)
Shot framing
Subject description
Subject movement (if any)
Camera movement (if any)

Graphics and background visuals must list everything to be shown and the framing for each item. Indicate the background, color, spacing, and texture. Double-check accuracy of telephone numbers, addresses, prices, and URLs.

Avoid abbreviations in copy to be read, and spell out words as they need to be pronounced. (*NASA* is as a single word, but *K-U-H-T* has each letter pronounced separately.) Phonetize unusual, non-English, and difficult-to-pronounce words. (Place the phonetized version in parenthesis before the actual word.) Spell out numbers to make them easier to read accurately and also to provide for an accurate word count. Use contractions only when a contraction would be part of a character's method of speaking. Avoid AM and PM. Use *morning, afternoon,* or *evening* instead.

Instructions for Single-Column Format Using Microsoft Word

Header

Same as dual-column, except single-column does not use a header on every page.

Setting Tab Positions

Set margins at 1 inch for the top, bottom, left, and right.

Place numbers for reference only, as illustrated below:

0   5   15   20   40   45   55   60
....

Make certain tabs are set for 5 spaces.

Automatic Formatting

It is recommended that ALL automatic features are disabled. Go to
FORMAT, pull down to AUTO FORMAT, and check OPTIONS for
the settings you want.

Using Tabs

Tabs are useful to move cursor from the left margin to the "5" and
"15" positions. You must watch for ending lines at the "45" and
"55" positions.

Using Centering

It is usually faster and more convenient to use the centering control for entering characters' names, the delivering mode, and in
some cases, the actual dialogue. As you type the delivering mode,
make certain it fits within the "20" to "40" space. Make certain the
dialogue fits within the "15" to "45" space.

Bottom of the Page

Make certain you do not split a scene at the bottom of the page.
Start at the top of the next page if an entire scene cannot fit on the
space left at the bottom of the page.

Radio Copy Instructions

Each line of radio copy needs to be numbered, even if the same character continues a speech. Margins for line numbers and character

CLIENT: Sam's Pet Shop   Sarah Jones
TITLE: The Doberman   2-15-04
30 Sec   Local, testimonial

---

1. INT   SAM'S PET SHOP INTERIOR LOOKING OUT TO STREET   DAY   1

    Wild sound auto doors open/close, store nat sound as floppy-eared Doberman
    enters with owners at his side, owner visible from waist down only.

DOBERMAN
I may not be Lassie, but you can believe me
when I say that Sam's Pet Shop is the best
pet store in town.

2. INT   INTERIOR OF STORE, DOG & OWNER WANDERING THE AISLES   DAY 2

    MS rear of Doberman and owner pushing shopping cart down aisle

DOBERMAN
They stock all the top brands of everything
a discerning dog needs and wants.

    CU large bag of dog food as it lands in cart followed by treats

DOBERMAN
Pedigree, Iams, Science Diet

Milkbones, Jerky Treats, Pig's Ears

    OS Doberman looking at toys as owner reaches for rope toy

DOBERMAN
Rubber balls, squeaky toys and rope !!!

3. INT   STORE CHECK OUT STAND DOG & OWNER LOADED CART   DAY 3

    Clerk checks contents of the cart, owner pays cashier reaches across
    counter and gives dog a treat.

DOBERMAN
And the best part of all – it's the only
store in town, where I'm welcome !!!

4. INT   SAM'S PET SHOP LOGO   DAY 4

DOBERMAN
Sam's Pet Shop – where pets are family too.

                                             FADE OUT

Figure 3.3. Single-column spot script copy is the same as dramatic script format. It includes dialogue and complete scene descriptions.

RADIO COMMERCIAL FORMAT

SPONSOR:	Star Stores	Length: 1:00
AGENCY:	Smith & Sons	RUN: Fall

1.	VOICE 1	Okay, you can start this Star Slurpee commercial now
2.	VOICE 2	Who are you?
3.	1.	I'm the truth-in-advertising watch dog
4.	2.	Uh-huh
5.	1.	I'm watching you
6.	2.	Right
7.	1.	So watch it
8.	2.	Right, OK, cue the birds,
9.	SFX	(BIRDS IN BG-UP AND UNDER)
10.	2.	Once upon a time in slurpee land, a million years ago
11.	1.	Don't exaggerate
12.	2.	Once upon a time in slurpeeland, a hundred years ago?
13.	1.	That's better
14.	2.	There was a beautiful fairy princess named Lorilee
15.	1.	Not believable
16.	2.	There was a girl named Sheila
17.	1.	OK
18.	2.	She just loved slurpin' slurpees
19.	1.	What's a slurpee?
20.	2.	It's a cold drink that's made outta ice. She found out that
21.		Star's were selling the 22 ounce cup of freezing cold treat
22.		for only 49 cents.
23.	1.	Is that true?
24.	2.	It's true, she went to Stars for a 49-cent slurpee and
25.		she loved it
26.	1.	True, true, and true

Figure 3.4. Radio spot script copy format uses a number of each line and wide margins.

names can be flush left, but the margins for copy to be read should be set at 1.5 inches from the left and 1.5 inches from the right. The wider margins make reading easier as the reader's eyes scan back and forth from one line to the next. Single-space for instructions, double-space between announcer lines, and if possible, triple-space between lines read by different talents.

Music and SFX may be underlined, but this is not necessary. Indicate whether music is up full, faded under or behind dialogue, or faded out completely. If you use music lyrics instead of dialogue, the lyrics must be transcribed and cleared with ASCAP or BMI. Be careful to avoid overpowering dialogue with music or SFX in the background. Do not describe something you cannot hear. Describe the sound effects so that they tell the audience what it will hear.

Production Values

Despite the best intentions of you as the writer and creator of a spot, you have little control over the final production or the production techniques used to produce your spot. Both are set more by financial matters. The budget allotted to produce the spot and the distribution methods both will affect the funds available to actually produce the spot. If the spot will be distributed locally, the costs will be less as compared to the same spot if it were to be distributed regionally across several states or in major cities. Regional spot budgets do not match budgets produced for a national marketing campaign. Most local spots, depending upon the size of the market, will be produced by a small agency, a local television station, a local production studio, or a cable outlet. The format choices will be between multi-camera in-studio video or single-camera electronic field production, recorded in either standard definition (SD) or 16-mm film. Each of these formats with today's equipment will provide the basis for a highly professional production at a minimal cost, depending on the complexity of the script.

Regional productions step up the quality by using higher-quality equipment and larger crews and by taking more time. The same basic formats will be used, with the addition of 35-mm film and medium-quality high-density (HD) recording, but more likely there is a greater chance that the final distribution will be through HD or 35-mm film.

National spots increase the budget, size of crew, and quality of equipment and may handle a much more complex script. Recording and distribution more than likely will be on an HD format or on 35-mm film. Each of the variables depend on two basic factors: the complexity of the script and the availability and size of the budget. As a writer, you need to be aware of not only the budget, but also of the plans for distribution and the demands of the client in order to meet their specific desires.

And the last hint: whatever you place on paper, your copy will not be the same as you thought it was going to be. By the time the sponsor, producer, director, and talent make their "suggestions," you probably will not recognize your work. But the possibility always exists that the final work will unfold even better than you had envisioned.

Summary

Spots, as aired on broadcast stations, cable channels, motion picture theaters, and on the Internet, fall into three categories: PSAs, promos, and commercials. PSAs sell the audience to support nonprofit organizations. Promos sell the audience to watch another program on the same channel or station. Commercials sell the audience products and services. The funds raised by selling commercials pay for production costs and airtime for programs distributed on visual and aural media. Promos are internal productions, so no cost passes within the stations creating and using them. PSAs are aired without cost as a public service of broadcast stations but are not required by cable or satellite operations. The three must sell a concept, a product, a service, a program, or a charity.

Avoiding unethical, deceptive, and obscene copy, and not defaming or invading the privacy of individuals or companies is critical to the business of writing spots. Copyrights, music licensing, and trademarks must be respected. Timing and targeting specific audiences is a necessity for success in spot writing. Script formats for writing spots vary little from standard dual-column, single-column, and radio formats. The scripts a writer creates for spot production seldom will be finished as originally written by the writer; they will be modified to please the client and to meet budget requirements.

Be Sure To...

1. Double-check all laws affecting your spot.
2. Make certain you are well within ethical and moral standards.
3. Make certain you are not deceiving the audience.
4. Make certain you are not breaking obscenity laws.
5. Make certain you have not defamed anyone or any corporation.
6. Make certain your have not violated anyone's privacy.
7. Avoid violating any trademarks or copyrights.
8. Double-check music, performance, and union clearances.

Exercises

1. Visit the local radio or TV station that has been on the air the longest. Ask if they have a history of the station: when it started broadcasting, what type of programs they aired, and how the programs were first paid for. Write a brief history of the station's changes in terms of how it paid for itself.
2. Record a half-hour TV sitcom or dramatic program. Break down the format of the program. How long before the first commercial, and how long is that break? How much time passes before the next commercial break and the third? Calculate the ratio of programming to commercial time.
3. Do the same as Exercise 2 with a TV newscast.
4. Do the same as Exercise 2 with an hour-long block of your favorite radio station.
5. Do the same as Exercise 2 with a cable sitcom or drama. Make certain it is *not* from one of the major TV networks, but rather that it originates from the cable network.

Additional Sources

Print

Day, Louis A. *Ethics in Media Communications: Cases and Controversies.* 2nd ed. Belmont, CA: Wadsworth Publishing, 1997.

Friedmann, Anthony. *Writing for Visual Media.* 2nd ed. Boston: Focal Press, 2006.

Garrand, Timothy. *Writing for Multimedia and the Web.* 2nd ed. Boston: Focal Press, 2001.

Hacker, Diana. *A Pocket Style Manual.* 3rd ed. Boston: Bedford/ St. Martin's Press, 2000.

Hilliard, Robert L. *Writing for Television, Radio, and New Media.* 8th ed. Belmont, CA: Wadsworth Publishing, 2004.

Kessler, Lauren, and Duncan McDonald. *When Words Collide: A Media Writer's Guide to Grammar and Style.* 6th ed. Belmont, CA: Wadsworth Publishing, 2004.

Lutzker, Arnold P. *Copyright and Trademarks for Media Professionals: Broadcast, Cable, Film, Internet, Multimedia, Satellite, WWW.* Boston: Focal Press, 1997.

Vale, Eugene. *Screen and Television Writing.* Revised ed. Boston: Focal Press, 1998.

Willis, Edgar E., and Camille D'Arienzo. *Writing Scripts for Television, Radio, and Film.* 3rd ed. Fort Worth, TX: Harcourt Brace Jovanovich College Publishers, 1993.

Zelezny, John D. *Communications Law; Liberties, Restraints, and the Modern Media.* 5th ed. Belmont, CA: Wadsworth Publishing, 2006.

Web

www.ammi.org
www.televisiontoys.com/Old TV spots

CHAPTER 4

News

The conflict between the men who make and the men who report the news is as old as time. News may be true, but it is not truth, and reporters and officials seldom see it the same way... In the old days, the reports or couriers of bad news were often put to the gallows; now they are given the Pulitzer Prize, but the conflict goes on.

—James Reston, U.S. journalist, 1966

News is the distribution of information affecting people or information of an interest to the largest audience.

Introduction

The passing of information to the general populace has a long and often confrontational history. People generally welcome good news, but bad news has to serve a specific purpose to be acceptable. Yet, one of the greatest attractions, as shown by the size of the audience and number of readers, is bad news; gory, bloody, violent, and yes, sex-filled news. The contradiction between what people should be interested in and the stories that attract the largest audience has yet to be resolved, but that fact affects the decision making in the gathering, editing, and delivering of news. It does not matter whether the medium is print, television, radio, or the Internet.

This chapter will be dedicated to the gathering, editing, preparation for, and the delivery of news at a professional level on electronic media, with the understanding that the reality of the financial support for the delivery of news is predicated on the audience's perceived likes and whims of the moment.

The Fourth Estate

Many of the traditions and highest standards of news reporting were established by the print industry. That does not guarantee that all print publications follow the same high standards today. A wide range of publication standards exist in the print world. The style and choice of delivery may be compared among the grocery store gossip peddlers, to the *New York Times, Washington Post, Los Angeles Times,* and *Chicago Tribune,* to the weekly news magazines like *Time* and *Newsweek.* Filling the gap in between are the dailies of smaller cities, weekly papers serving rural areas, and national publications like *USA Today.* The consistent high standards of print media did not occur overnight, but rather over a period of several centuries of fulfilling the responsibilities of what became known as the *Fourth Estate.* Originally, the other three estates were the aristocracy, the church, and the common people. Today, it is felt that the other three are the three branches of the modern democratic system: the executive branch, the legislature, and the judiciary branch. The Fourth Estate is expected to act as a watchdog over the actions of the other three. This places journalists in a confrontational position that would not work if it were not for the First Amendment in this country. The very responsibility of the Fourth Estate to report corruption, misuse of power, and the mistreatment of the less powerful and the poor places them in direct opposition to those in power and those wanting to gain power by illegal or unethical means. The general public often does not want to or cannot understand the complexity of our legal system, our economic system, and the general workings of the world. To overcome ignorance depends on truthful and accurate reporting from journalists, even though often the reported news is misunderstood or misinterpreted by the audience that most needs accurate information.

The burden to fulfill the Fourth Estate's responsibilities falls on all news media, regardless of the tradition, the level of perceived professional standing, or the method of distribution.

Print Newswriting Basics

In-depth description of writing and reporting for the print media will be left to specialized print journalism texts. The author assumes that a journalist preparing for a career in any one medium eventually will be required by convergence to work and write in any one or all of the other media. Therefore, at least a cursory knowledge of all reporting methods prepares a reporter for any future career opportunity.

As in all of the media, someone has to investigate, research, and gather information before a story may be written. In print, that job falls to the reporter. Print reporters tend to specialize and often are assigned specific areas called *beats*. Some reporters are general-assignment reporters and are assigned whatever story needs to be covered as the day proceeds. Regardless of the assignment, the reporter must gather information. The information may come by telephone, the Internet, on the street from personal contacts, from the organization's morgue (the repository of all published stories and archival information), the research staff, or from personal files maintained by the individual reporter. Police, city, state, national files, and corporate files (if accessible) also become sources for story information. Regardless of the original or primary source, in some manner, all information must be checked and cross-checked to make certain of its accuracy. In the print world, there tends to be more time and people available to achieve that certainty of accuracy than in the electronic world. All media must face some type of deadline, but in print there is more flexibility available for research and certainty in the facts of the story.

Once written, one or more editors then take over the process of checking not only facts, but also grammar and the company's style, the style as documented by the Associated Press (AP, the international press information organization), or both. The AP provides its subscribers with a constant flow of information gathered and edited by their staff scattered around the world. The copy from the AP is called *wire copy,* from the days when that information was telegraphed to the AP home office and then on to the papers. The AP is a nonprofit news cooperative owned by its members who provide news coverage to newspapers and radio and television stations around the world. The *AP Stylebook and Libel Manual* is the bible of the news business,[1] providing a guide in grammar, spelling, punctuation, and usage of the English language.

An interesting set of editing and proofreading symbols become the code between the editor and the writer. The codes indicate

---

[1] The Associated Press Stylebook and Briefing on Media Law, 2004.

EDITING AND PROOFREADING SYMBOLS

The same symbols are used for copyediting and for print media as well as electronic media. The difference between copyediting in print and electronic editing here is one more chance to make a change before the copy is set to be printed.

The following common symbols are used universally.

_℮_   Delete; take it out

⊂   Close up; write some thing as one word

_℮_   Delete and close up

∧   Insert word, letter or punctuation with a caret

#оα| Insert a space (or insert a space)

⁋   New paragraph

STET   Let it stand as written

∿   Transpose; the change order

SP   Spell out an abbrev. Or a figure, as (200)

⹀   Set in capital letters

/   Set in lowercase letters

ITAL   Set in italic

BF   Set in boldface

∨   Insert apostrophe

∧   Insert comma

⊙   Insert period

⊙   Change a comma to a period

⊙   Insert colon

∨ ∨   Insert quotation marks

RUN IN Run in

⌐   With preceding words

Start a new line

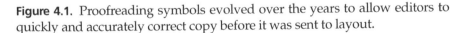

Figure 4.1. Proofreading symbols evolved over the years to allow editors to quickly and accurately correct copy before it was sent to layout.

corrections that need to be made in the copy. All news operations, whether print or electronic, use the same symbols, with minor variation depending on the specific newsroom operation.

The writing of the story for print follows the traditional inverted triangle format. That is, the most important fact comes first, followed by increasingly less important information to fill out the story's detail. The first line, the *lead*, is critical. It must grab the readers and motivate them to continue to follow the story. The five "Ws," and sometimes "H," should be answered as early as possible in the story: *who, what, when, where, why,* and *how*. Both *why* and *how* need to be handled carefully since both must rely on at least a minimum level of conjecture or opinion. Some publications have moved away from a strict use of the triangle to create "interesting" stories rather than fact-based stories. Readers often find the inverted triangle difficult to read to the end once they have absorbed the key information in the lead and first few sentences. The inverted triangle serves a useful purpose for the editor and layout of the paper; the story may be trimmed and shortened easily by cutting copy from the end of the story since the information at and near the end is the least important.

Most daily newspapers must compete with local and network television stations reporting national, regional, and local news carried on their afternoon newscasts. Few afternoon papers have survived that competition and have switched to a morning delivery to avoid direct competition with afternoon television newscasts. Newspapers allot more time and staff to preparing their reports than television or radio. As a result, most print stories tend to be more accurate and comprehensive than stories reported on radio and television. The electronic media do not have the time or newsrooms staffed with the resources to match print operations.

Layout of the Print Copy Page

The layout of a story on the page as it leaves the reporter's computer varies with the operation of individual companies. But there are some basic standards that are fairly common and are universally followed. Each story starts on a new page. At the top, usually on the left corner, are the reporter's name, the date of submission (and sometimes the edition of the publication), and most importantly, a *slug*. The slug is a one- or at most two-word title of the story. It needs to be descriptive to separate it from any other similar story, yet as brief as possible. The slug follows the story from its inception until it is filed in the morgue.

A0401
Rm

AM CONGRESS 50

A new 5-cents-a-gallon gas tax is law.

President Bush signed the bill authorizing the tax

while vacation at his ranch in Crawford, Texas.

The additional tax will help balance the budget and encourage

people to conserve energy.

Figure 4.2. The format for the print news copy page includes the story, a slug, and identifying information such as the date, edition, and reporter's name.

Electronic Newswriting Basics

Writing news copy for electronic transmission, radio, television, or the Internet does not vary in basic journalistic content as much as in the form and methods of delivery. Broadcast stories are complete units that stand alone. Unlike print, which uses the inverted pyramid to allow editing from the bottom up, the broadcast story should be written to fit within a designated amount of time. Because broadcast stories are measured in time (minutes and seconds), they must capture the audience from the very first words. In addition, the broadcast reporter may have only 15–30 seconds to tell the story. Every item in broadcasting must be timed to the maximum of each story's allotted time in the typical newscast, which airs approximately 22 minutes of actual news. Two ways of accomplishing this are either through unusual phrasing or by loading the first line with facts. Therefore, the inverted triangle of print reporting is not necessarily followed in electronic media.

An example of a first line written with unusual phrasing might be:

> "The lame duck keeps limping along. Congress met for the third day of its lame duck session today. It failed to act on the president's tax proposals."

An example of a first line loaded with facts could be:

> "The 5-cents-a-gallon gas tax is law. President Clinton signed the bill authorizing the tax today while visiting New York City."

A common structure for developing and creating a broadcast news story is called *dramatic unity*. The three points of the story are *climax*, *cause*, and *effect*.

Climax	Give the point of the story in the same way that a headline introduces a story.	HISD students start class an hour earlier next year.
Cause	Tell why an event happened and the circumstances surrounding it.	The Houston Independent School District Board voted last night to lengthen the school day 50 minutes at all elementary schools.
Effect	Give the context of the story and possibly some insight into what the story means.	This is another effort to raise test scores. Board members also expressed the hope that this will ease the burden for single working parents.

Newswriting Guidelines

Every news story has, at its heart, a conflict. Person against person, people against nature, nature against people, or groups of people against other groups make up the usual conflicts. Conflict is the basis for drama; without opposing forces there is no dramatic force. You do not need to invent the conflict—just find it. Research is a matter of opening your eyes, ears, and mind to the neighborhood. Crimes such as murders, rape, robberies, and assaults obviously have the conflict of victim against criminal. But the same story may have a deeper conflict that needs to be brought out by looking at the cause and by looking for the effect.

The second reporting guideline answers the five "Ws," and sometimes "H." *Who, what, when, where, why,* and maybe *how* ask the questions to be answered. The answers to as many of those questions in the lead and next sentence of a story may be all that are needed, especially in short newscasts. The lead is the first sentence; in the example above, the climax. That first sentence is the most important of any story and should be considered as carefully as any other. The *why* is important in longer stories: Why did the event happen? Next in importance is the *how:* How can the event be avoided? Each may add important dimensions and interest to the story. Remember, every story has a beginning, a middle, and an end. The lead-in from the anchor and the tag at the end of the story complete the story.

The story must be written in a conversational (but not slang), clear style. Avoid popular terms and language unless a word signifies an important element in the story. Such common terms as *guy* or *gal*, when referring to a man or women, do not belong in a news story. Also, be aware of when the age of a female subject changes from *girl* to *woman*. Generally, after age 16, she is a woman. This may vary with the stylebook of the particular newsroom. The same holds true of a young man. After 16, he becomes a man in the news, even though he may not be prosecuted as such until age 18. Some newsrooms now use *teen* or *teenager* for both genders from ages 13–19.

Do not bury important information deep in the story.

Accuracy is paramount. If a fact is not absolutely known, do not guess; do not use it. Remember, a reporter is neither a judge nor a jury. A person's guilt or criminal charge can only come from an officer of the law. But that means the opinion of a police officer is not a fact unless it is reported as the opinion of the officer as a quote. Also, care must be taken in the use of *allegedly*. It is a lazy reporter's way of saying, "I don't have the exact facts, but the following is close." Unless information is known and confirmed, do not use it. *Allegedly* should be used to describe a person if he or she has been arrested but not charged or found guilty of a crime. *Apparently* also is a lazy word. If the facts are not known, then do not write a sentence that requires an imprecise adverb. Be precise or do not report.

Use titles of all subjects when available. Titles and identifications come before the name in most cases (e.g., Secretary of State Condoleezza Rice). Stories from field reporters, but not from the anchors, generally end with a signature that may include the reporter's name, location, and often the station's call letters or channel identification.

Be aware of trademarks and copyrights. Use *tissue*, not *Kleenex*; *copy*, not *Xerox*; *adhesive bandages*, not *Band-Aids*; *soft drink*, not *Coke* (except in Texas, where everything is *Coke*); *appliances* or *refrigerator*, not *Frigidaire*; *transparent tape*, not *Scotch tape*; and *plastic flying disc*, not *Frisbee*. If in doubt, check the AP stylebook or your own operation's stylebook. (See also Chapter 3.)

The Sins of Poor and Bad Newswriting

Avoid Passive Writing

First, avoid using any form of the verb "to be," including *is, are, were,* and *was*. They offer no action and no meaning, and they usually end up placing the subject after the object, making for a very confusing sentence for the audience. Instead of "The condition of Jane's car was assessed by the insurance company," it is better to write, "The insurance company assessed the condition of Jane's car."

Write in the Present or Future Tense

Past tense is no longer news, but history. The sentence, "A service station was robbed last night" is written as a factual account but is both passive and past tense. How about instead writing, "The service station bandit now rests in jail following his midnight holdup on Main Street." Some stories may have to be written in the past tense, but avoid this by tying the story to its present condition or effect.

EXAMPLES OF ALTERNATES TO PASSIVE STATEMENTS

attitude is a breath of fresh air	attitude provides a breath of fresh air
the field will officially be changed to	the field officially becomes
these actions are exactly what she received	these actions illustrate exactly what she received
scratched rims were a few car details	scratched rims revealed a few car details
the teams are looking for	the team looks for
they are still willing to spend	they still will spend
she was unavailable for comment	she had no comment
it was 6 months ago when it happened	six months ago it happened
he was faced with the option to continue	he faced the fact he must continue
students have been utilizing laptops	students utilized the laptops
job security is an important factor for a secure future	secure future depends on job security
in 2005 other activities have been added	since 2005 they have added other activities
is referring to the crisis	refers to the crisis
is a new graduate from college	graduated from college
mothers are working to balance	mothers work to balance
but for her it was a matter of being an unwilling	but for her she became an unwilling
the condition of her car was assessed	the insurance company assessed the condition of her car
he said it was on of the biggest days	one of the biggest days became

Figure 4.3. Avoiding passive verbs adds excitement and detail to sentences.

Sentences Need Subjects

In an effort to write short sentences, you may omit the subject and use a passive verb. Consider the sentence "George was run over." Yes, there is a subject, but "George" actually should be the object of the action, if there were an active verb. Better, "Sam ran over George." The best way to avoid such mistakes is to follow the golden news rule, **"Who Does What to Whom."** Follow that rule, and you will seldom either write a passive line or forget the subject.

Avoid Run-On Sentences

In an effort to cram as much information as possible into the lead sentence or to avoid extra sentences, you may tie several different thoughts or actions together without thinking about how confusing that run-on will be to the audience. An example of a run-on is, "The soldier was struck by two bullets fired by a sniper who was captured by the lieutenant after a brief search." Better phrasing would be, "The sniper fired two shots. Both hit their mark. The lieutenant searched and found the sniper, putting him out of action. The soldier recovers at the local aid station." This makes a longer lead and could be shortened by removing some information: "A sniper shot and wounded a soldier, bringing about his own downfall." Not a great lead, but better than the original.

Suggestions to Avoid Poor and Bad Writing

Write short, direct-to-the-point sentences. Do not ramble or write complex sentences.

Avoid backing into sentences. Start with a subject, and use an active verb with accurate but easily understood modifiers.

Avoid the use of indefinite pronouns; better to repeat a name than to leave the listener confused about who or what you are describing.

Avoid splitting infinitives or separating adverbs from modifying verbs.

Avoid ending a sentence in a preposition. It has become acceptable, but it may read awkwardly.

Never use slang unless it is truly necessary and appropriate.

Learn the differences in the uses of *that*, *which*, and *who*.

Learn proper usage for words that sound the same: *they're, there,* and *their; two, to,* and *too; your* and *you're;* and *whose* and *who's.* (See Chapter 1.)

Spell check, spell check, spell check—but your computer spell check will not correct the previous series.

Understand the differences among positioning prepositions, including *on, in, from,* and *of.*

Hyphenate letters that are pronounced individually (e.g., N-B-A, F-C-C, and K-P-R-C), but not if the initials are pronounced as a word (e.g., NASA).

Spell out numbers except as follows:

When two numbers occur together (e.g., He had twelve 20-ton trucks.)

Use figures for years (e.g., 2004 or 2-thousand 4), time of day (e.g., 4:30 or 4 to 7), and most sports statistics (e.g., 102 to 99—Be sure the "to" appears between the numbers).

Use figures for phone numbers, but hyphenate between numbers (e.g., 5-5-5-4-2-7-9-8-9-1).

Round large numbers to easily understood figures. Use "Nearly five million" instead of "four million, nine-hundred thousand, two hundred" or use a combination of numbers and letters, such as "4-million, 9-hundred-thousand."

Never write "a million" because it sounds like "8 million"; instead write "one million."

In script copy, do not use quotation marks, bold type, italics, or all uppercase font unless the stylebook or format instruction call for such modifications.

Brevity marks the best quotations. Find the key statement in the entire statement for use in a story. Do not change the meaning of the statement by cutting too tightly, but the power of a good quote is a simple, straight-to-the-point comment. A short quote is better than a paraphrasing of a long statement, but if no single short sentence expresses the truth of the entire statement, then careful and accurate paraphrasing is called for. If an actual recording of the quote is not available, then verification must be conducted to make certain the quotation is accurate and reflects the meaning of the statement.

Interviewing

A professional interview begins with research. This includes a study of the interviewee, a study of the topic, and, most important, a study of the ramifications of the potential effect of exposing the information in the interview. Despite the best intentions of deep and vigorous research, you must be prepared for the unexpected. Either the subject will offer information beyond your knowledge, or the subject may refuse to reveal the necessary information you need for the story. The solution to the former is to be a good listener. Without prior knowledge of new information, you must lead the subject into explaining in detail the new topic. You can avoid such a nightmare by being well prepared. If probing, prodding, and repeated questions from all angles on the subject cannot open the subject to provide the answers needed for your story, then cancel that interview and find another subject.

Avoid at all cost asking questions that may be answered *yes* or *no*. Starting a question with *do* or *does* automatically allows the subject to give a simple one-word answer that destroys the value of the interview. If questions begin with the five "Ws" and "H," an explanation must be made by the subject to answer the question. Ask the subject to explain and define the topic or the individual points of the interview. The more opportunity a subject has to add personal ideas and thoughts, the better the interview. Do not answer your own question by starting the question with the answer. Sportscasters violate this rule often by starting the question with a statement and then stopping, expecting the subject to decide what to say. This makes both the interviewer and the subject look ignorant, or worse. This error often comes from the interviewer wanting the subject to react to a specific topic rather than leaving the question open-ended. If you write a well-researched and well-worded question, you will avoid the problem without offering the answer first.

With permission, always record an interview. File the tape, both for reference when writing the story and as a defense against future litigation if a charge of libel or misquoting is filed. Write out a list of questions in advance. View the list as possible questions; the act of assembling the list will build a store of knowledge for you on the subject. Never start an interview with critical or defensive questions. Ease into the interview by letting the subject know you are knowledgeable but sincerely want the subject to answer fully and from his or her own perspective. Listen carefully and build a positive relationship, indicating an empathy for both the subject and the topic. If a confrontational question must be asked, save it until near the end of the interview because an antagonistic question could abruptly end the interview. Remember, you are asking a favor of the subject to take the time to talk to you. It may give the subject an opportunity to reveal his or her own thoughts through the media, but you still need the subject's voice to make the story.

Although interviews provide a source of information, information from an interview may not be reliable. As with all sources, an interview also needs some type of reliability crosscheck with at least one other source. The same holds true for any information gained through research on the Web or any other Internet source.

Research, research, research: make certain your research is accurate in terms of names, addresses, terms, titles, and details. Do not assume anything. Check and double-check all aspects of copy.

Know Your Stylebook—Objectivity and Fairness

No absolute hard-and-fast fairness rules exist in newswriting. Reporting the news means every story is different and must be approached and dealt with differently. The difference between pre-story bias and pre-story research depends on an open mind toward the subject at hand. You must reach an understanding of the topic and its potential while gathering all available information and making the selection necessary to avoid overwhelming the audience with unimportant or redundant information. Understanding the basic conflict and the impact on the listener based on potential interest provides a key perspective in choosing the words that tell the story.

One of the most difficult aspects of newswriting is the maintenance of objectivity and fairness. Understanding the difference between balance and fairness requires a sense of critical judgment. A news story cannot be absolutely balanced. Depending on the story, there may be only one side of the story that is important. Fairness requires the writer to provide all information needed for the audience to understand the story and its reason for occupying the valuable and limited airtime within any one newscast. An example would be the reporting of the number of deaths of American soldiers in battle. Balance would require reporting the number of deaths on the opposite side of the battle. That figure might be important, but it would not be necessary if the point of the story was the rapidly escalating number of dead American troops. In covering an automobile wreck, it is impossible to give a truly balanced story. In fairness, you should give all of the information available on who was in the wreck, the result of the wreck, and, if available, what may have been the possible cause of the accident occurring. That would be fair, but not balanced. If all stories were absolutely balanced, there would no reason for a newscast.

The second mitigating aspect of attempting to maintain objectivity in newswriting is the pressure existing due to the nature of the American commercial broadcast system. It is impossible to totally eliminate bias in any form in many different factors of the broadcast business. Although most operations attempt to maintain a distance between the sales and news departments, subtle operational factors intrude on that distance. Advertisers pay for the operation of the station through the commercials they purchase. The advertiser would prefer that the newscast reflect at least a portion of their attitudes, despite the policy of no communication between advertisers and news management.

As an example, a subtle type of arrangement exists with transportation advertisers. If an airline, railroad, or bus company purchases a spot in a newscast, and if a major airline, bus, or railway accident occurs, especially if there are fatalities, the contract calls for the spot to be pulled from the newscast if the story of the accident is scheduled in that newscast. That places pressure on the newscast producer and news director to decide whether the story is important enough to lose income for the station and, indirectly, income to the newsroom by carrying the story. Instead of judging the story on its merits of news value, the story now must be judged on the basis of financial value. This is just one of the political, social, and economic attitudes of the community that affect the news operation.

Personal biases of newscasters, producers, and news directors often are leveled at news operations. Most newscasters try their best to avoid personal bias, but when a writer has covered years of stories on poverty, unethical big business, and illegal acts of politicians, a certain level of personal feeling about the world in general may very well take place. At the same time, the personal, political, and social biases of the highest level of management who have not been exposed to anything but their own rarified social strata have their own effects. Upper-level management control the wages, hiring and firing policies of the news staff, and operational budgets of the news department. In theory, the differing views of reporters and management would eventually balance in the delivery of the news.

Financial pressures also act in the choice of stories and the methods of treating stories. When audiences show their preferences for yellow journalism rather than balanced, thoughtful reporting, the pressures to follow the audience are placed against the news operation rather than in continuing to provide quality news if income continues to drop. At the same time, producers follow the temptation to fill the newscast with soft, human-interest stories that do not offend anyone.

Another subtle form of anti-objectivity arises from the nature of the beast of broadcast news itself. The relentless broadcast schedule requires a newscast to start and stop within a fraction of a second. Commercials, lead-ins, and promotions squeeze hard news into the remaining 22 minutes in a half-hour newscast. With newscasts airing several times during the day, each demanding some new stories or, at least, rewritten stories with some new information, there is not enough time to research, double-check all facts, and perform the required in-depth study to truly learn all of the information and report a story completely.

Radio Newswriting

Radio news may be broken into three categories: the "all-news" stations, quick 1–3-minute on-the-hour summaries, and the lowest form, the news integrated into the programming, usually in the form of off-color and ribald morning DJs.

Radio news could provide a major service to the communities from which it draws its income by producing accurate, timely, and informative news designed for the listener's ear only. This partially exists in two forms: the National Public Radio (NPR) stations that carry NPR morning and afternoon news as well as their own carefully gathered and written local news, and, to a lesser degree, the all-news commercial radio stations. On NPR, the stories run as long as it takes to cover the material properly without skipping important details. Their interview programs are well researched and fulfill the obligation of introducing the audience to interesting people, happenings, and history of value. The during remainder of the broadcast day, local NPR stations carry music, generally classical, jazz, or folk.

NPR may be compared with commercial "all-news" stations that purport to cover the news 24 hours a day. In reality, most all-news commercial stations offer blocks of news covering the morning drive time and the afternoon drive time. In between, the early-morning and late-night broadcasts consist of talk shows, more often than not with a strong political or social bias designed to initiate heated conversations with rabid listeners. They also may allot a major portion of their broadcast day to sports reporting, especially if the market supports professional teams. Unfortunately, much of the news is repeated over and over, barely rewritten, since in-depth research and gathering of news is labor intensive and costly to produce.

As convergence continues, some radio stations rely totally on television news departments, especially if both radio and TV stations are owned and operated by the same company. Another approach to cost savings uses a local independent news-gathering operation that provides periodic weather updates, traffic reports, and some local news coverage. Such an operation will serve more than one station in the same market; in fact, most offer their services to as many stations in the same market as possible to survive financially. The end result is a homogenization of news coverage throughout the day and across the market. It severely reduces the opportunity for listeners to be able to access a variety of coverage, as well as the possibility for employment in the field of radio news.

At one time, radio stations prided themselves on their news departments; small as they were, at least they were staffed by trained professional journalists who would cover the local market as best they could within the limits of their operation. Such stations usually offered short but complete newscasts on the hour or half-hour, and generally at some time during the week they would produce a public affairs program to discuss important issues in the community, as the FCC once but no longer specifically required. Instead, music radio stations may break for a brief 1–3-minute condensed newscast on the hour or half-hour, with what can only be described as headlines, a quick weather report, and the top sports story of the day. If the newscast actually originates from the station, it serves the minimum requirement of a news service. But too often now, such a newscast may originate from a centrally located station many miles, or even states, away, feeding the same newscast to many stations owned by the same company, regardless of the need for a local aspect to the coverage.

The next step downward in radio news operation consists of a reader reciting news copy written with the intention of giving the DJ, whose music show the newscast has interrupted, an opportunity to make a joke of the story. Worse yet, the story may be twisted and distorted to grasp for a humorous aspect, regardless of the pain or anguish that such distortion may cause the subject of the story. The reader more than likely is not a trained or a professional journalist, but rather is more of a comedy writer whose major responsibility is to ferret out news stories that fit the level of humor presented within that particular broadcasts segment. Needless to point out, this type of operation causes stations more lawsuits than any other programming technique other than lewd or pornographic discussions and stupid DJ on-air tricks.

Writing Radio News Copy

Writing for radio is uniquely different from writing for the rest of the electronic media in that the audience uses only one of the five senses to comprehend the information in the story, the sense of hearing. Print sources, television, and the Internet access both sight and sound in their newscasts, but radio must rely solely on the audience's sense of hearing. Radio does have an advantage. That is, it may, if properly produced, utilize the audience's imagination. From the beginnings of radio, the ability to reach audiences through their imaginations has benefited radio dramas, commercials, comedies, and even newscasts. If written precisely enough, listeners may place themselves within the story and imagine what they cannot see. This makes radio writing depend on careful and critical selection of each word to maximize the vision of the story in the mind of the listener. Imprecise or nondescriptive words do not belong in radio news stories.

The use of sounds other than words also may help develop the imagination of the audience. A story on Afghanistan or Iraq with the sound of a helicopter passing in the background, distant sounds of gunfire, or strains of music of the location of the story may bring the story greater imagined visual power. Of course, it is better if the reporter is actually on location, but even studio newscasts may benefit from sirens in the background during a police chase story or the sounds of fire engines and pumpers working during a fire. Care must be taken that such effects do not create a docu-newscast instead of an actual newscast.

Your radio newswriting must be precise and simple without writing down to the audience, but rather writing in clear, straightforward sentences that may be understood on the first and only hearing. Short sentences using words of fewer than three syllables carry meaning more accurately than long, drawn-out sentences with complex phrases and multi-syllable words. Numbers need to be simplified and rounded to the closest, largest denomination. "Nearly 4 million," rather than "3 million, nine-hundred thousand," makes more sense to the ear.

Your use of *actualities* (i.e., *sounds bites*) is important for the listener to actually hear the person in the story speak. The actualities should be kept short, using only the critical words that explain the part the person played in the story, without lengthy explanations. Make certain to properly and accurately introduce the speaker, with a correct title or the part the speaker played in the story.

Both your writing and the delivery of the script should sound as if one person is sitting on the other side of the window, listening. If the station targets a specific audience demographic, and most radio stations except all-news stations do target their niche demographic, then some consideration may need to be made in the language and choice of words in the news copy. Slang and off-beat words and phrases should be avoided in an effort to maintain a reasonable level of professionalism and to act as a model in speaking clear and understandable English.

Radio Script Format

Today, no one professional script format exists in the radio news business. Partially due to the many different delivery formats of radio news, no single page layout of copy fits all newscasts. The best format to follow, unless instructed otherwise, includes the following:

1. All copy to be read is typed in uppercase and lowercase letters. All instructions, sound effects (SFX or EFX), music cues, or names of newscasters are typed in uppercase letters (e.g., CAPITALS).
2. Double- or triple-space all copy to be read.
3. The copy to be read is typed in a column about 4 inches wide down the middle of the page. Set margins from 2–2.5 inches on each side of the news copy.
4. Instructions should start at the normal (i.e., 1-inch) margin on the left.
5. Each story starts on a separate page. If a story runs longer than one page, place "(MORE)" at the bottom of the page.
6. Avoid splitting words at the end of a line, and avoid splitting a sentence at the bottom of a page.
7. Methods for labeling the page vary, but the following is a good rule to follow: place the slug, writer's name, date, and intended air time or program at the top left corner of each page. Page numbers are seldom used since stories seldom are written in the order they will appear in a newscast.
8. The headlines segment, if one exists, is typed on a separate page since it may be rewritten often before airtime.
9. Any recorded inserts (e.g., tape, CD, or digital file) carry a slug title, an accurate length, a few of the first words as an *in-cue*, and several of the final words as an *out-cue*. In- and out-cues

help the production staff make certain they have the correct insert and make a clean cut out at the end of the insert. If the insert is less than 10 seconds, all of the recording should be transcribed as in- and out-cues. The slugs and cues should be typed in caps so that the newscaster knows the copy is prerecorded and not to be read. In some operations, the entire insert may be recorded and transcribed in the script: in case a technical problem prevents the insert from playing, the newscaster then can paraphrase the recording to save the story.

RADIO NEWS FORMAT

Taxes (Slug) :30
Jones
9/16/07
7AM

BOB   The Mayor wants to raise your taxes but

                           City Council says no. Mayor William Anderson

                           insists cuts in the police and fire departments

                           will be made unless citizens are wiling

                           to provide additional revenue to the city.

                           With election less than a month away

                           the council members up for reelection

                           hesitate to upset the community with

                           more taxes.

INSERT: Mayor :20   IN-CUE: THE CITIZENS...

                           OUT-CUE: ...FULLFILL RESPONSIBILITIES

                           The mayor hopes to reach an agreement

                           by next week's council meeting.

---

* Note—any sound bite under :10 should be completely written out.

Figure 4.4. Radio news copy format presents the copy and instructions in a simple, easy-to-read format.

Radio Production

The amount of production actually performed by radio news reporters depends on two factors: the size of the news operation, and the
level of digitalization of the news operation. Smaller operations rely
on reporters to perform their own production, interviewing, recording, writing, editing, and preparing of recorded material for airing.
Larger news operations may assign some of the production functions to specifically trained audio production personnel, relieving the
reporter from time-consuming production activities. If the operation
has moved to total or nearly all-digital equipment, many of the production functions may be completed by you easily, quickly, and with
less technical knowledge required. Basic understanding of sound,
acoustics, and audio recording, regardless of whether the medium is
analog or digital, still needs to be grasped by you, even if you think
of yourself as a writer and not requiring technical production skills.

Production techniques for radio news are comparatively straightforward as compared to television or Internet news-gathering techniques. Since audio is the only consideration, environment, lighting,
visuals, and even crowd control do not generally affect a field report
or the gathering of information for radio. On the other hand, as a
field reporter, you must be self-reliant. You will not have a producer
to locate and arrange for someone to interview, nor to do any field
research, much less find a you parking spot or locate a safe position
for you to work. If technical problems or equipment failures occur, it
is up to you to repair them, to find another means of accomplishing
their work, or to contact a technician to suggest a solution since a
technician will not be closer than a possible telephone call. It is critical that you know intimately your equipment, its operation, and basic
field repairs, especially dealing with batteries and cables. Even if you
are sitting at your desk in a newsroom, you may be the only person
present or the only person not committed to another assignment,
leaving you to solve the problem on your own.

Alphabet Soup for Radio Newswriters

A set of jargon furnishes reporters with a means of communicating
accurately, in a minimal amount of space on a script and in as few
words as possible. The following compose the basic terms.

Actuality	A live story or clip
AP	Associated Press
Bite	A short sound clip
Lead	The first section, usually the first sentence of a story
Morgue	Archival files of old stories and information
NAT	Natural, wild sound
Raw stock	Unused tape or discs
RENG	Radio electronic news gathering
Slug	Title, label of story, tape, disc, and other sources
SNG	Satellite news gathering
Soft lead or Tease	Partial story information to promote a story later
Stock	Footage purchased from a provider
VO	Voice over

Gathering Information

The most convenient, but not always the most accurate, manner of gathering information requires using the telephone. Always take notes while listening, including notes of your own questions. With permission, record the conversation (depending on local state laws on telephone recording). Record both sides of the conversation for note research and also for accuracy.

The recording media may be (depending on the station's equipment) one of the following:
Reel-to-reel (highly unlikely)
Analog cassette (if wired to the phone)
Mini-analog cassette
Direct-to-disc
Digital miniDV
Direct-to-computer hard drive
An MP3-type medium
Cell phone memory

Information gathered in the field provides the best source of personal explanation of a story. Field recording depends on an additional production factor of microphone techniques. A unidirectional mic works best in the field. The mic needs to be held so that both you and the interviewee speak directly into the mic. You must move the mic back and forth before each statement is made to catch all of the audio as each person speaks in turn. You must be aware of background noise that might diminish the quality of the recording. When possible, a separate take of environment ambiance should be recorded to be used as a transition or to add background "reality" in the editing process. Taking notes while recording provides a reminder of where on the recording important information is located so that you can find that information during the editing process. Wear an in-ear head phone to monitor the recorded audio to make certain you are recording usable material.

Editing Radio News Media

The first stage involves downloading either all of the recorded material or only those segments from notes taken during the interview that are important to the story. Assemble the story on a computer, choosing the best statements that tell the story in the shortest time without leaving out or distorting critical information. Additional copy of your voice needs to be added to the computer to be included in the final story. Editing on a computer loaded with an audio editing application is as simple as editing using a word processor on a computer. Once the story reaches its final form on the computer, it may be duped to a playback medium or fed through a local area network (LAN) to the producer for integration into a newscast or for archival for later newscasts.

Live on Air

Deliver copy as if speaking to one or two people. Generally speaking, radio audiences are made up of individuals listening by themselves or in small groups, most often in an automobile. Speak clearly, using correct pronunciation and proper grammar. Radio depends on the individual style of reporters, but style should not overwhelm the main function of radio news: to deliver clear and concise, easily understood information to a large and demographically varied audience.

Television Newswriting

Television news grew from and inherited characteristics, both good and bad, from print and radio. Professionally operated television news departments follow the disciplined guidelines of print news operations, treating news as a unique service to the public that must be both fair and accurate, at all costs. Unfortunately, the corporate pressures of the business side of television have created news operations that have become as concerned with the effect on the sales department of the station as with reporting the news.

Types of Newscasts

Local network-affiliated stations generally follow a specific pattern of scheduled newscasts that fit within the network's programming schedule. An early-morning, 5-minute newscast sandwiched in between half-hour blocks of network morning shows give the local audience a smattering of news from the night before. Some local stations schedule a full half-hour of news following or preceding the network morning show.

Most local stations devote a half-hour of "home" news during the noon-time break between network programs. The mid-afternoon newscasts fall between afternoon talk and game programs and the evening network-produced newscast. The local news block may be an hour in length, a half-hour before and another half-hour following the network news, or a combination of news blocks to fill the programming schedule until the beginning of prime time network programming. A locally produced half-hour follows the end of primetime network programming and preceding the network's late-night program block. This same newscast may be recorded and repeated following the network's late-night program, at midnight or later.

Independent or nonaffiliated local stations broadcast limited or no formal locally produced newscast. The station may rebroadcast a sister station's newscast or segments from a 24-hour cable channel's newscasts.

The four national broadcast networks that maintain full news staffs and news programming spread their newscasts across the daily program schedule, starting with an hour or two of a morning show that uses segments of news, weather, sports, and interviews of general interest to the audience. Too often, these programs become more entertainment-oriented than news-oriented despite the quality of the news operations. The key network newscast, which determines much of the income and ratings of each individual network, is fed to the affiliated stations to be broadcast live or delayed, depending on the local station's programming requirements. Generally, these newscasts are aired at 6:00, 6:30, or 7:00 PM, depending on the time zone. Eastern and Pacific time zone stations generally broadcast the news at a later time than Central and Mountain time zone stations. The broadcast networks also schedule special late-night and weekend newscasts, generally as an interview format.

Some areas of the country have organized local cable 24-hour news channels, generally operated by a chain of stations with a common owner. The news staffs of the stations augment the newscast and story coverage of the cable operation and share stories to avoid redundant coverage. These cable news channels usually cover a two-to-three-state region, increasing the potential audience across the area. The schedule usually consists of alternating short newscasts, weather reports, sports, and interview segments. Often, segments are repeated to fill time and to reach a new audience as the day progresses.

Nationally distributed cable news channels program news around the clock. The 24 hours are filled with short to half-hour newscasts, weather segments, and sports reporting, along with interview program segments. Often, segments are repeated to fill time later in the day. Entertainment, business, and government reporting segments also compliment the hard news of the day. In addition to the 24-hour news cable channels, specialized channels report on areas of news such as sports, weather, entertainment, and the continuous operation of government reporting channels.

Some entertainment cable channels schedule their own version of news to supplement and compliment their specialized music, drama, and children's programs.

Writing Television News Copy

All the basic rules of radio and print newswriting pertain to television newswriting, with the added consideration of writing to and for the power of visuals. Production becomes more important than radio in TV newswriting because as a TV newswriter, you must understand the scope and limitations of the production operation within a given company.

You must also understand how visuals may be created and the importance in a story of using visuals or not using visuals. The audience may gain as much information from the audio as from the visual, but it is attracted to and tends to concentrate on the visual. Therefore, the choice of visuals is critical. The visual should tell the key parts of the story without distracting the audience with unnecessary information. The visual should match the copy read by the anchor or reporter, but it should add to the copy, not redundantly duplicate the copy; nor should the copy duplicate the visual.

The concentration on people makes it imperative to identify each person with keyed names. Locations and important facts should be illustrated by graphics to explain what is not obvious. Every story should have a graphic of some sort, or at least something visible over the shoulder of the anchor. It could be necessary to create a multiple-frame visual showing different aspects of the story, but the visual should not be so complex that the audience cannot instantly understand what you are showing and why it is important to the story.

As a writer, you will have to use what you have been given or have collected. The videographer should have provided a variety of shots, from among which you may choose the best to create a series that tells a logical story with a beginning, a middle, and an end, just as your copy should do. If there are shots available in the morgue, use them. Fill in gaps by using previously shot footage to contrast, compare, and illustrate changes in location or even in people. A good TV newswriter must think visually to capture and hold the audience's attention, especially if the story is complex.

Television News Script Format

Just as in radio copy formatting, television news formats vary from station to station. There exist some basics that, once learned, newcomers to the field will adapt to whatever format is prescribed on their next job. The script page is split into two columns. The left-hand column contains all visual descriptions and instructions. The right-hand column is reserved for audio-only copy and instructions.

The video instructions and all other copy that is not read by the anchors is entered in capitals *(caps)* and is single-spaced. All copy to be read on air is double-spaced and entered in uppercase and lowercase letters. If an audio instruction is inserted in the right-hand column, it must be in caps and single-spaced to avoid being read on air.

The philosophy of entering copy to be read in uppercase and lowercase letters is controversial. Some anchors, especially those with many years of experience with older prompters, insist on having all of their copy entered in caps. This comes from a mistaken notion that all caps are easier to read from a prompter. But many readability tests have shown that uppercase and lowercase copy is easier to read and allows fewer errors than all-caps copy. If the anchor insists on all caps, then instructions need to be entered in uppercase and lowercase letters to differentiate from the copy to be read.

Triple-space between stories and between inserted instructions to assist anchors in reading their copy. Some portions of a TV newscast script may still be in preparation as the newscast begins. The anchors may not have had the opportunity to read the copy before air and must sight-read as the newscast progresses. To assist the anchors, make the script as clean and uncluttered as possible. Make the instructions obvious and in logical locations and format. A TV news script will contain fewer video instructions than commercial, dramatic, and documentary TV scripts because much of what occurs during a newscast has been organized ahead of time and because the crew knows what to expect and is prepared to move forward without detailed scripts.

```
                                              SH-SCHOOL
                                              (SH-SCHOOL)

              PG 5


              TALENT=BILL

                                              (BILL)
                                                 CALVIN BELL.. THE
                                              HOUSTON MAN WHO
                                              WOUNDED TWO POLICE
                                              OFFICERS DURING A
                                              SHOOTING SPREE AT
                                              PINEY POINT
                                              ELEMENTARY SCHOOL..
                                              IS ON HIS WAY TO A
                                              PSYCHIATRIC
                                              HOSPITAL.
              ENG= NAT SOUND: 06              (***VO***)
                                                 BELL WAS RECENTLY
                                              ACQUITTED OF ALL
                                              CHARGES IN THE
                                              SHOOTING.. BUT HE WAS
                                              ORDERED TO UNDERGO
                                              NINETY DAYS OF
                                              PSYCHIATRIC
                                              EVALUATION.
              ENG=UP FULLRUNS=: 07


              CG=CALVIN BELL - INNOCENT BY REASON OF
              INSANITY

                                              OUT Q=.. DOING
                                              BETTER.
```

Figure 4.5. Television news script format follows the two-column format, but it is simplified to clarify copy for the anchors and to leave room for the director's own script markings.

```
5PM RUNDOWN                 17:29:25                          dis
ChannelTwoNews at 5                                           07
     SLUG         TAL    CAM SOURCE   TYPE    SS      ARCH# RUNS  NOTES
---------------------------------------- SEGMENT 1 ----------------------
1    BREAKOPEN               VTR      VTR     57:35         0:19
2    HOTOPEN      BILL       D-ENG    VO                    0:32
                  JAN        W-ENG    VO
                  BILL       W-ENG    VO
3    5SH-BELL     B-J        UNIT#27  LIVE                  1:59 HUGGINS/PE
                             ENG-1    PKG           3049
5    SH-SCHOOL    BILL       ENG-3    VOSOT      3053 1:08 RAYMAN
6    TREERESCUE   BILL       ENG-4    VO         3054 1:12 OVERCASH
7    TX-FLOOD     JAN        ENG-5    VOSOT   FL-TIME 3074 0:01 AUSTIN
                                             FL-NUMB
8    FATTUESDAY   J-B        NEWSROO  LIVE                  2:06 REGAN/BARO
     P-fattuesd              ENG-6    PKG           3052
4    M-HEIGHT     JAN        ENG-2    PKG           3051 1:56 ROSTODHA/S
     P-m-height
9    PITCH1       J-B        VTR                            0:25
                             VTR
                             LIVE     1st-WX  1ST-BN
------------------------------------------------------------------------
10   BREAK1                                                 2:05
---------------------------------------- SEGMENT 2 ----------------------
11   COMPAQ       JAN        ENG-7    PKG           3080 1:42 BEBE/TREAI
     P-compaq
12   NASAJOBS     BILL       ENG-8    VO                    0:31 FILE
14   SCORPIONS    JAN        ENG-9    VO                    0:46 NC 2:30 NA
14B  MICKJAGGER   BILL       ENG-10   VO                    0:35
15   PITCH2       J-B        VTR                            0:13
                             VTR
------------------------------------------------------------------------
16   BREAK2                                                 2:06
---------------------------------------- SEGMENT 3 ----------------------
17   SPORTS       3SHOT      SET      WORDS                 3:05
17-1 HOWE         CRAIG      ENG-11   SOT
17-2 OILERS'      CRAIG      NEWSTAR  LIVE    DBL-BOX
                             ENG-12   PKG
17-3 COWBOY       CRAIG      ENG-13   PKG
18   PITCH3       B-J        VTR                            2:10
------------------------------------------------------------------------
19   BREAK3                                                 2:01
---------------------------------------- SEGMENT 4 ----------------------
20   WEATHER      3SHOT      SET      WORDS                 2:27
21   PITCH4       J-B        VTR                            0:02
------------------------------------------------------------------------
22   BREAK4                                                 1:46
---------------------------------------- SEGMENT 5 ----------------------
23   6PROMO       2SHOT      NEWSROM  LIVE    BX-COMI       0:25
                             ENG-14   VO      VTR-AT6
```

Figure 4.6. The television news rundown sheet lists every video and audio source, their origination, and the order in which they will appear in the newscast. A timeline back-timing the newscast occupies one column of the sheet.

Production Instructions

One method of preparing the crew for a newscast consists of creating a *rundown sheet* (also called a *format sheet)* prepared hours before the newscast and listing everything that goes into the newscast. Individual columns of information indicate the order of the stories, what visuals go with each story, who reads the story, and an indication of the length of time for each segment. This document is updated periodically during the day as the assembling of the newscast progresses. It must be accurate, and everyone involved in the newscast must have updated copies at all times, especially as the newscast hits the air. The sheet is filed on the local area network (LAN) computer so that everyone in the newsroom can keep up-to-date on changes by viewing the rundown sheet on personal desktop computers.

The organization of a newscast depends on several variables and station policies. Depending on the time of day, a newscast may be organized starting with the most important story, followed by less important news. Or the organization may follow a geographical pattern, leading with international news, following with national, regional, and then the lead local stories. A newscast may be written to cover a specific topic from many different angles.

Figure 4.7. The home page of a newspaper Web site will list the headline or lead of the stories published in that day's edition, with links to the full story.

The rundown sheet binds a newscast together, bringing a solid performance out of possible chaos. Both sound and pictures for a television newscast originate from at least four to as many as a dozen different sources, beginning with the two to four studio cameras on the floor of the studio providing pictures of the anchors. An anchor seldom sits with a plain background; a graphic of some sort appears over the anchor's shoulder to highlight or visually explain the story. The graphic could range from a simple name identification of the anchor on the lower third of the frame to a complex series of graphics over the shoulder. The graphic may be a single frame or even an animated series or else a full-screen graphic replacing the anchor in the frame.

Complete stories, as well as segments of stories, originate from the field, transmitted to the control room by microwave, telephone circuits (including cell phones), or satellites. The satellite feed may originate from a local field news unit, the stations chain's regional or national bureau, or a foreign country. Prerecorded segments may originate from videotape, disc, hard drive, or directly from edit suite servers.

The coordination of all of these sources depends on the organizational skills of the program's producer, who must create the rundown sheet, relying on the accuracy, timing, and quality of the written scripts. Without an accurate rundown sheet, the director will be handicapped in calling a flawless live newscast.

Television Production

The earliest television newscasts consisted of an announcer, later to be titled *anchor*, sitting in front of a camera, with a painted background, reading copy directly from a script, often ripped from a wire service teletype machine. Prompting devices mounted on the front of the cameras came along later. The earliest visuals were created by the small staff or by the anchor himself who would draw on a blackboard in the studio. Sixteen-millimeter news film helped, but it took time to shoot, process, and edit before airing.[2] By the late 1950s, smaller video cameras and bulky portable video tape decks allowed live or immediate coverage. Thirty-five millimeter slides,

---

[2] Cronkite, Walter. *A Reporter's Life.* New York: Alfred A. Knopf, 1996, p. 160.

4×5 inch opaque (telop) graphics and more sophisticated switching equipment increased possibilities of visualizing stories.

Today, you must maintain a certain level of technical knowledge without being responsible for the continuous operation, repair, and maintenance of equipment. You should carry and operate comfortably an audio recorder of some type, whether it is an analog or a digital cassette recorder, a disc recorder, or a solid-state recorder. You need to be able to research material and to record interviews, background sounds, and your own copy, if needed. Digital equipment generally is lighter in weight, requires batteries that last longer, and offers a higher-quality recording for downloading into a final edited piece. A stopwatch or digital timer is handy to time segments, narration, and video clips. A cell phone is now a necessity, not only to maintain contact with the studio, producers, and crew in the field, but also, if necessary, it may be used for a live audio feed or the audio portion of a full video feed.

Many newsrooms now require their reporters carry a video camera. The new small, lightweight digital cameras operate easily with a minimum of video production knowledge if operated within reasonable limits. Such footage provides substitute video if a videographer is not available. In addition, you may be required to act as a backup, or B-roll, shooter during a complicated or fast-moving story. Learning to shoot news video to be edited quickly and accurately takes some time and experience to reach, but the basics of shooting video are the same, whether the camera is an analog video camera, a still camera, or an advanced digital camera. The shot must be in focus, exposed within a range of usable and viewable picture, and framed to show the audience whatever needs to be seen. An added skill allows shooting the type of footage that enables the editor to create the best and most accurate series of shots into a meaningful story. Knowing when wide shots (WS), close-ups (CU), cutaways, and cut-ins are needed makes a world of difference in the final edit of a story.

In an emergency, you may need to be able to operate a microwave feed or a satellite feed, to find and connect power for a truck, or to connect to telephone lines for audio and communication feeds. When digital equipment fails, there are seldom any easy and quick repair fixes. In some cases, a part may be substituted, but generally a damaged or inoperative digital piece of gear is out of service until returned to the studio.

The sophisticated level of today's video equipment offers few limits to the creativity of the newswriters and producers to tell and show the story. High-quality digital cameras and recording media, rapid digital editing, and limitless computer graphic possibilities require some knowledge and appreciation for the operation of such equipment to sufficiently utilize the production values of that equipment.

Alphabet Soup for Television Newswriters

Alphabet soup for television reporters includes all of the abbreviations used in radio, plus many more specific to video.

Actuality	A live story or clip
AP	Associated Press
CNN	Cable News Network
Bite	A short sound or video clip
Lead	The first section of a report, usually the first sentence of a story
NAT	Natural, wild sound
Morgue	Archival files of old stories and information
Stock	Footage purchased from a provider
Raw stock	Unused tape or discs
ENG	Electronic news gathering (probably should be renamed DNG)
DNG	Digital news gathering
RENG	Radio electronic news gathering
SNG	Satellite news gathering
Slug	The title, label of the story, tape, disc, and other sources
Soft lead or Tease	Partial story information given to promote a story later

VO	Voice Over
VOT or VT	Voice-over tape (even though the recording may be from another digital source)
SOT	Sound on tape (or another synchronized source)
CG	Character generator
Lead-in	The first line of a story, often delivered by the anchor before switching to the field reporter
Wrap-around	A story briefly introduced by a reporter, followed by a sound bite, which is followed by the reporter ending the story
Tagline	The final line of a field story
Stand-up	A story told by a reporter in the field, standing at the scene of the story; the story is often live and may include interviews
Signature	The final line of a field story, usually with the reporter giving his or her name, followed by the location of the story
Package	A complete story, beginning with the anchor delivering a lead-in that introduces the story and reporter. The complete story is prerecorded, including voiceovers, sound bites, interviews, and stand-ups, ending with the reporter's signature
Microwave	A straight-line method of feeding a video and audio signal from a field location
Satellite	A method of feeding a video and audio signal from a field location to a satellite and back to the station; now replaces microwave feeds in most cases

The constantly changing technology in the world of electronic media will bring about changes in all aspects of media reporting. But accurate and thoughtful reporting will not change just because the equipment has changed. The technical changes may make the process of reporting operate differently, but the final product must still be based on factual and thoroughly researched newswriting and reporting.

Sports Newswriting

Covering sports offers you a fixed location and a fixed time to cover a story, except for triathlons and cross-country bicycle races. Ratings indicate a large percentage of the audience is a sports fan, concentrating on favorite teams or competitions. That requires you to develop a knowledge of the sport and the participants greater than the most dedicated fans. Reporting the results of sports even tests your ability to give a balanced and fair report, especially if one of the teams or contestants may represent the local area. You often must write sports copy during or immediately after the contest. This means you must write from your personal store of information that you carry with you, either in your memory or on some type of portable filing system. Often your copy will be delivered close to air time and will not be edited or must be delivered as an ad-lib story by the reporter. It remains then for you to make certain you have your facts straight and that you write accurately and interestingly. Scores may tell part of the story, but you must provide more than a series of numbers to please the sports fans. They want to know why someone won, lost, or failed in the attempt. The danger of allowing personal bias to become the basis for your writing must be avoided if possible. If sports writing is to be considered newswriting, then the rules for newswriting should be followed.

Sports writers tend to be highly specialized and to center their interest and knowledge on a specific sport, if not all competitive sports in general.

Weather Newswriting

Most weathercasters prepare their own broadcasts, with the possible assistance of one or more staff trained in meteorology. Writing weather is a highly-specialized field, combining science and fortune telling. Most weathercasters are certified with a meteorology association, which requires both formal study of atmospheric conditions and years of experience reporting weather. Weathercasters generally deliver their portion of the news by memory, without the aid of a prompter. They then must have all of the specific data in mind and recorded on the graphic fields, which will be chroma keyed behind them while they are talking. Since the board behind the weathercasters is either a blue or green screen, the talent must read the combined picture from a monitor mounted on the camera, plus several located beyond camera range but easily viewed by the talent as he or she moves back and forth in front of the camera.

Writing for a weathercast means collecting all of the data, organizing it in a series of logical patterns, and then delivering the information to the graphics department to enter into the system, which will allow the director to key that information and the camera shot of the weathercaster together for airing. The data may be entered directly into the graphics system from the weather department's computers, along with the visuals provided by weather services.

Often, the weather department also reports on environmental and natural disaster stories like global warming, sunspots, eclipses, floods, tornados, and volcano eruptions.

Specialized Newswriting

Larger news operations in major markets often assign writers and reporters with medical or science training to cover these specialized fields. The same holds true for reporters and writers with skills in the economy and politics. Newsrooms may use a senior anchor or reporter to deliver periodic commentaries or editorials. The stories covered generally include sensitive topics and must be written following careful research and consultation with an in-house editorial board, including management representation.

Stations whose audience covers a wide geographical area may assign a reporter and writer to a bureau located at the edge of the coverage area while still including sources for stories of interest to the metro area. This crew operates much like a small newsroom, with a minimal staff but with the capability to feed stories to the stations when the story warrants this.

Internet Newswriting

Over 2,000 newspapers, an equal number of other periodicals, and a like number of broadcast stations duplicate their news copy in some manner on the Internet. Originally, print operations turned to the Internet to protect their readership from abandoning print for the Internet. They discovered the Internet was not only a means of keeping some of their readers using both media, but that the Internet also showed promise for a financial return without a major additional expenditure by their news operation. Hiring reporters capable of writing and, more importantly, thinking in Internet terms proved financially feasible and profitable. Some newspapers and magazines now require writers to automatically prepare two sets of copy, one for the Internet for immediate publication, and the other for print, to meet the print deadline. The Internet has no deadline since it operates 24 hours a day, 7 days a week. As soon as a story is written and edited, it belongs on the publication's Web page.

The style of writing or preparing copy for the Internet varies with publications. Some newspapers simply reproduce their print copy in the same format for the Internet page. The long-time readers of those publications feel at home with that format called *shovelware*. Most other publications specifically design their pages to maximize the benefits of Internet communication. Stories are condensed, salvaging print's inverse format, but entering only the headline, the lead, and at most, a brief second sentence, often incomplete. The concept is that if readers wish to read the rest of the story, they click on the link and read what they want to from the publication's server before returning to the home page. This system allows readers to quickly scan the home page, choose the stories they care about, and skip those that do not interest them. This takes advantage of the Internet's nonlinear construction. Often a publication will list previous stories, which are held in a type of Internet morgue so that a reader may go back and review or reread a previous story.

A second advantage of Internet format allows the reader to skip detailed explanations. If a term needs defining or a biographical note needs to be included, a link is written to lead to those tidbits, and the reader chooses the option of going to the link for more detail or simply going on without the special information.

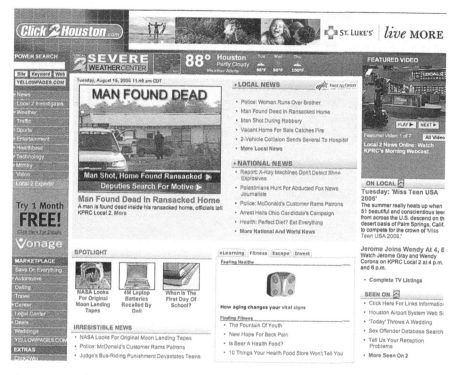

Figure 4.8. This television station's home Web site lists the key stories of that day, as well as links to information supplementing those stories that were not aired. Also, a list of stories from previous newscasts can be found if the reader wants to go back in history to check a previous story.

You need to be able to write in both styles for print operations that maintain full Web pages. You also need to be visually aware since print Web pages are using more and more photos, graphics, and even moving video. As a Web page writer, you need to have a visual sense equal to that of a television writer, director, or graphic artist.[3]

Television news operations that also maintain a Web page find the Web allows shorter stories aired within the newscast the opportunity to provide the audience with full and complete detail on the Web page. The page also gives the sales department one more avenue of maintaining a revenue steam for the station. The sales

---

[3] Examples of publication Web pages may be found at www.ajr.org and www.newspaperlinks.com/voyager.cfm.

Figure 4.9. A radio station's new Web page may list stories broadcast with links to additional information and promotional activities of the station.

department may sell commercials within programs duplicated on the Web site and also may sell Web advertising on the site's pages.

Radio stations found a new means of communicating with their audience by using the Internet and maintaining a Web page. Now they can tell their story "visually" by including photos and even moving visuals and animation to enhance their pages. Again, full-time news radio stations or even rip-and-read stations can expand their news coverage with a Web page to take advantage of showing their radio audience something it cannot see on radio, for example, sports scores, business information, and constantly updated traffic and weather information. The question is, how are radio listeners going to read a Web page? Laptop computers, some cell phones, and handhelds may be able to download the Internet and reach Web pages. Again, the sales department of a radio station now has new available space to sell, either as a package with their airtime, or by selling space on a Web page by itself.

Beyond reproducing the standard electronic news media as a Web page, the Internet offers anyone the opportunity to distribute "news" as they see fit on a personal news blog. The danger of invalidated, unsubstantiated information transmitted as news, without warning the reader of the lack of reliable research, clouds

Mama & Me from PDX
We miss all of our family and friends in Jackson, Miss., but Portland's home now.

Monday, August 14, 2006
Stay tuned for more of Casey's visit, followed by the return to our apartment.

Y'all are great to take a look at these photos. Thanks to those who've e-mailed me and to the two who've commented. That's such fun. I like this technology when I can get it to work. In the next few days, I'll add more photos and the rest of the tale of Casey's visit to Portland. Then I'll start in the apartment again. Bye for now.

posted by Lynette @ 9:54 PM   0 comments

We interrupt the info about Casey in PDX for a movie trailer of sorts

Thursday at work we got an e-mail telling us that Morgan Freeman and Greg Kinnear would be a few blocks up Hawthorne filming a movie, at the Lucky Labrador Pub. The reason we got the e-mail was that some of the production trucks would be using the top floor of the parking garage. Anyway, I thought I'd just mosey up Hawthorne at my breaks and at lunch so I could check it all out.

Friday morning I saw someone with the look at a production

About Me
Name:Lynette
View my complete profile

Links
◇ Google News
◇ Edit-Me
◇ Edit-Me

Previous Posts
◇ Stay tuned for more of Casey's visit, followed by the return to our apartment.
◇ We interrupt the info about Casey in PDX for a movie trailer of sorts
◇ We interrupt our tour of the apartment for a visit from Casey Parks!
◇ Here's our perfect bookcase and the wall behind it, plus the dining area
◇ We like our front wall and window
◇ That's all for now ...
◇ Here's the last piece on the living room interior wall
◇ My brother Howard says we've got way too much on the walls!
◇ Let the tour begin ...
◇ You've made--here's the front door.

Figure 4.10. A blog Web page may be the source of information unavailable elsewhere, but the dangers of unsubstantiated information make using information obtained from a blog suspect.

the definition of *news* to the point of placing legitimate news in the same category as Internet news.

Blogs and other personal Web sites may give readers the feeling that they are receiving valid information based on facts rather than filled with unsubstantiated personal biases, attitudes, distortions, and libelous materials. The target of such misinformation is not even aware of the attack and has no means of contradicting or defending against the attack. Means of controlling such actions are under study by legislators, but reaching a balance between First Amendment rights and protecting personal rights will be difficult.

The eventual outcome of how to control those who use the Internet for their own personal bigotry may take years and changes in communication laws that may also impinge on other long-held freedoms of expression.

Summary

The background of the development of reporting information to the public follows a long and, at times, strenuous relationship between those who make the news by their activities and those who must report the news to the public.

Print news led the development of news gathering with a long tradition of accuracy and fairness based on diligent research on the part of the reporter and careful review by editors.

Electronic newswriting evolved from print. When time, finances, determination, and facilities allow, radio, television, and Internet reporting may match print in quality. But such convergence seldom occurs in electronic media. As in print, each story should answer the five-Ws and H when possible. The conflict in each story is the heart of the story and needs to be explained fully, clearly, and simply for an audience that will be exposed to the information only once, and then briefly.

Good writing avoids the sins of poor writing in any form, print, electronic, or digital. Proper use of the English language, avoidance of slang, and appreciation of the targeted audience builds the basis of good newswriting. Information must be gathered, and the reporter needs to develop skills in interviewing techniques that allow the interviewees the opportunity to state their attitude and knowledge of the story.

Fair reporting means accurate reporting with the knowledge that balance is a goal, but also with the knowledge that all stories cannot be perfectly balanced without losing sight of the meaning of the story.

Radio newscasts fall into three basic categories: all-news stations; short 1–3-minute hourly casts; and integrated news within the station's programming as an adjunct, providing humor from news. Radio news copy must be written to appeal to the single sense of hearing. Therefore, it must be simple, direct, and uncomplicated. Radio news copy is entered in a single column down the middle of the page with wide margins and double or triple spaces between lines. Radio production concentrates on sound, and the reporter expects to be the writer, producer, and editor of the story. Computer editing simplifies the process for radio as it does for television and the Internet.

Television newscasts range from 5-minute breaks within other programming to half-hour, hour-long, and even 2-hour-long blocks of news originating from local stations, television networks, and cable news networks. Television newswriting combines both visual and audio aspects of the story.

Television newscast copy is organized into two parallel columns. The one on the left contains all instructions and visuals; the one on the right, all audio, including the copy the anchor reads, entered in uppercase and lowercase letters. All instructions and inserts are entered in capital letters. In order to produce complex television news, the writer must maintain a level of technical competence in order to understand what can and cannot be efficiently integrated into a live newscast.

Internet newswriting still has yet to be fully developed and systemized. The very freewheeling nature of the Internet leaves the well-organized, trustworthy Internet newscasts open to criticism.

The methods of preparing and delivering Internet news borrow from all predecessors since the Internet may use print, graphics, video, and audio in presentation.

Be Sure To...

1. Work at improving your writing with grammatically correct English.
2. Compare broadcast news operations by watching and comparing all electronic news media.
3. Learn to write accurately, with as little personal bias as possible.
4. Take care when interviewing subjects—record accurately both your questions and the answers.
5. Practice listening to people to determine what they actually mean from their phrasing and choice of words.
6. Practice looking and actually seeing what occurs in front of you, to be able to report accurately what happened.

Exercises

1. Choose a short (6–10-inch-column) story from the newspaper. Write a radio news story that could be read in 15 seconds, and another version in 30 seconds. Add sound effects and music if the story requires such enhancement. Use at least one actuality in the 30-second version.
2. Use the same story in Exercise #1 and write a 30-second television news story with visuals. DO NOT use the same audio as the 30-second radio story.
3. Write a story that you might have seen on the Internet, using the same information. Use as many production techniques as possible that fit the story.
4. Write a news story from information you gathered from your immediate environment (e.g., school, home, or work). Prepare the copy in both radio and television format. Make the stories as interesting as possible, and use all of the production techniques that you believe fit the stories.

5.   Use Web search engines to gather at least two competing sources on the topic of the First Amendment as it has been applied in the past 4 years.
6.   Interview someone you do NOT know personally. Research what that person does and why a news audience might be interested in what that person has to say. Write both radio and televisions stories. The radio script should run 30 seconds, and the television script, 1 minute, 30 seconds (1:30). Use as many possible production techniques as needed to make the story complete and professional.
7.   To provide a direct comparison among media, record a radio newscast and a television newscast, and research the same story in a daily newspaper and on a blog. Compare the length of each story and the amount of detail covered, and explain the difference in accuracy among the media.

Additional Sources

Print

Auletta, Ken. *Backstory: Inside the Business of News*. New York: Penguin Press, 2003.

Baker, Bob. *Newsthinking: The Secret of Making Your Facts Fall into Place*. Boston: Allyn & Bacon, 2002.

Brooks, Brian S., George Kennedy, Daryl R. Moen, and Don Ranly. (The Missouri Group.) *Telling the Story: Writing for Print, Broadcast, and Online Media*. Boston: Bedford/St. Martin's Press, 2001.

Callahan, Christopher. *A Journalist's Guide to the Internet, the Net as a Reporting Tool*. 2nd ed. Boston: Allyn & Bacon, 2003.

Hausman, Carl. *Crafting the News for Electronic Media: Writing, Reporting, and Producing*. Belmont, CA: Wadsworth Publishing, 1992.

MacDonald, Ron. *A Broadcast News Manual of Style*. 2nd ed. New York: Longman Publishing Group, 1994.

Martin, Shannon, and David Copeland, eds. *The Function of Newspapers in Society: A Global Perspective*. Westport, CT: Praeger Publishers, 2003.

Sammons, Martha C. *The Internet Writer's Handbook*. Boston: Allyn & Bacon, 1999.

Shook, Fredrick. *Television News Writing: Captivating an Audience*. New York: Longman Publishing Group, 1994.

Wallis, David, ed. *Killed: Great Journalism, Too Hot to Print*. New York: National Books, 2004.

Web

www.anywho.com/rl.html
www.bartleby.com
www.census.gov/sdc/www
www.eznews.com
www.fcc.gov
www.fema/listsrv./htm
www.infoplease.com
www.law.emory.edu/FEDCTS
www.lcweb.loc.gov
www.mapquest.com
www.pac-info.com
www.people-press.org/index.htm
www.rtnda.org
www.spj.org
www.switchboard.com
www.whitehouse.gov

CHAPTER 5

Documentaries

The documentarist has a passion for what he finds in images and sounds—which always seems to him more meaningful than anything he can invent. Unlike the fiction artist, he is dedicated to not inventing. It is in the selecting and arranging his findings that he expresses himself; these choices are, in effect, comments. And whether he adopts the stance of observer, or chronicler, or whatever, he cannot escape his subjectivity. He presents his version of the world.

—Erik Barnouw, Professor Emeritus, author, historian, writer and producer of documentaries

Documentaries are produced to capture fragments of actuality, the creative treatment of actuality, the interpretation of recorded images and sounds, and the selection of a socially important topic for clarification.

A documentary is a film that deals with the relationships between people and their environment, people and their work, people and other people, and any combination of those relationship as seen in any society existing at the time of producing the film.

Documentaries make drama from life through the interpretation of actuality and by using the perception of symbolic equivalents to make a socially emphatic value judgment.

Introduction

Each of the definitions of a documentary listed above indicates the range of what may make a media production a documentary. The range of definitions is one of the sources of confusion about documentaries; another is the evolution and changes that documentaries have passed through in the century of their existence. As a writer of a documentary, it is critical that you reach an understanding of what you are attempting to accomplish. A documentary must be produced to make a point, to win an argument, or to solve a puzzle about a socially important topic. Once that goal has been reached, the production technique used is not as important as the method of capturing the reality of the subject and the choice of material used in the final program.

Background

The first documentaries were created accidentally. Photographs from mid-19th-century wars in Europe and the United States Civil War became comments on the price of war, in suffering and in death. Unintentionally, the photographs graphically created an emotional anti-war documentary.

The earliest motion pictures were "documents" of reality. The films showed people leaving a factory, families interacting, and the activities of the city. But without a specific point of social comment either for or against an issue, these films were not documentaries, but merely archival recordings of human activity. Robert Flaherty has been credited with producing the first true documentary with his study of man in and against his environment in *Nanook of the North*, produced in 1922. John Grierson of England, and later Canada, followed with his intense studies of people in their environments and the social issues of living within those environments.

In the 1930s, radio first explored issues raised by the news of the world with the Voice of Time, Harry Von Zell, leading a cast of actors, a full orchestra, and sound effects technicians recreating key stories of that week on the radio newsreel *Time Marches On*. The less sophisticated audiences of that time, with limited access to alternate news sources, accepted the radio recreations as actualities. Since the writers worked for Henry Luce, the publisher of *Time* magazine, the liberal political point of view was the key to the documentary stories.

Earlier film had explored the issues of the daily news in silent newsreels produced in England, France, and Germany. In the United States, newsreels were shown in theaters between the feature and the animated short. *The March of Time* film series connected short subjective news stories of the lives, problems, and activities of people throughout the world that could be reached with a film camera. The liberal social and political attitudes of the producers contributed to classification of many of the shorts as documentaries. By the late 1930s, the German government had found film documentaries as the ideal propaganda tool to sell Nazism through such documentaries as Leni Riefenstahl's *Triumph of the Will*. Both Russia and the United States followed the German propaganda lead with less success until late in World War II.

The term *propaganda* acquired a negative standing in communication, although the term simply means a communication method used to manipulate public opinion to gain support for a specific cause. In many ways, a documentary may use propaganda techniques to win an argument.

Following the war, newsreels continued in the theaters until block booking ended the monopoly control of film distribution by the major studios. Before 1945, the major film studies also owned the distribution and theaters that exhibited the films. Both their own and independent theaters leased films in a package. If a theater wanted to show a new major release, they also had to take a set of a short, a newsreel, and an animated cartoon, as well as a series of "B" lower-quality movies. A lawsuit against the major studies in the mid-1940s required the studios to divest either the distribution or the exhibition part of the combination. They chose to release the theaters. This act did not totally end block booking, but it diminished the power of the major studios to determine what the theaters could use to make up their programs. By the middle of the century, exhibitors cut the animated cartoons, short features, and newsreels to increase the number of times a feature film could be run each day.

Fortunately, television opened new distribution channels for all genres of film, including documentaries and animation. The early TV documentaries tended toward information and travelogues without hard-hitting social values, but each examined some aspect of the human social milieu and the problems therein. Classic examples include the hour-long live (before videotape) *Wide, Wide World*, produced by NBC. The program featured live segments from around the county using microwave connections to feed individual segments to the New York control room. Each program and segment investigated a particular part of American life, from changes in the railroad business to psychological counseling.

In the 1960s, CBS, ABC, and NBC produced series that investigated the human condition. *CBS Reports*, ABC's *Closeup*, and NBC's *White Papers* looked at humans in action and how they reacted to their environment, including careers and family life. Some were very powerful and controversial, especially those produced by Fred Friendly and Edward R. Murrow of CBS. The conflict with the red-baiting Senator Joseph McCarthy, civil liberties, and segregation were topics subjectively covered to reveal specific points of view. The 1960s also saw the increased use of cinema verité techniques using small handheld film and video cameras without an imposing presence to reach subjects.

The 1970s produced a mixed bag of quality documentaries. Murrow was replaced with Don Hewlitt's *60 Minutes*, a collection of short subjective analyses of current topics in the news, not unlike the original *March of Time*, but more sophisticated and subtle. Documentary subjects began to fight back with lawsuits filed based on privacy and libel laws. In most cases, the suits were settled or thrown out of court, but the effect was to indicate to producers and especially networks that some caution had to be shown, depending on the subject and how close it came of concern to a major sponsor. Since the income to produce documentaries depends on sponsors paying for commercials, a documentary that annoyed a leading and major-spending sponsor could stand less of a chance being produced or aired. During this time, networks refused to air independently produced documentaries, so the control of the sponsors shut off such documentaries investigating and promoting fuel-efficient automobiles and alternate power sources.

As society changed, so did documentaries. During the 1980s, feminists, homosexuals, and racial and ethnic minorities become sources of topics. During the late 1980s and the 1990s, the collapse of the Soviet Union, as well as repressive governments in Asia, Africa, and South America, provided fodder for a new wave of documentaries. Cable and satellite operations provided distri-bution opportunities for biographical, travel, and informational documentaries, as well as some topics too violent and sexually oriented for broadcast television.

The first decade of the 21st century found documentaries examining as prime sources for topics large corporations, their financial problems, and relationships with both consumers and employees; the Gulf Wars; and the threat of international terrorism.

Types of Documentaries

Despite the wide range of topics covered throughout the history of documentaries, three basic formats have developed that allow the freedom to make the necessary value judgments and points and, at the same time, maintain the feeling of actuality and realism necessary for a documentary.

Dramatic   Uses an emphasis on actualities of the people or the action of the topic. The more the camera and microphone show what is happening without narration, the greater the dramatic impact. But the documentary must rise and fall through a series of crises, following the dramatic storytelling pattern. The climax may be social or personal in nature, but the argument must be presented in resolving the crisis.

Biographical   Relies on either the subject talking about and showing his or her life, or close friends, relatives, and experts on the subject discussing the subject. When possible, show how the life of the subject was important, and clarify either the positive or the negative aspect of that life to reach a conclusion to the argument.

Compilation   May be a combination of both dramatic and biographical, but more importantly, it is a collection of everything possible to illustrate the point being made about the subject through the ups and downs of the personality's life or the societal of the argument. Often archival and news footage, photographs, and interviews are all are edited together to tell the story.

Script and Production Patterns

The basis for the production of documentaries allows, if not requires, unique means of assembling information and carrying out production techniques. Despite the need for in-depth research before shooting a documentary, the actual creation of a formal script may take a variety of forms. The forms may vary from no written script at all to detailed shooting scripts with complete narration, sound effects, and music prepared before shooting begins.

No Formal Script

Once the basic concept and point of the argument of a documentary has been worked out and locations are determined, shooting may begin in an effort to capture as much information on film or tape as possible. The recordings then become the secondary source from which the complete program may be assembled in the editing room. If the wild and natural sound recorded with the visuals is powerful enough to maintain the flow of the story and to carry the meaning intended, then no written narration is necessary. This type of documentary must be based on extremely powerful and meaningful visuals and sounds, or the audience will miss the argument being made.

Figure 5.1. The point or argument of a documentary should be made with actual footage shot on location of real people and events.

Post-Shooting Script

Again, if the shots and material recorded carry the message strongly enough, a production may proceed without a formal script until the editing process begins. Once the editing has been completed, the wild and natural sound may be supplemented with a minimum of written narration to fill gaps not fully explained with the visuals. Also, such a production may have a complete narration written, to be added after the editing has reached the final cutting stage.

Post-Shooting Script Outline

Another system may be followed by creating an outline after viewing all of the footage shot. Watching the footage and choosing the best available shots gives the producer/writer and editor the means to assemble the program without a formal completed script until after editing has finished. The outline then will guide the editing process. Once editing is completed, narration may be added if needed.

DOCUMENTARY SCRIPT FORMAT

VIDEO	AUDIO
28. MONTAGE OF JEWELRY WORKBENCH, BEADWORK	28. BOBBY BLUE VO: Tells of wanting to work on his own naïve art. Explains how he opened his shop starting with bead work, then added jewelry
29. SHOW COMPLETED COSTUME, HEADDRESS	29. BB VO: Talks about getting interested in costumes and then dancing.
30. DISS: ECU DRUM STICK BEATING DRUM, ZOOM BACK SHOW FULL CIRCLE OF DANCERS	30. BB VO: Talks about importance of Pow Wows in bringing Native Americans together and to show non-natives what a real American Indian is like.
31. VARIOUS SHOTS DANCERS END ON MCU OF BOBBY	31. WILD SOUND: DRUMMING, DANCING, AND SINGING
32. DISS: EXTERIOR NATIVE AMERICA CENTER	32. WILD SOUND: SEGUE TO FLUTE

Figure 5.2. A documentary script may only indicate in a general manner the writer's concept, which may or may not come to fruition in the completed edited production.

A second method would be to view the footage, write the script, and then edit the material, adding narration as needed.

Pre-Shooting Script

After a complete script is researched and written and the shooting schedule is assembled, then the visuals, interviews, and narration are recorded. All of the material then moves to the editing suite, where the production is assembled in its final form, following the script with modifications that occur because of changes in the material that finally arrives in the editing room.

Another method of scripting is based on recording the interviews and then writing the script from the interview material. Cover shots are recorded to illustrate the topics of the interviews, and then these are integrated with the interview footage in the editing suite.

Sponsored Documentaries, Biographies, and Docudramas

These pseudo-documentaries should be fully scripted well before production begins. These types of semi-documentaries need approval from several sponsoring or funding sources before actual production may begin to make certain the information included satisfies the sponsors or funding agencies. These productions also tend to be shot as dramatic productions and generally require full preproduction stages, with larger casts and crews than a typical documentary.

For-profit and nonprofit organizations may commission sponsored documentaries to confirm or supplement their public vision and presence. The danger for you as the writer to avoid is creating a lengthy infomercial without any socially redeeming value.

Depending on who commissioned a biographical documentary, it may only promote the person, leaving the audience without any specific judgment of the person's social significance or value to or against society, giving them an ego-centered puff piece.

Docudramas

The expense of producing feature-length documentaries with no assurance of a return, much less profit, discourages writers and producers from investigating topics that may turn audiences away rather than attracting them to the theater. The solution has been to modify documentaries by adding dramatic touches to create the genre of docudramas.

Docudramas take two forms:

1. An actual historical event, time period, or incident, dramatized using people who may only represent the actual participants in the incident
2. An actual single person or group of people placed in a created series of events that represents what may have happened at some point in time

The first often are based on ancient or very early historical events, such as depicted in the film *Troy;* the event happened and some of the people depicted may have existed or took part in the event, but the dramatic aspect of the relationships between the people provides the basis of the story. Battles and other action sequences may be added to enhance the story, but the reality is based only on the event. *The Killing Fields,* set in more modern times, follows the same pattern of basing a dramatic story on an incident, filling the plot with relationships of people who may or may not have actually existed.

The second type of docudrama is biographically based. The film tells the story of a real person, such as Howard Hughes, as revealed in the film *The Aviator* (among several similar films of his life), using some events tied together with the person's relationships with other people. Much of the story is based on recorded facts, but the story depends on dramatizing the events surrounding the subject, rather than a chronological historical review of the subject's life.

Television series and one-off specials also have produced both types of docudramas. The long-running *M*A*S*H**, originally a feature film and then TV series, was based on the mobile medical troops of the Korean War. *Brian's Song* related the story of a sports figure, and *Judgment: The Court Martial of Lieutenant William Calley* added the Vietnam War to history of another war.

Some productions defy absolute categorization as to whether they are a documentary, a docudrama, or a dramatic feature. *Good Night and Good Luck* falls into that nebulous category; it is in many ways all three. It is a detailed look at the career and times of a single person, Edward R. Murrow, the world events surrounding and involving him, and his battle to defend personal freedom against a bigoted politician.

Documentary Preproduction Process

Before cameras or recorders may roll, several steps of the production process should be completed.

1. Research comes first. You must thoroughly investigate the topic. You must know both sides of the question before decisions can be made as to what interviews and scenes are important to proving the point of the topic.
2. Your preproduction conversations and interviews provide detailed background information, names of possible participants, and historical information important to the topic. You may or may not record your preliminary conversations at first, but you may record them later as on-camera interviews when specific questions are better framed through your research.
3. You must carry out site surveys of possible locations to determine equipment needs and possible production problems to be solved before the crew arrives. This should be accomplished with the producer, the director, and the key crew chief.

4. Permissions must be obtained from all owners of property, including civil units such as city, county, and state sites. If possible, obtain signed releases from anyone interviewed, shown on camera, heard, or whose property is visible in any shot, whether or not that sequence is used in the final production.

Documentary Formats

Short Forms

The earliest short-form documentaries made up the balance of the segments filmed for presentation within the newsreels, especially the *March of Time*. This series began as radio programs and motion pictures shorts during the 1930s. Although the production techniques made the program appear to be straight reporting, those topics covering politics, the economy, and other socially significant stories were intentionally aimed at revealing a specific point of view. Through the years, the newsreels, including those of *March of Time*, degenerated into reporting on the latest in fashions, new buildings, and entertainment culture.

Today, the most often used short form documentaries are segments within full-length programs such as CBS's *60 Minutes*, NBC's *Dateline*, ABC's *Close Up*, and PBS's *Wide Angle*. These hour-long programs consist of two to six stories, each ranging in length from 7–20 minutes. These documentaries must make their point quickly, sharing some of the writing techniques of hard-hitting news stories. The audience often cannot discern the difference between short documentaries and in-depth news reporting. The difference is determined by the point of view clearly stated by the documentary and the attempt at balancing a story in a news report.

Radio long since has given up on producing accurate documentaries, except for NPR. The thoroughly researched and well-edited programs under the title of *Watching Washington* delve deeply into topics of social and political significance. Programs based on highly opinionated talk show hosts do not qualify as documentaries, despite their one-sided coverage of the topic at hand. Those types of programs are intended to be controversial just to attract an audience by eliciting emotionally heightened responses without studied and accurate research or valid socially significant solutions.

Periodically, television networks and some local stations will produce individual programs that may be categorized as documentaries. The constraints placed on broadcasters by sales policies and, more often today, pressure groups make writing and producing documentaries that clearly define a social issue and a solution without attempting to please all segments of the audience very difficult, if not impossible. In the past, CBS's *Selling of the Pentagon* and ABC's *All the Children Were Watching* did succeed in making the type of statements required of quality documentaries. Both generated heated responses, and in the case of *Selling of the Pentagon*, the government attempted interference and legal action.

Cable channels such as the Sundance Channel proved brave enough to take on a challenging topic and give it a full and pointed coverage, as it did with the history of surfing, *Riding the Giants*. The History Channel's programs vary from balanced historical narratives to documentaries and docudramas. This mixture confuses the audience unless the program is clearly labeled as using restaging and reenactments instead of actual historical footage to describe the incidents that make up the story. Reenactments are used in documentaries when needed to fill gaps in available scenes but not to add dramatic value as in docudramas.

Networks have produced and aired series of documentaries on an irregular basis, as opposed to series that run for a specific length, called miniseries. The PBS science and nature series *NOVA* has a long history of accurate and specific coverage of topics that may or may not be controversial. Instead, it takes a specific point of view of a scientific breakthrough, investigating the topic in depth to leave the viewer with the opportunity to accept or reject the information provided to make the producer's argument. Each episode of the *Ted Turner Documentary* series, such as "Avoiding Armageddon," makes a strong argument based on the information presented.

Long Forms

On the other hand, the networks that produce and schedule mini-series that run for a length shorter than a normal season but longer than a single episode alternate between a documentaries, such as PBS's *Baseball,* and docudramas, such as *Roots.* Each may make a strong argument. Although *Roots* told a lengthy story based on historical facts, it was highly dramatized to hold an audience over several nights during the time of its scheduled run.

The production of full feature-length documentaries for theatrical distribution has had limited success. Exhibitors reserve their screen time for features that will show a promised profit, starring leading actors and directed by successful directors and telling stories that people want to see (as shown by ticket sales). Audiences looking for escape or entertainment generally do not look to thought-provoking controversial documentaries. The recording of the 1970s music festival *Woodstock,* which exemplified the time and social changes of the period, held a young audience it needed to be a film success. In the past few years, two unusual types of documentaries surfaced, again as a reflection of the early 21st-century times and social attitudes. Morgan Spurlock's *Super Size Me* and the anti-war *Why We Fight* reflect a growing dissatisfaction with the corporate and military worlds. The other aspect of the population's concern appeared in the support for the nature documentary, *March of the Penguins,* which filled the theaters and won an Academy Award.

Writing a Documentary

All of the confusion and abstraction swirling around the documentary genre leaves you, the writer, with a true conundrum as how to proceed. The following are five suggested steps to be taken:

1. Develop or create a clear argument as the basic concept. You may take a stand against or for a topic, person, or event, but your writing must eventually say to the audience, "I believe the following is the correct way to interpret a socially important subject."

2. Research is a critical stage in documentary writing. It is important that you are totally aware of all of the possible information on the subject, both for and against your view. To take a stand, you must know both your view and the opposing view or views. You must have at your fingertips enough information that, as you gather your material, you will know what will support your view and what information may need to be countered to avoid losing your advantage. The research must be accurate and complete. What you did not find out in the research stage may destroy your argument in the long run.

3. Gathering footage, interviews, historical materials, and creating graphics and other supporting visuals as well as music and sound may lead you toward or away from your first concept. You must know your material well enough to be able to adapt and change your plan as you approach the actual writing stage.

4. Depending on the type of documentary, as indicated earlier in this chapter, the script and scriptwriting stage may vary from nonexistent to a script that is completely detailed, word for word, shot for shot. But the more you have worked out in writing in advance of shooting, the better prepared you will be to take advantage of what you have gathered and what becomes available to you during the production stage. You probably will discard much of your original research by the time you have finished editing.

5. Once the editing and assembling stage begins, then the final decisions will need to be made. Material supporting your argument needs to be assembled in a logical and coherent manner so that the audience will understand and most importantly accept your argument. The story and available material will determine how precisely you edit the production, but do not make the mistake of using everything you have recorded. Be brutal in editing out anything extraneous; use only the best you have available. Do not fear using counterarguments to support your concept. Often, an opposing view makes the best argument for your stand, depending on how you control the editing.

Final advice—do not lose sight of trying to win an argument. Use all legitimate persuasive techniques within ethical standards of the genre to convince your audience of the validity of your point of view.

Summary

Documentaries over time evolved from single-issue archival representations to powerful investigations of complex and controversial social issues. Radio, film, television, and motion pictures provided the media needed to reach audiences over the years. The three basic types of documentaries—dramatic, biographical, and compilation—give the writer wide latitude in program design and concept. Script formats range from virtually nothing on paper before recording and editing to complete, detailed scripts with narration and all shots accurately described. Sponsored documentaries, biographies, and docudramas vary the level of presenting documentary material without precisely meeting the criteria of a documentary.

Producing a documentary depends on thorough research of the topic, the people involved, and the locations for shooting. The controversial nature of documentaries suggests that you follow careful legal advice and make certain all permissions and releases have been obtained. Documentaries vary from short segments of earlier newsreels and today's television programs to full feature-length films and TV series.

Writing documentaries requires a clearly articulated argument, thoroughly researched to determine all available material both supporting the argument as well as contradicting the argument. The completed project depends on the availability and access to the people involved, written records, and historical materials. The writing process of a documentary begins with a concept and ends with the final edited production, ready for distribution.

Be Sure To...

1. Develop a clearly definable argument.
2. Completely research your topic from all angles.
3. Collect all available material both for and against your argument.
4. Keep an open mind to discover and use material or information beyond your original concept.
5. Edit carefully to include only the best material that will win your argument, including the voice of the opposition.

Exercises

1. View a copy of an early documentary such as *Nanook of the North* or *The River*. Outline how the argument is developed and what visuals were used to explain the writer's point of view.
2. View a copy of a more recent documentary such as *Super Size Me*, and compare the techniques with the documentary viewed for Exercise 1.
3. Watch a historical program on the History Channel and determine if it clearly falls within the definition of a documentary or a docudrama.
4. Do the same as Exercise 3 with a historical feature film now running in theaters.
5. Choose an event in your family's history and write a documentary about the event or the key person in the event. Keep in mind that you are going to convince the audience of your point of view.
6. Find a copy of one segment of the PBS series *Jazz* and determine if it is a documentary or a docudrama.

Additional Sources

Print

Barnouw, Erik. *Documentary: A History of Non-Fiction Film*. New York: Oxford University Press, 1974.

Bluem, A. William. *Documentary in American Television: Form, Function, Method*. New York: Hastings House, 1965.

Carroll, Raymond. *Factual Television in America: An Analysis of Network Television Documentary Programs, 1946–1975*. Ph.D. Dissertation, University of Wisconsin-Madison, 1978.

Cumings, Bruce. *War and Television*. London: Verso, 1992.

Edmonds, Robert. *About Documentary: Anthropology on Film, A Philosophy of People and Art*. Dayton, OH: Pflaum Publishing, 1974.

Fielding, Raymond. *The American Newsreel, 1911–1967*. Norman, OK: University of Oklahoma Press, 1972.

——. *The March of Time: 1935–1951*. New York: Oxford University Press, 1978.

Hammond, Charles Montgomery Jr. *The Image Decade: Television Documentary 1965–1975*. New York: Hastings House, 1981.

Jacobs, Lewis, ed. *The Documentary Tradition*. 2nd ed. New York: W. W. Norton & Company, Inc., 1979.

McCann, Richard Dyer. *The People's Films; A Political History of U.S. Government Motion Pictures*. New York: Hastings House, 1973.

Musburger, Robert Bartlett. *An Analysis of American Television Docudrama: 1966–1982*. Ph.D. Dissertation, Florida State University, Tallahassee, FL, 1984.

Rosenthal, Alan. *The New Documentary In Action: A Casebook in Film Making*. Berkeley, CA: University of California Press, 1971.

——. *Writing, Directing, & Producing Documentary Films*. Carbondale, IL: Southern Illinois University Press, 1999.

Rotha, Paul. *Documentary Diary*. New York: Hill and Wang, 1973.

Snyder, Robert L. *Pare Lorentz and the Documentary Film*. Norman, OK: University of Oklahoma Press, 1968.

Web

www.archivalfilmresearch.com
www.archive.org/details/movies
www.der.org/about
www.docurama.com
www.environmentalmediafund.org
www.lib.berkeley.edu/mrc/videographymeno.html
www.pbs.org/pov
www.rihs.org//grcollfilm.htm
www.uaf.edu/museum/depts/docfilm/index.html

CHAPTER 6

Informational Productions

Training is everything. The peach was once a bitter almond; cauliflower is nothing but cabbage with a college education. I have never let schooling interfere with my education.

—Mark Twain, American humorist, novelist, short story author, and wit (1835–1910)

Informational productions provide the quickest and most efficient systems to communicate a consistent, accurate message to a large number of people at a single time for the purpose of increasing a specific audience's knowledge.

Introduction

Corporate and educational media productions share many techniques and goals, but as private media (as opposed to public media of radio, television, and motion pictures), their techniques are unique and narrowly targeted rather than aimed at a mass audience.

Writing for instructional media, whether for a corporate or an educational audience, requires you to assimilate quantities of technical, scientific, and other detailed and accurate information and to turn that information into exciting entertainment that will motivate the viewer to absorb, understand, and remember how to apply the important information.

Such writing requires you to maintain an intellectual curiosity and a willingness to become a "semi-expert" in a new field for each production. This curiosity leads you to areas of knowledge of which you may not have even been aware, much less interested in, until the assignment requires the research necessary to write intelligently and accurately on the topic.

You must be able to write in visual media style, not print. Although many corporate media units may be part of a public relations department, the writing must be different from brochure and press release writing. Instead, you will be concentrating on taking advantage of all possible visual means: computers, slides, Power Point, still photos, graphics, video, and large multiscreen auditorium presentations, as well as film or video.

Since distribution will be through a variety of analog, digital, and live presentations, you will not be limited to any one medium or format. You will choose your medium depending on the requirements of the assignment, the available budget and facilities, and your own creativity. One of the advantages of informational production is the lack of restrictions on the length of the production and the freedom of using your creativity to its maximum. Final productions may be released on DVD, tape, film, or through the Internet. The framing, graphics, and amount of information within each frame must be usable, whether viewed on a 30-inch HDTV or a 2-inch screen on a cell phone.

There is a greater possibility of full-time employment for you in corporate and instructional media than any other media form except news and possibly commercial copywriting. Stable and creative work conditions are the norm for corporate media, more so than broadcasting, which depends on ratings and the whims of sponsors and audience.

Background

As in much of the history of all forms of media, the actual beginning of this form or the first informational production may never be known for certain. Corporate and educational media developed separately but in parallel throughout their histories. Both used the same type of equipment and, in some cases, equivalent distribution systems.

Corporate Media

Late in the 19th century, a company that manufactured magic equipment, Magic Introduction Company, also manufactured cameras and projectors and produced short films to market their products. A portable projector was sent with a salesman to client offices, where they were treated with the unique novelty of watching a demonstration shown on motion pictures. The means to project films at any time in any location was reached when 16-mm film stock and a portable projector were originally developed by the White Lily Washing Machine Company in the early 20th century. The basic design led to the JAN (joint army-navy) projector, used by the armed forces throughout World War II and for many years after by educators and corporations.

As early as 1914, Henry Ford started a film production unit within his company, assigned the responsibility of producing training films and archival films of his operations of Ford Motor Company. In the years following, as corporations and their work forces became larger, the need for internal and external communication and training became much more important. By the middle of the 20th century, following recovery from World War II, most of the larger companies in the United States either organized in-house media operations or contracted independent outside studios to produce their film projects. By the beginning of the last quarter of the 20th century, corporations employed more people in media production than the broadcast industry. With comparable or better wages, stable working conditions, and opportunities for projects as creative as network television programs, many writers, directors, and crews went to work in the corporate world.

The end of the 20th century saw a drop in the number of in-house media operations as projects were reduced or were outsourced to independent studios, often owned and operated by the same people released by the corporations. As digital equipment became smaller, less expensive, and capable of higher-quality productions, both corporate and educational informational projects were written and produced by a wider range of personnel. This gave the freelance writer and other production crews the opportunity to display their talents by working for a large number and variety of different corporations. Today, corporate communication production units use the same type and quality of equipment as broadcasters. In some cases, the facilities are superior to local operations and are equal to or surpass network and cable operations.

Educational Media

Early in the history of radio, despite the Federal Radio Commission (FRC) ignoring the possibilities of using radio for educational purposes, the state of Ohio broadcast classes to rural school districts as early as 1928. By 1940, pressure on the FCC forced the allotment of one-eighth of the available frequency modulation (FM) channels for educational use. In 1945, the number of FM channels for educational use was reduced to 20. Seven years later, the FCC allotted 242 channels on the new TV band for educational purposes. In 1953, KUHT at the University of Houston began the first educational broadcast service to help alleviate the overwhelming number of new students attending school on the government issue (GI) bill. The most popular class was Introduction to Psychology. A year later, WQED in Boston joined KUHT, but as a community-owned and operated station not directly affiliated with a university.

In the early 1960s, six midwestern states were served educational courses by a DC-3 flying in circles over Indiana, since at that time there was no practical means of delivering TV programming to widely scattered markets. Two years later, the National Education Television system began bicycling programs between stations, first on kinescope films and later on videotape. Before videotape, kinescope recordings provided the only means of recording and distributing live television programs. A 16-mm film camera focused on the image of a TV monitor tube (called a kinescope). As the live TV production proceeded, the black and white image was recorded on 16-mm film. The laboratory processed the film, made copies, and distributed the films as kinescope recordings. In 1969, the Children's Television Workshop (CTW) produced and distributed *Sesame Street* as the first educational series intended for in-home, instead of in-school, viewing. By 1970, educational programs were distributed by satellite. By this time, educational radio had disappeared; those nonprofit stations still operating were used for school system public relations or as training facilities for students interested in careers in broadcasting.

The nonprofit television stations originally organized to broadcast classes changed their programming to drama, interviews, public affairs, and programming designed to attract the general public interested in quality artistic programs. Many of the programs were delivered through the Public Broadcast System (PBS), with funding from the Commission for Public Broadcasting (CPB). In-class media productions generally were produced by individual schools for their own curricula, to be distributed by local networks or videotape, and later by digital media such as DVDs and digital videotape. In some cases, closed-circuit networks using microwave or fiber optic circuits, or both, carried programs between buildings and various campuses of one or more school systems.

As a corporate or educational media writer, your function would be to work with a content specialist or professor to create an interesting and accurate script to be produced either by in-house media production departments or by students operating as production units for credit within a school or department of communication.

Writing Corporate Media Scripts

Writing methods for corporations may be as simple as orchestrating the recording of a speech written and presented by a major officer of the corporation, or as complex as a training series involving a group of content experts and complicated production techniques and locations around the world. Regardless of the complexity of the project, 10 basic steps have been developed to ensure maximum quality and minimum costs, as follows:

1. Project requirement analysis (PRA)
2. Research
3. Content outline
4. Treatment and budget
5. Timeline (i.e., production schedule)
6. First script drafts and revisions
7. Approved final script

8. Production
9. Postproduction
10. Evaluations

Project Requirement Analysis

Before any commitment should be made toward a media production, a thorough analysis of the desired goals, accomplishments, audience, and basic design of the project needs to be run by assembling a PRA. The PRA describes in specifics the goal of the project, including what knowledge the audience members should be exposed to and, most importantly, what knowledge should be imbedded into their minds by the end of the viewing session. The precise audience demographics, as well as the question of who exactly will be watching or listening to the material, must be included in the PRA. The potential audience's education, their personal background, and the part they play in the operation that they are being taught are critical factors to be considered. The number of people watching at any one time also is important. An audience's reaction differs between a large auditorium presentation and a small group of less than a dozen. You also need to consider whether there will

Figure 6.1. One of the best uses of corporate training media is to show nonprofit organizations' successes to their members and supporters.

be a moderator present to answer questions following the presentation and if there will be printed handouts provided after the presentation. It is best never to hand out printed material before the presentation. If the material is in hand during the presentation, the audience will try to follow the printed material rather than paying close attention to the information in the media presentation.

There are five traditional reasons for producing corporate media productions, as follows:

1. To train staff
2. To analyze work procedures

Mother of Mercy Church 75 Years of History 6-12-03	Gibbs Media Group, LLC Linda Gibbs

VIDEO	**AUDIO**
1. PAN ACROSS HOUSTON SKYLINE	1. VO: Houston, Texas, the nation's fourth largest city – home of skyscrapers and oil wells
2. DISS: CU MOON	2. VO. NASA
3. DISS: AERIAL MEDICAL CENTER	3. The home of the world's largest medical center
4. DISS: FRONT OF CHURCH	4. WILD SOUND: CHOIR SINGING
5. DISS: PAN OF CHURCH SYMBOLS	5. CHOIR CONTINUES
6. DISS: OPENING TITLE: OUR MOTHER OF MERCY CATHOLIC CHURCH: 75 YEARS OF HISTORY IN THE MAKING	6. CHOIR CONTINUES
7. DISS: INTERIOR OF CHURCH DURING MASS – TILT UP, SHOW CONGREGATION	7. PRIEST: LEADS CONGREGATION IN MASS
8. DISS: TWO SHOT, PRIEST AND ACOLYTE	8. PRIEST CONTINUES WITH MASS

Figure 6.2. A corporate script needs to be accurate, but it also may need to be modified as the production moves forward.

3. To recruit staff
4. To educate consumers
5. To advertise products or services

The primary reason for creating media productions has been to train workers at all levels in a corporation. The technique is especially beneficial in training workers with limited background or preparation for a specific function that needs to be performed in a precise manner. Factory workers, food preparation workers, health care technicians, and even some clerical workers who perform repeated, semi-skilled jobs without variations in the end product are typical targets for media training. A well-made media production will serve in analyzing and completing complex operations that are difficult or dangerous to view or work close to, yet must be precisely carried out.

Corporations wish to provide the best image for potential employees, and at the same time, to explain in detail benefits, duties, and operations expected of a new employee. These facts and duties can best be shown using a media production that may be viewed in a group setting, with a human resources employee present to answer questions, or as a take-home recording. Web sites also now are used for distribution of such programs.

Productions designed to show a consumer the proper manner of using a product or service, how to operate a new device, or the benefits of a service also may be distributed by recordings on tape or DVD or through a Web site. Such recordings help alleviate unnecessary service calls and consumer dissatisfaction due to a lack of understanding of the product or service and its operation.

Some corporations prefer to produce their own commercials to be aired on television, cable, or closed circuit, or to be made available for downloading to a cellular phone or other portable media device.

An interesting media phenomenon developed by corporations to increase positive information about their product and or about the company is recordings delivered to broadcast stations and cable outlets called video news releases (VNR). The production unit within the corporation will create a segment that appears to be a news story. The topic of the story is positive information about the company or the company's product, but it is recorded with narration that sounds like a news story. Often, the segment is constructed without an on-camera talent so that the local station may use the visuals and have their own anchor voice the story from the copy provided by the company. Some stations with small news staff will use such releases to fill their news block or to give the newscast a professional appearance. The audience is not aware that the VNR actually is a news-segment-length commercial disguised as a news story. The most common VNRs are produced and distributed by pharmaceutical companies touting their latest nongeneric, expensive medicine.

Crisis writing is a specific type of writing used by corporations when an oil spill occurs, an airliner crashes, or a chemical spill is caused by a train wreck. The corporation involved must send a positive message to the public as quickly as possible, avoiding the negative facts. The public relations (PR) message will carry as much positive information as possible, called *spin*. The goal is to assure the population affected that there is no danger or that the company is taking care of any problems that may have been caused by the accident. Governments use the same technique when political, diplomatic, or battle problems go awry.

Research

Corporate or educational media developed partially as a result of the research and use of media during wartime. Propaganda studies during World War II indicated the powerful effect media (at that time, radio and some films) had on training and informing both the citizens of the nation and those of the enemy. Two key factors continue to be used in training and information productions. The first is called *filtering*; that is, communicating only the information that supports the goal of the production. In training, this means concentrating only on what the trainee needs to know to complete the function, and possibly not communicating any other aspect of the job or where the employee fits into the larger picture of the operation. The second factor is for propaganda purposes for our own population, communicating only positive information on the progress of the war, the correct decisions of the government, and the part each citizen must play to help in the war effort. Not included are the failures of the government's decision making, the success of the enemy in battles, or how the war may be affecting the citizens on a long-range basis, such as paying the taxes to fight the war.

For educational productions, the same philosophy follows, filtering to concentrate on only what the student needs to learn from a specific topic without causing confusion by offering too much information on related topics.

The first research step is a study of the potential audience and the reason for targeting that particular audience. The development of the basic concept will depend on whether the audience is made up primarily of employees, potential employees, members of the trade, potential customers, or the general public audience.

The next step is to become as thoroughly knowledgeable as possible with the topic to be covered. A content expert should be assigned to the project from the unit requesting or inaugurating the project. That person must be an expert on not only the subject of the item, but also on how it is to be used and the reason for the project.

The research also will include site surveys of the locations for the recording, as well as transportation, lighting, sound, and traffic problems to be solved in advance of the crew arriving at the location. Be careful to avoid writing locations that require complex permissions (city, county, state, and national properties require very specific permissions forms to be signed and filed). No private property may be used without permission; even if a building is recognizable in the background, the owner most agree in writing to allow the image to appear in the production.

Content Outline

From the assembled research information, you write a content outline, which begins the preproduction paper trail. Each specific point to be made in the project is included; how those points are to be

shown or discussed, the order and method of carrying out the concept of the production, whether humor will be used, whether there
will be an on-camera talent, voice-over narration, special effects,
special music, and location requirements all must be listed. You
must decide every detail of the production at this stage of the process. You will decide the following well in advance of the presentation: what sort of media will be used, including slides with audio,
videotape, film, multiscreen, or a digital interactive of any variation
of media productions; the length of the program; who will be on
camera; what music and special effects will be used; what genre
will be included; and what part music and special effects will play
in the story line. Once the general concept, goals, and design have
been determined, then the next important step begins.

Most importantly at this stage, the content outline that you have written with the assistance of the content specialist must be approved and
signed by any and all members of management who may have the
right to authorize changes or the final approval of the project. Without
this signed approval at any stage from this time on, unexpected or
irrational changes made by management will not only increase the
cost of the production, but more importantly, also may destroy the
original concept, creating a worthless and ineffectual production.

Treatment and Budget

You are responsible for the treatment, but the budget more likely will
be the responsibility of the producer. Keep in mind that whatever
you as the writer put on paper will affect the cost of the production.
Writers need to be aware of budgeting only as an overall variable
of the production, not as a means to inhibit the creative completion of
the concept.

The treatment is a narrative description of the project. It is not a script,
but it should follow the order of a script. It is written in narrative
form, not script form, and generally is without dialogue or narration
unless a specific line is critical to making a point that cannot be
made in other manner. The treatment must fully describe the action,
movement, visuals, graphics, and type of dialogue, without specific
shots or transitions. If a special shot or special effect is critical to the

production, it should be described. The idea behind the treatment is to create a document that may be read and comprehended by a nonmedia person who, once finished reading the treatment, should be able to visualize and understand what the production will look and sound like. This document also must be approved and signed by all who may have any authority over the finished work before proceeding to the first script drafts.

Budgets for all productions follow the same pattern as far as you are concerned. Complex and expensive locations should be avoided unless there is a budget specifically set up for such locations. A fly-by of Mount Fuji in Japan may sound like a clever idea, but unless stock footage may be found, it is beyond most any corporate budget unless that company has an office sitting in front of the mountain. Helicopter, underwater, military vehicle, and military personnel shots raise major budget problems and should be avoided if possible.

Corporations and some educational organizations use two methods for maintaining control over production costs. In the first method, the production unit is a self-contained, individually budgeted unit within the company. The unit fulfills requests to complete productions on an as-available basis until the production unit's budget for the year has been expended. This places the production unit in an awkward position of either accepting a single creative but expensive project and rejecting several simpler and cheaper productions or producing the run-of-the-mill daily shows and ignoring the expensive creative productions. Generally, such production units are controlled by and the selection of projects come from a higher level of management who must make the decisions of setting priorities for project selection.

The second method, the *charge-back system*, is a method of "paying for" a media production unit within a company. Each department that needs or wants any media production work done must submit an request for proposal (RFP) stating what they want done. The production unit then studies the request, performs preliminary research, and issues a proposal, treatment, and budget. The proposal goes through several stages of negotiation, and once everyone is satisfied, the production goes forth and funds are transferred from the requesting department to the production unit. This allows the production unit to work only on productions that a department really wants or needs and can afford. It also equalizes the responsibility between the requester and the producer. The more productions that a department needs or wants and can afford, the larger the production unit may become.

Script Drafts and Revisions

Once a commitment of acceptance has been made on the treatment, you can write the first draft of the script. The genre may be straight narration (which tends to be boring), a dramatization (which can be creative, but must be realistic), humorous (which is the most difficult of any genre), or more commonly, a combination of all three, depending on the needs of the subject. The most important genre to avoid is a lecture, either by a professional performer or by a member of the administration of the company. Audiences of today, regardless of their background, now have become so sophisticated that a media presentation must be interesting, creative, and gripping to sustain interest until the end; it must also be entertaining, even if the subject is serious or critical.

Humor has advantages in the entertainment area, but it is the most difficult genre to write and to perform professionally. If the joke or sketch is not really funny, the audience will not only be bored but also will be turned off. Humor also is closely tied to social mores, habits, and ethnic humor not shared by all cultures. A joke or catch phrase or even a hand sign may mean something to one nationality but may mean the exact opposite or worse, an insult to another culture.

The key to keeping the audience involved is to capture and hold its attention by concentrating on single events or descriptions at a time and thoroughly show and describe each event before moving on to the next step.

Although the director will determine specific shots, keep in mind that static shots are dull. You may suggest moving graphics, if properly designed and integrated within the frame, to provide a means of impressing the audience with specific facts, numbers, directions, and other critical information.

The choice of location should be as realistic as possible. If necessary, you should plan to shoot on location in the factory, office, or other corporate location. That choice may involve gaining permission from company departments to disturb its operational pattern while you record the shots needed, but in the long run, the realism is worth it. Setting up and finding enough space and lighting on location may require some modification to the original concept of the setting for a scene, but those problems are the director's to solve.

Dramatic writing is covered thoroughly in Chapter 9. Corporate drama must be subtle: not as emotional as soap operas, not as tense as a mystery, nor as frightening as a war or horror film. Instead, the drama needs to draw the audience's attention to specific actions illustrated by the dramatic action. A good use of the dramatic form is to produce comparison scenes. First, show the actors doing something the wrong way, and then contrast that scene with the actors showing the correct way to complete an action. The audience's attention should be concentrated on the actions that show the difference between the two scenes.

Script Format

The vast majority of corporate and educational scripts are written in the two-column format (see Chapter 2). On rare occasions, the single-column drama format may be used if the entire production is a single drama. Never mix the two formats. Often, a third column may be added to the two-column format. The third column shows a storyboard for each shot. The storyboards may range from simple stick figures showing general framing and composition of the frame to prints of digital photographs taken during site surveys or rehearsals to show precisely how each shot is to be framed and composed.

Approved Final Script

Expect your work to pass through several rewrites. Each level of management and all departments involved in a corporate production will expect to have their input, some of value but many

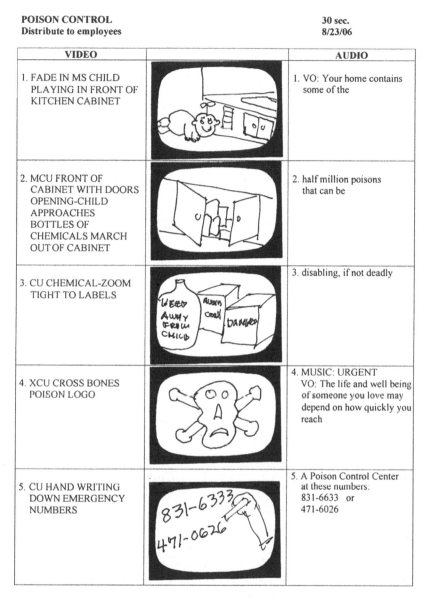

| POISON CONTROL | | 30 sec. |
| Distribute to employees | | 8/23/06 |

VIDEO		AUDIO
1. FADE IN MS CHILD PLAYING IN FRONT OF KITCHEN CABINET		1. VO: Your home contains some of the
2. MCU FRONT OF CABINET WITH DOORS OPENING-CHILD APPROACHES BOTTLES OF CHEMICALS MARCH OUT OF CABINET		2. half million poisons that can be
3. CU CHEMICAL-ZOOM TIGHT TO LABELS		3. disabling, if not deadly
4. XCU CROSS BONES POISON LOGO		4. MUSIC: URGENT VO: The life and well being of someone you love may depend on how quickly you reach
5. CU HAND WRITING DOWN EMERGENCY NUMBERS		5. A Poison Control Center at these numbers. 831-6633 or 471-6026

Figure 6.3. Storyboards integrated on the script page show everyone on the crew and in the cast what the concept calls for, shot by shot.

worthless. The producer will need to fight for what is of value and to try to bypass the useless. Again, once the final script is completed, it must be approved and signed before releasing the script to the director to start rehearsing and recording.

Production and Postproduction

Unless you also are the producer, once the final script has been approved, your responsibility ends unless the director specifically wants you to be on set or location to help make script modifications as needed. Often, regardless of how well a script has been researched, approved, and rewritten, some changes inevitably will need to be made during the recording and the postproduction process. These changes also should be made with the confirmation of whomever has final approval of the production.

Evaluations

The stage most writers and producers dislike most is the evaluation stage.

There are three reasons for performing evaluations:

1. To find out what the audiences does NOT know before viewing.
2. To find out what the audience learned after viewing.
3. To prove to management that your production was valid.

First, there is no point in creating a media production if the audience already knows everything there is to know about the topic, especially in a training production. The difficulty for you as the writer is to write an evaluation pre-test that will reveal what the audience already knows and, most importantly, what it does not know without telling it what you are trying to find out. A comparable post-test must be written to accurately examine the audience's learned knowledge, again without telling them what you are trying to determine. The two tests, pre- and post-, must be fairly matched so that the results will be valid.

The final test comes from the report that you write for management revealing the comparative results of the two tests. If you and the production have accomplished what you had set out to do as indicated in the project analysis and content outline, then management ought to be satisfied. The best proof of success, of course, is for

(PRE-TEST)

PROTECTING YOUR FAMILY FROM POISONS

Answer each question honestly and fully on the attached sheet. This exam is to determine what you know about the subject and is not graded, and it will not affect your personnel file.

1. Which room in your home is the most dangerous to your family?

2. How do you store sharp instruments like knives and scissors?

3. What chemicals do you store under your sink in the kitchen?

4. What chemicals do you store in your bathroom?

5. What is Syrup of Ipecac?

6. What is the most effective way of treating accident poisoning?

7. What does a Poison Control Center do?

(POST-TEST)

PROTECTING YOUR FAMILY FROM POISONS

Answer each question honestly and fully on the attached sheet. This exam is to determine what you learned about the subject and is not graded, and it will not affect your personnel file.

1. Where should chemicals be stored?

2. How can normal household liquids hurt someone?

3. How is Syrup of Ipecac used?

4. List one of the Poison Control Center's phone numbers.

5. How soon after someone ingests a possible poison should you act?

6. Where is you closest Poison Control Center located?

7. How can you poison proof you home?

Figure 6.4. The difference between the pre-evaluation and post-evaluation tests must show a positive change in knowledge to indicate that the project was successful.

the employee who viewed the production to then report to work and immediately begin to operate as instructed in the production, without error.

Since there are so many different types of corporate media productions, there is no one best manner of writing evaluation tests. The differences between instructing new employees on how to operate complex machines, as opposed to teaching new employees what their retirement and insurance benefits include, require totally different approaches to the test-writing and evaluation process.

Writing for Teleconferences

Writing scripts or other material for teleconferences presents a different challenge for you as an informational writer. Teleconferences combine face-to-face conversational meetings with mass media distribution of ad-libbed comments and multimedia displays of audio, video, and graphics to accentuate the two-way communication links that may encompass locations around the world or down the hall. Teleconferences may be viewed by the participants in a conference room or auditorium, or in individual offices viewing the conference on desktop computer monitors. The rationale for holding teleconferences rather than gathering all of the participants in one room at one location is based primarily on cost savings. With travel costs rising and the expenses of housing and feeding participants in hotels, a more economical means of passing information in an interactive manner has become critical to some businesses. Using microwave, satellite, and today, most economically, the Internet or closed-circuit digital networks, such meetings may be held at a much lower cost and in comfortable and familiar settings.

Some teleconference participants require complete, well-researched scripts to guarantee accuracy, security, and legal protection, as well as to help maintain schedules. Since information will originate from more than one location, your minimum writing will include a format sheet describing which location will offer which information and in what order, where the visuals will be fed from, and what order each location will be allowed to offer contributions to the program.

A project manager, who may or may not write all of the material used in the conference, guides professional teleconferences. But one person must be in control of such a complex operation as a teleconference. Each remote location also should have a manager to make certain that facilities are properly prepared and operating and that the participants are gathered and prepared for the conference. Some gathering of information and preparation of that information in written form for the participants may be performed by you as a staff or freelance writer.

In addition to multi-source discussions and presentations, teleconferences also serve as distribution systems for distance learning and training. The training programs produced for such distribution must meet the highest-quality standards in addition to being created for interactive communication between the primary information source location and the remote sites receiving the training. Again, the writing required beyond that of the specific training scripts involves organizational scheduling to make certain the program runs smoothly. Usually, teleconference feeds are reserved for live programs since other information, including training programs, may be recorded and distributed for viewing at the convenience of the participant.

Writing Educational Media Scripts

Educational media productions integrate subjects into formal school curricula in addition to providing educational material for consumption by the general public or by specialized audiences. The development of educational media, especially the use of television, paralleled that of the development of corporate training media. The major difference existed in a cost differential. Corporations, once convinced media training was practical, invested whatever the price demanded, but in the educational world there have been limited financial resources to properly fund the development and experimentation required to reach a successful level of achieving all educational goals.

A certain level of confusion over how television could be used to teach at various grade levels also held back the process of using media for teaching purposes. A distinct disdain existed among educators for television; similarly, television producers felt no special respect for educational psychologists or curriculum developers who were critical of using television techniques successful in selling sugar-coated cereals to children as a means of teaching positive values to children.

Much of this negative environment was dissipated by the success of the Children's Television Workshop's (CTW) *Sesame Street*. CTW forced a combination of educational psychologists and professional television producers to work together to use the best of television's techniques, guided by research and experimental cognitive techniques, to achieve a common goal of teaching children the basics of the education they needed at the targeted age levels.

For writers of educational programs, *Sesame Street's* success provides the guide for careful research and consideration of what exactly to attempt to teach and at what level. The production technique must concentrate on a specific point of the lesson; too many different techniques may distract the student from absorbing the critical information of the lesson. At the same time, TV production techniques may better illustrate and channel the viewer's concentration on that specific point by using close-ups, split screens, zooms, or any other technique that properly fits the specific scene. The use of dialogue balloons, graphics, color and music coding, puppets, and animation may draw the attention of the student to the point being made better than any live classroom situation or technique.

For you, then, a thorough knowledge of media production techniques and how those techniques may be used, guided by the research of the educational specialists, indicates a winning combination to achieve a positive learning goal for the students.

Summary

Using media for informational purposes began over a century ago. The concept of using media evolved from both corporations and educational institutions needing a method of distributing detailed information to large groups of people as economically as possible. Using media proved that audiences of mixed educational backgrounds could be taught and trained to learn new skills and working methods. The same system works well in disseminating information to employees in widely spaced locations in small or large gatherings. Distributing the same information on a take-home basis also has proved to be successful.

Writing informational scripts requires the study and determination of the need to be fulfilled, research of the topic, and a study of the audience's prior knowledge. Scripts may use drama, humor, and narrative styles, but they must keep the audience interested and entertained. The value of the project will be determined by comparing the results of specifically written pre- and post-evaluation tests. If the post-test results indicate an increase of knowledge or skill in comparison to the pre-test, then the project was a success.

Be Sure To...

1. Set specific goals.
2. Carefully research topics.
3. Work with content experts for accuracy.
4. Write accurate and detailed scripts.
5. Receive written approval at each step of the process.
6. Design pre- and post-evaluation tests to determine value.

Exercises

1. Visit a corporation that uses an in-house production unit. Determine their process for setting project goals.
2. At the corporation in Exercise 1, determine their budgeting system—charge back or by department budget—and explain why that system is used in this case.
3. Write a PRA for a training project, following through with each step up to production.
4. Write pre- and post-evaluation tests for the project in Exercise 3.
5. Visit a corporation that uses teleconferences. Tour the facilities and interview the project manager. Ask to follow a project from conception to completion.

6. Write an educational project for a subject that you find difficult to understand.

Additional Sources

Print

Bucy, Erik P. *Living in the Information Age: A New Media Reader*. Belmont, CA: Wadsworth Publishing, 2002.

Burder, John. *The Work of the Industrial Film Maker*. New York: Hastings House, 1973.

Campbell, Richard. *Media and Culture: An Introduction to Mass Communication*. 3rd ed. Boston: Bedford/St. Martin's Press, 2003.

Croteau, David, and William Hoynes. *The Business of Media: Corporate Media and the Public Interest*. Thousand Oaks, CA: Pine Forge Press, 2001.

DiZazzo, Ray. *Corporate Television, A Producer's Handbook*. Boston: Focal Press, 1990.

Hiebert, Ray Eldon, Donald F. Ungurait, and Thomas W. Bohn. *Mass Media VI: An Introduction to Modern Communication*, New York: Longman Publishing Group, 1991.

Lesser, Gerald S. *Children and Television: Lessons from Sesame Street*. New York: Random House, 1974.

Orlik, Peter B. *The Electronic Media*. Boston: Allyn & Bacon, 1992.

Portway, Patrick S., and Carla Lane, Ph.D. *Guide to Teleconferencing and Distance Learning*. 3rd ed. New York: Advanstar, 2000.

Rhodes, John. *Videoconferencing for the Real World: Implementing Effective Visual Communication Systems*. Boston: Focal Press, 2001.

Web

www.aaim.org
www.alliancecm.org
www.atsp.org
www.cma.org
www.current.org
www.educause.edu
www.icia.org
www.imtc.org
www.mediachannel.org

www.mediaed.org
www.mediafamily.org
www.mediaownership.org
www.mediaweek.com
www.mmcf.org
www.usdla.org
www.veronissuhler.com
www.wict.org

CHAPTER 7

Animation

...in spite of bending the laws of space, time, and reason to the limits of imagination, animated films tend to come over larger than life. This is because, above all other film techniques, animation allows concepts to be isolated, analyzed, reinforced, and presented in a direct form that is immediate and obvious.
— Stan Hayward, award winning animation writer,
producer, and director

Animation creates the appearance of inanimate objects moving.

Introduction

Animation knows no limits as to what the process may accomplish; therefore, animation may use nonobjective and nonlinear plots and action sequences that live action finds difficult or impossible to complete without resorting to computer graphics imagery (CGI), which also is animation. Even though animation stories should have a recognizable form, the pattern of the beginning, middle, and ending format of normal dramatic structure is not as necessary. Audiences readily accept a more abstract pattern of animation storytelling than they do of live action.

The definition of animation for the purposes of this text includes such items as puppets, collages, sand and clay figures, found objects, painting and scratching on film stock, pin boards, and of course, cel and computer animation. This broad definition is both a blessing and a detriment to analyzing and understanding animation. Traditionally, a group of objects that could be shot on film at the rate of one or two frames at a time constituted animation. But today, with computer applications and digital equipment, no clear delineation exists between reality and a computer creation. For you, it just means there are no limits to your creativity.

Writing animation requires you to concentrate on visuals rather than dialogue. Again, a balance between the two must be maintained for a quality production. One of the advantages of animation is its ability to transcend language barriers when properly produced. Well-produced and well-conceived visual aspects tell the story in any language and culture, without narration or dialogue.

Animation depends upon characters as the basic building blocks of the story. Maintaining a balance between character development and the entertainment value of the story requires careful consideration of each in relation to the other. Animation characters must be strong, larger than life caricatures, with exaggerations of their personalities and actions. Voices also may add to the development of those characters, especially unique or unusual voices. But you must be careful to avoid letting characters and their personalities overpower the story.

Background

Using motion picture film to animate objects coincided with the development of film itself. Many of the earliest films were produced in order to exhibit so-called mysteries and special effects. In order to do so, single-frame exposure of action, drawings, and double exposures created those effects. The fundamentals of animation comprised these techniques.

In the past, the animator was the director, producer, and often even the actor and the writer (since there were few scripts actually in place on paper). Animation was, and still is currently, an auteur medium. Although during the earliest days of animation all of the writing aspects of the production process were completed by one or two people for any single production, the process of assembling the information needed to reach a completed film remains the same today, regardless of who actually writes the script.

The first addition to the writer's duties was to create storyboards, or at least sketches, of each scene before the cels were drawn. For some writers, drawing storyboards was not a problem, but with time, storyboard creation became an art in itself. The writer then concentrated on developing characters and action scenes, leaving the drawing of storyboards to artists hired for that function. Disney developed the "factory" system of producing animation beginning in the 1930s by creating individual departments, including separate scriptwriting and storyboard departments.

The storyboard artist then assumes some of the responsibilities of the director, interpreting the script, drawing each scene, and even drawing key frames and individual cels. The storyboard artist may also decide on the movement of both the characters and the camera. The ability to draw boards and to maintain the vision of the writer is critical for quality animation productions.

At the same time, groups of writers began writing by committee in gag meetings. A gathering of three to a dozen writers, led by a producer, work out story lines, character development, and the gags that build the action and the progress of the plot. With increased use of computers to create animation, the separation of writing and drawing became even more clearly defined. The value of quality writing in developing strong characters and stories that capture and hold the audience separates good writers from poor. All stories will be based on some kind of a conflict, but violence is not as important as the use of action that propels the audience into the story. Humor is crucial in most animation, even if a scene or two become heavy with dramatic action. The success of the Pixar animated films and Disney's early features and shorts illustrates the value of well-constructed stories populated by believable characters, as opposed to the weak stories of some direct-to-video and television animation of today.

Today's quickly produced television animation tends to depend on dialogue rather than visual action because it is cheaper to let the characters tell the story rather than to show the action, which requires more time and effort, raising costs. Music, sound effects, voice-over narration, and dialogue without lip synchronization describe the story, rather than acting out the action to show the audience the story.

Making certain voices match lip synchronization also becomes an increased financial commitment.

The Production Process

The production process varies depending on the length of the production, the type of animation used, the size of the studio, and the budget. The independent animator today may raise the funds needed, write the script, draw the cels or use a computer program, assemble the story, and prepare it for distribution. But even if all of the work is accomplished by one person, the production process follows a reasonably parallel path regardless of whether the product is the simplest or the most complex.

Sound

Once the concept has been fleshed out and a complete script written, then production may begin. Recording the soundtrack must be completed first. Once recorded, the track is carefully analyzed and timed, word by word. A dope sheet lists each frame to be created, along with the three accompanying tracks: dialogue, music, and sound effects (SFX). The dope sheet consists of a chart based on scenes broken down into increments of 1/24 of a second. Film and some digital recordings are normally exposed at the rate of 24 frames per second. Most animation uses exposures of two or three frames per cel, rather than one cel for each frame. This reduces the number of cels needed without decreasing the flow of the visual.

Drawing

Backgrounds and key frames are drawn separately. Depending on budget, the inbetween frames are completed within the studio or drawn overseas, where lower labor costs help maintain budget levels. The images are entered into a computer file that parallels key and inbetween frames of a cel-drawn production. In a 3-D computer production, 3-D wire frames are constructed within the computer or are captured from a motion capture (MoCap) process or from digitally photographing 3-D models of characters.

EXPOSURE (Dope) SHEET

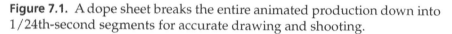

| TITLE | | SCENE | ANIMATOR | | SHEET # | |

FRAME	ACTION	SETTING	LAYERS						CAMERA
			4	3	2	1	BG		

Figure 7.1. A dope sheet breaks the entire animated production down into 1/24th-second segments for accurate drawing and shooting.

In cel production, the outline of the character or object is drawn in black on the front of the individual cel, and then painters add the color on the backside of the cels, frame by frame. In the computer world, each space is labeled a color, and that space will carry that assigned color in each frame wherever that shape appears. In 3-D, texture mapping creates solid surfaces and surface textures.

Once the painting process has been completed in the cel production, then the cels are photographed, sandwiched over a background. Each movable part of a character appears on a separate series of cels that are changed for each new camera exposure. A parallel process occurs in computer animation by assembling individual scene files into a final and permanent form.

Each of these same stages is followed if the production uses dimensional materials (e.g., sand, clay, or paper cutouts) instead of cels or a computer program, except that each frame is a physical set-up. Once the characters and objects are arranged on a dimensional set, they must be lit. Then the camera operator shoots individual frames before moving each character or object and making the next exposure.

One of the most difficult animation techniques, regardless of the medium, is creating and maintaining synchronization between the sounds, especially voices and the movement of the character on screen. This process is called maintaining *lip sync*. Each set of vowels and consonants requires a different shape of the mouth for a realistic action, and the changes of the shapes must match the voice on the track.

Postproduction

The postproduction stage may consist of simply printing a copy of the edited film combined with a mix of the soundtracks or a frame-by-frame recording, adding visual effects and rearranging shots to remove unwanted images, such as power lines, or unwanted

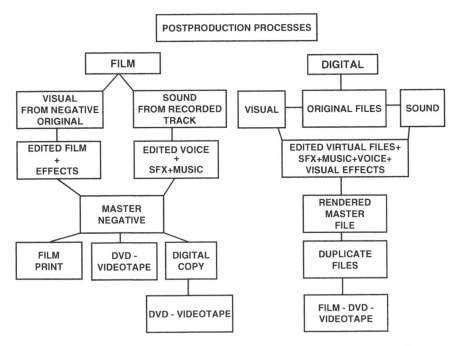

Figure 7.2. The postproduction process for film and digital formats follows a parallel but differing path from raw footage to finished product for distribution.

sounds. The final stage for computer production involves *rendering* the original virtual files into a conformed final file that may be duplicated or converted to film or videotape.

The Writing Process

The exact process used in writing for an animated production will depend partially on the size of the production, the budget, the crew, and the client's desires. But the following step-by-step process covers the critical areas, regardless of the complexity of the product. Several of the steps may be combined, again depending on the type of production.

An Idea

A basic concept of what the production is to do or say has to start with a simple idea. It could arise from within an experience, from an observation of the world about you, or from brainstorming with others. Other sources may come from modifying an existing story by reversing images or characters, or else from modernizing a myth, fairy tale, or traditional story. And there is always the possibility of you adapting a published work if you can gain permission from the copyright holder.

The Premise

Another name for the premise is the *log line*. The premise must state in one sentence the entire concept, without dialogue or narration. Reduce the idea to its simplest form. From this point, then your idea can be developed and expanded without losing sight of the original concept. If the idea cannot be summarized in one concise statement, then the you have not accurately thought through the concept.

A Proposal

At some point, you must decide who will pay for the production. Even if is self-produced, you must worked out a budget, at least tentatively. If it is not self-produced, then someone else will need to be convinced to provide the funding. Your proposal is a sales tool to provide the potential bankroller a rational for loaning the funds for the production. The proposal should be no longer than two pages. It should describe what the production will look like, without dialogue or narration, and the briefest of scene descriptions. An approximate budget should included a timeline, outlining the progression of the production day by day, from scripting through to the completed film or computer file.

SAMPLE LOG LINE AND PROPOSAL

LOG LINE

Two young androgynous space creatures explore a new planet to find adventure, action, violence, and humor.

PROPOSAL

Two gender-neutral space creatures, Itsy and Bitsy, take off in their space ship to explore a new planet. They manage to crash-land their rocket without harming themselves. They unload their space rover to explore the new planet. They must find a way through a big mountain to find a suitable location for a picnic lunch. On the way they meet and try but fail to capture a large butterfly. The search for a picnic site leads them to a lake full of fish, which they try and fail to catch. Fortunately, they brought along their lunch and manage to consume it before it is time to return to their space rocket and find their way back to their home planet.

Each of the four 3-minute episodes will be filled with different levels of humor, violence, and action as the basis for a study of the reaction of young children to the three stimuli.

A budget of approximately $4,000 will cover the cost of materials to create cel animated episodes. Labor costs will require $10,000 and finishing another $2,000. The project will be completed within 9 months of final acceptance of scripts and approval of financing. Writing the scripts will require approximately six months from approval of the treatment. The episodes will be shot on film or distribution via either film or a digital medium.

Figure 7.3. A log line defines the project; the proposal explains in more detail what the animator has in mind to create.

An Outline

Once the concept is firmly in mind, then you must list the scenes addressing key plot points of the production, acting as a guide to establish characters, locations, and basic actions. The outline may be expanded to provide a storyboard frame for each item of the outline.

The Bible

A tool that determines many aspects of an animated production is the *bible*. The bible is a listing of characters by name; a fairly complete description of their appearance, characteristics, personality, and type of voice for casting; and, most importantly, the relationships among the characters. You must also create a list of locations, scene descriptions, music, and SFX required to provide the basis for planning backgrounds and other settings and props needed during the production. And, finally, you will need model sheets for each of the characters. A model sheet consists of pencil drawings of a character in different poses viewed from different angles, as well as close-ups (CU) of the head, hands, and other distinguishing body parts. The model sheet guides the many different artists involved in the production to maintain consistency in drawing each character.

The Treatment

Once all of the characters and details of the production are known, then a complete description of the production should be written in narrative form, without dialogue, avoiding technical media or animation terminology. The treatment accompanies the proposal to the pitch.

A pitch is a meeting with the potential funding source, who listens to you describe in detail the entire production, often with you reciting the dialogue and acting out some of the action. The proposal and treatment are left with the funding source as a reminder of where their money is about to be spent until a firm contract is written. The treatment provides the second step in the funding request sales presentation.

SAMPLE TREATMENT

In order to better test the relative response of children to various elements in television cartoons, it is necessary to produce a specific controlled series of cartoons, rather than using cartoons presently being telecast. In order to produce such materials, it is important to make them as close as possible in appearance and quality as those presently telecast.

This project will produce four 3-minute cartoons using the same story line, but varying the activities of the characters to create one episode that has no action, violence, or humor. The second will use action without gratuitous violence or humor, the third will be based on children's humor without action or violence, and the fourth will feature gratuitous violence without any humor or action aside from the violence.

The treatment for the neutral episode follows:

A small planet appears and a space ship approaches from a distance. Itsy and Bitsy are sitting at the controls. They discuss the likelihood of landing on the planet and decide it looks safe. They remember to buckle their seat belts and the space ship lands on the planet. Once the space ship comes to a full stop they drive out in the Space Rover, a two-seat vehicle designed for exploring planets. They discuss which way to go and agree on a direction and away they go. They are pleased with the beauty of the passing mountains, rivers, and a lake. They decide the lake will be a good spot to have their lunch. They pull up to the lake, get out, and Itsy spreads a blanket for a place to eat. While they are eating a large butterfly flutters right by them as they sit on the blanket. They admire the butterfly and then decide to find some dessert. They discover a nut tree and decide if they shake it gently some nuts will fall out of the tree for their dessert. They pick up some nuts and find them crunchy and delicious. Suddenly they see a fish jumping in the lake. After watching the fish for a while they decide it is time to return home. They load up the Space Rover and head back to the space ship. Once the Space Rover is inside the rocket they take off and fly into the sunset.

Figure 7.4. The treatment describes the entire production in greater detail than the proposal, using a narrative format without technical jargon. The treatment should tell the story as if it were a short story without dialogue.

The Storyboards

An important stage in an animation production rests with the accurate creation of the storyboards. Storyboards must be drawn, even if just simple stick figures are used to indicate characters, movement, and framing, along with accompanying dialogue for each board. With storyboards as a guide, you can approach the critical facet of animation: the visual approach to the story. With individual boards drawn, you may pin them to a wall to show the progress of the story, particularly where scenes begin and end. If necessary, you may rearrange them if the original plan does not work. It is

PRODUCTION PRODUCER	WRITER DATE
VISUALS	**AUDIO-DESCRIPTION**

Figure 7.5. Storyboards may take different forms, but they must show the accurate frame aspect ratio for the chosen medium.

important for you at this stage to think *visually*. You need to think about what the frames are going to look like, what the pictures will tell the audience, what will happen in the action, and how the action will move the story forward.

Figure 7.6. The final frame reached after shooting may not appear as described in the original script.

Full-sized storyboards work better if drawn on separate sheets from the script. Eventually, the storyboard frames will be separated and pinned on a wallboard or other surface for rearranging and modifying as the production process moves forward. The storyboard frame should be accurately drawn to indicate either the 3×4 aspect ratio of standard 16-mm, 35-mm film, and NTSC video or the 9×16 aspect ratio of wide-screen film or HDTV. Each frame should be numbered to match the shot, with notes indicating pans, zooms, tilts, and other movements, and if necessary, the background arrangement as well as matching audio.

The First Draft

Writing the rough draft follows the completion of the storyboards. The written script now is critical in order to develop the sound of the production, including the dialogue, narration, music, and SFX. Once you complete the first acceptable draft, the voice track may be recorded. After the voice track has been recorded, individual cels and the number of cels needed to cover the track may be calculated.

```
           CELL LIST- ITSY AND BITSY

      BG's lrg   #1     Space with planet on right
                 #2     Landing zone
                 #3     Land plus lake on right
                 #4     Larger lake

           sml   Space ship interior
                 Land Rover interior (head on)
                 Palm tree

★ New, coll #
        0001     Space ship in upper left, very small,
        0001A
        0001B
        0002
        0002A    Moves downward, to the right
        0002B
        0003
        0003A
        0003B
       ✦0004     getting larger
        0004A
        0005
        0005A
        0006
        0006A
        0007     more detailed
        0008
       ✱0009
        0010
        0011
       ✦0012
        0013     passes past camera on right
        0014     I & B looking foreward in space ship cabin
        0015     I looks at B, I talking
        0016     B looking at I, B talking
        0017     I & B looking at each other
        0018     Space ship large on left
        0019
        0020
        0021     moves to right
        0022
        0023
        0024
        0025     gets smaller
        0026
        0027
        0028
        0029
        0030     out of frame on right
        0031  ----
        0032  ----
        0033  ----
        0034  ----
```

Figure 7.7. The two-column script format must accurately list all sound sources, as well as accurate sequence descriptions.

The Final Draft

Corrected and final drafts follow as changes are made during the production. In some cases, an actual final script will not be written until after the postproduction stage has been completed.

Writing Techniques

The very nature of the variety of different materials used to create animated productions demands different formats in script and storyboard layout.

Script Formats

The script format may be either patterned after the two-column television format or after the single-column dramatic film format. Because animation is more visually than aurally dependent, the two-column format allows for greater space and alignment of visuals for animated productions. The visuals are listed shot by shot in a column on the left side of the page, with the audio aligned with the matching shots on the right side of the page. All visual and production instruction, SFX, and music are entered in capital letters (caps), whereas all dialogue is entered in uppercase and lowercase letters. A column of storyboard frames, if included in the same page, is usually aligned down the center of the page. Two pages of finished script may equal approximately 1 minute of screen time.

The structure of an animated story will vary with the intended length. Animated shorts commonly run 7, 11, or 22 minutes long. Three 7-minute, two 11-minute, or one 22-minute short make up a half-hour of television programming. Animated features run from 60–90 minutes long.

A 7-minute short consists of one act. A crisis is established and then resolved, with a quick gag saving the hero. An 11-minute short moves with two acts. During the first act, the crisis or problem is introduced, with the hero reacting, setting the first action. A short second act may contain a new crisis, but all problems are resolved by the end of that segment. A 22-minute short consists of three acts. The first is longest, to establish characters, location, and the basic story line. The conflict must be paramount in the first act. During the second act, the immediate crisis may be resolved, but unexpected changes in action introduce the major problem or a new crisis. The third act builds to a climax, followed by a resolution of all of the crises.

Features follow the same pattern as a 22-minute short, but each act lasts longer and becomes more complex as the story progresses, with increasingly more important or dangerous crises building to the final climax and resolution. The action rate must increase as the plot progresses; since animation is action and visually oriented, the pace of action is important, if not critical. A feature should include several subplots, some involving the main characters and some with secondary characters for added interest and comic relief. The action of features occurs in several different locations. Each change of location adds new interest and plot possibilities. A feature also will require many more characters than a short, with different levels of importance to the plot and to the action. But each character must be defined and have a reason for existing in the production to help move the plot forward, directly or indirectly.

Direct-to-video productions vary from features originally released for public theaters in that they are produced with smaller budgets, often are shorter in length, and have lower production values to short, low-budget features produced specifically for direct-to-video sales. As studio marketers become aware of the income value of direct-to-video, the production values and the care taken in the producing these quick-to-market animation features and packages of shorts may improve.

Internet animation generally uses shorter formats and less-complicated production techniques. Internet animation will be discussed in Chapter 10 in greater depth.

Developing the Plot

Before a story may be told, you must write a central concept. You concentrate on a hero or a heroic action or incident. The plot and story develop around the hero or key character as the center of the action. The plot and characters must match or mesh, or they will distract the audience from following the plot. Write an outline or plot a graph showing each key scene and how each sequence relates to other sequences. In moving the story forward, follow the golden rule of KISS, "Keep It Simple and Succinct"; do not overwhelm the audience with words, but rather use the power of visuals to show the audience your story. Show the audience what is going to happen, with hints of coming actions before they occur so that the audience can be expecting something to happen and will be prepared to understand the gag.

Another approach to plot development depends on a pattern of alternating dynamic and static sequences. As an example, a story starts with the characters in happy, satisfied relationships, with all going well (a static position); then, suddenly, something happens that destroys or threatens the relationship. It can be the intrusion of a new character or an old competitor, or even a physical change such as an earthquake. The plot now is in a dynamic position, and the protagonist must move the story to a new static position. Alternating between static and dynamic positions makes for an interesting manner of approaching and solving crises. A story may start in total dynamism, leaving you the challenge to create stativity by the end of the production. Stativity does not necessarily mean a happy ending, but rather just an ending that satisfies the audience with resolution of the primary crisis.

Pace, Tempo, Rate, and Rhythm

The perceived feeling of the passage of time in animation depends on a sense of rapid motion. Animated productions control time better than live-action production because you control time with each individual frame. Therefore, time and the sense of passage of time in animation become critical. Time is subjective, but the perception of time is controllable. To one audience member, a scene may appear to be moving rapidly; to another, time passes at a much slower rate. A method of measuring time factors considers pace, tempo, rate, and rhythm. Pace is the perceived speed of an overall production: fast, medium, or slow. Tempo is the perceived speed of individual sequences or scenes. Rate is the speed of individual performance, such as the shot length and the comparison of adjacent shot lengths. A series of shots are short if the series ends quickly and the audience perceives a sense of a rapid rate.

Rhythm develops with variations in pace, tempo, rate, or a combination thereof. Rhythm gives the audience a sense of the flow of the action within individual scenes, sequences, and an entire production. Rhythm may be calculated in *beats*. A pattern of beats is a combination of the lengths of individual segments and the number of segments that make up a sequence.

Character Development

Even though action, movement, and the visuals provide the key to pleasing an audience in animation production, you must properly develop characters that the audience wants to believe in, or at least believes fit the plot. In every drama, including animation, whether the plot is serious or comic, a conflict must exist or be created. The conflict depends on the relationship between an antagonist and a protagonist. The antagonist may be a natural event, a human, or a machine, depending on your decisions and the direction of the plot. The antagonist will oppose the protagonist, the main character or the hero of the plot, providing the crisis or the conflict necessary for a drama.

Animated humanized characters, animals, creatures from space, or mythological figures must communicate among themselves as if they were humans so that the human audience can relate to the characters and understand why the relationships exist and why the actions develop as they do. There must be recognizable, strong personalities that are good, bad, or (preferably not) in between, but they also must be characters that the audience can accept as existing within the story line of the production. Some characters will dominate the plot, and others will be subservient or even just neutral, but all characterization must be clear enough for the audience to understand exactly what type of personality a given character exhibits.

All characters must be recognizable to the targeted audience. Whether the audience is children watching morning or afternoon television, prime time or late-night adult viewers, or casual viewers, the character must make sense to the audience. The direction the character moves in the story and the motivation for that movement lets the audience feel part of the story through its understanding of what is happening and what might happen next. Anticipation keeps an audience interested and tuned to the program. The characters also must grow to show a change in how they have felt, learned, or reacted to others in the cast and to the actions that occur to them as individuals.

Some of the basic recognizable traits of characters are age, physical size, strength, appearance, gender, and relationship to others as a leader, follower, or sidekick. Animation productions depend upon at least one character taking a leadership role. An animated series requires a leader plus a leader's sidekick or buddy. That sidekick may be a goof-off, a devoted friend, or an idiot, but the story's action needs to show a contrast between the lead character and the supporting character or characters.

A three-dimensional character will show intelligence, stupidity, likeability, loyalty, destructiveness, dejection, supportiveness, uncooperativeness, aloofness, friendliness, unpredictability or predictability, or a combination of several of these traits. Without such recognizable traits, the characters become a two-dimensional cardboard cutouts.

Stereotyping

One danger in developing strong characters may depend on stereotyping. Stereotyping uses the technique of counting on the audience's preconceived notion of what a person or location will do because of appearance, gender, ethnicity, religion, or economic and social status. Especially in animated shorts with limited time to develop three-dimensional characters, you may use stereotyping to quickly establish a portion of a character's personality. The danger comes from using stereotypes in a negative manner, creating a character based on the worst negative characteristics of a group. Negative stereotypes must never be used. Instead, use stereotyping to quickly establish a location or some aspect of a character, but remain with positive characteristics, not the negative. Avoid depicting any member of a group as having the same actions or personality characteristics attached to a group by bigots.

Humor Versus Drama

Humor, the basis of most, but not all animation, is a subcategory of drama. All of the rules of dramatic structure hold true for humorous animation, as well any other genre of drama. In many ways, writing humor is much more difficult than writing straight drama. In addition to all of the other requirements of a well-written drama, a humorous production, including animation, must also appeal to the funny bones of the audience. The audience may be carried along with the strength of the animated characters, the believability of the plot, and the excitement of seeing crises develop and disappear, but most importantly, the audience must want to laugh, or at least be highly amused.

Writing animation requires an understanding of human and animal physiology and movement, as well as a strong sense of visual creativity.

Summary

The definition of animation in this text is intentionally broad to include all media productions that meet the criteria of inanimate objects seeming to move. The history of animation began with the beginning of motion pictures as an early production technique, and it continued as a format unique from live action.

The production process starts with the preproduction steps in writing, beginning with the idea expressed in a premise, continuing on through stages including the proposal, the outline, the bible, storyboards, and a more-detailed treatment and drafts of the script. Preproduction paperwork of animation needs to be more detailed than live action since each frame is shot individually. Once a script is written, storyboards and the soundtrack determine the progress of assembling the individual cels, frames, or shots of dimensional characters.

Strong stories, recognizable character development, interesting and exotic locations, and stimulating actions in animation provide you and the director with unlimited possibilities for creativity. Any action or description may be created in an animated form, from photorealism to the abstract, and animation may encompass any material that may be manipulated, including cels, clay, sand, toys, collages, and 2-D and 3-D computer frames.

The scriptwriting process follows the traditional dramatic writing structure, with the added requirement of making the audience laugh. A conflict of some sort must exist to develop the plot and to give the characters a reason for their actions.

Be Sure To...

1. Think your story concept through completely.
2. Create strong, contrasting characters.
3. Rely on humor and action instead of violence.
4. Think visually and create accurate storyboards.
5. Carefully consider your target audience.
6. Avoid negative stereotypes and use positive stereotypes judiciously.

Exercises

1. Write a log line and a proposal for a 7:00 short. Provide all details needed to sell the idea and an approximate budget.
2. Write and record the soundtrack for your proposal. Then analyze how many frames will be needed to complete the animation.
3. Create a bible for your proposal, including character descriptions and a model sheet.
4. Draw simple storyboards for each sequence (stick figures will do).
5. Explain how you will use stereotyping in a positive manner in your character development.
6. Using the original proposal, rewrite the log line so that the production may be completed without using any violence—only action.

Additional Sources

Print

Barrier, Michael. *Hollywood Cartoons: American Animation in its Golden Age.* New York: Oxford University Press, 1999.

Beck, Jerry, ed. *Animation Art: From Pencil to Pixel, the History of Cartoon, Anime & CGI.* London: Flame Tree Publishing, 2004.

Bendazzi, Giannalberto. *Cartoons: One Hundred Years of Cinema Animation.* Bloomington, IN: Indiana University Press, 1994.

Canemaker, John. *Storytelling in Animation: The Art of the Animated Image, Vol. II.* Los Angeles: American Film Institute, 1988.

Furniss, Maureen. *Art in Motion: Animation Aesthetics.* London: John Libbey & Company Pty. Ltd., 1998.

Hayward, Stan. *Scriptwriting for Animation.* New York: Hastings House, 1978.

Kanfer, Stefan. *Serious Business: The Art and Commerce of Animation in America from Betty Boop to Toy Story.* New York: Scribner, 1997.

Maltin, Leonard. *Of Mice and Magic: A History of American Animated Cartoons.* 2nd ed. New York: New American Library, 1989.

Noake, Roger. *Animation Techniques: Planning and Producing Animation with Today's Technologies.* Secaucus, NJ: Chartwell Books, Inc., 1988.

Patmore, Chris. *The Complete Animation Course: The Principles, Practices, and Techniques of Successful Animation.* Hauppauge, NY: Barrons Education Service, 2003.

Peary, Gerald, and Danny Peary, eds. *The American Animated Cartoon: A Critical Anthology.* New York: E.P. Dutton, 1980.

Scott, Jeffrey. *How to Write for Animation.* Woodstock, NY: The Overlook Press, 2002.

Webber, Marilyn. *Gardner's Guide to Animation Scriptwriting: A Writer's Road Map, the Secret to Writing Successful Animation.* Fairfax, VA: GGC, Publishing, 2000.

Winder, Catherine, and Zahra Dowlatabadi. *Producing Animation.* Boston: Focal Press, 2001.

Web

www.aardman.com
www.animationguild.org
www.animationjournal.com
www.animationstudies.org

www.asifa.net
www.cartoonnet.com
www.digitaljuice.com
www.looneytunes.warnerbros.com
www.mag.awn.com
www.pixar.com/index
www.researchandmarkets.com
www.teachingcomics.org

CHAPTER 8

Games

The pervasiveness of games—in cultures ancient and new, among people of all ages—suggests they are of more than casual importance. On a social level, games are often associated with ritual occasions, just as today's sporting events often occur on key religious and national holidays. On an individual level, there are games for almost every stage of life, from childhood to old age.

—Domenic Stansberry, award winning writer
and interactive designer

For the purposes of this chapter, a game is an interactive computer activity produced for a personal computer or an arcade console. A game may be distributed by a ROM cartridge, CD-ROM, DVD, HD-DVD, Blu-Ray Disc, or the Internet, for one or more simultaneous players.

Introduction

For as short a time as the game industry has existed, its impact on the electronic media field has startled the leaders of both businesses. With greater detail, increased settings, and complex characters and objects, the games of today attract a growing number of adults. The average age of game players is approaching 30, with both men and an increasing number of women as old as their early 40s attracted to game playing. The shift in age means games must offer more than simple plots and repetitive violence and gratuitous sexual attacks against women. For you, the challenge then is to maintain the feeling and historical challenge of new games without driving away potential audiences of either the young fans or the older players.

Not only are sales of games and game machines rising, but the increased number playing the games have become a target for advertising embedded in the games. By 2010, approximately $2 billion will be spent on game advertising. This represents roughly 6% of the available advertising dollars in the United States. Microsoft recently entered the game advertising business by purchasing a privately held company that specializes in advertising in nontraditional media.

Artists and writers who create games have begun to receive recognition equal to others in their profession. Games are attracting computer graphic artists, systems designers, and writers from the motion picture and broadcast industries. Games now are considered a powerful medium for artistic expression in all of the areas of writing, in vocal and motion-capture acting, and in computer coding.

Background

Despite its apparent short history, computer gaming may trace its history to as early as the late 19th century, when a Japanese playing card company, Marufuku, began manufacturing cards for the Western world. In 1951, that company changed its name to Nintendo, which means "leave luck to heaven." On the other side of the world, Gerard Philips in the Netherlands established a company to manufacture electrical products of all kinds. Within 20 years, Matsushita established Panasonic. A few years later, a Russian immigrant, Maurice Greenberg, distributed leather products to shoemakers under the name COLECO. The company moved to manufacturing plastic items by 1940. Following World War II, Harold Matson and Elliot Handler produced picture frames and manufactured doll furniture under the name Mattel. A few years later, following Japan's recovery from World War II, Akio Morita and Masaru Ibuka started Tokyo Telecommunications Engineering Company, manufacturing battery-powered miniature radios under the name Sony, from the Latin *sonus* (meaning sound). Following the Korean War, Davis Rosen began exporting coin-operated games to Japan. He named his company SEGA, short for "SErvice GAmes."

In the 1960s, a series of young electrical engineers and a variety of companies and universities experimented with computer games. In the late 1960s and early 1970s, Ralph Baer developed a chase game, a tennis game, and a gun to shoot light at a screen using a platform called *Odyssey,* and Ted Dabney and Nolan Bushnell designed and built the first *Spacewar.* In 1972, Bushnell started Atari (meaning "check" in Japanese chess), and *Pong* was born. By the mid-1980s, a rash of companies entered the field. COLECO received the first FCC permission to operate with radio frequency (RF) controls. The Fairchild Camera and Instrument Company produced the first programmable home game console using cartridges. At the same time, the game *Death Race 2000,* based on a movie of the same name, raised the first of many public outcries over violence in games. Atari was sold to Warner Communications and opened the first Pizza Time Theater.

In 1 year, 1978, Nintendo released *Othello,* Atari released *Football* using a trackball, Midway imported *Space Invaders,* Atari tried to sell computers to compete with Apple (but failed), Magnavox released *Odyssey 2* (with a programmable keyboard), and Cinematronics released *Space Wars,* which used vector graphics. Until 1982, the computer game business boomed, and then the bottom fell out with releases of badly designed games, poorly built consoles, lawsuits, bankruptcies, and too many games on the shelves, forcing price cuts below costs. In the following 3 years, the field began a slow recovery as Nintendo, NEC, Atari, SEGA, and Sony dominated the field.

The 1990s saw new technology developed, which increased the quality, playing time, and complexity of the games, and contributed superior graphics. In 1994, the Entertainment Software Rating Board (ESRB) was established by the industry to set ratings to overcome increased criticism of the violent and sexual content of many games offered to young people. Arizona tried but failed to outlaw violent and sadistic games. Congress accepted the ratings, but it blamed the retailers for failing to police purchasers. By 1996, Atari was out of the game business, and Nintendo, Sony, and SEGA were fighting a price war. By the end of the century, SEGA entered the field with Dreamcast, and Sony was talking of PlayStation2. Everyone released pocket units, like Nintendo's Game Boy Light. Florida tried but failed to pass a law banning violent games, and Wal-Mart refused to sell 50 of the most violent and sexist games, but retail sales were up, and the arcade business was dying.

The beginning of the 21st century found Sony unable to keep up with demand for the PlayStation2 (PS2). Small operations began to close, but Microsoft announced the Xbox for 2001. Sears, Wal-Mart, and Kmart pulled violent and mature games from the shelves.

Indianapolis passed the first law designed to protect children from playing mature games, but the law was found to be unconstitutional by the Supreme Court. The Federal Trade Commission (FTC) released a study showing video game companies were intentionally targeting young children for their violent games. The United States Army licensed *Rainbow Six: Spear Game* for training exercises, but many games were modified after 9/11, removing references to New York City, the World Trade Center, or other topics that touched on comparable terrorist incidents. The Xbox, GameCube, and PS2 all sold well as prices dropped. The FTC founds teens were still buying mature games from as many as 75% of retailers. To keep gamers happy and in an attempt to revive console game sales, Sony released PlayStation3, followed by Microsoft's Xbox360 and Nintendo's Wii.

Two competitors to console gaming suddenly appeared with advances in miniature technology games for cell phones and other small handhelds, offering new distribution outlets. The expansion of Internet gaming created an attraction for new multi-player games. Realistic, science fiction, war, and sport games lead in popularity as the first decade of the 21st century draws to an end.

Types of Games

Games may be classified in one of several different ways, either by content or by their delivery system. Content classification may include arcade, strategy, adventure/fantasy, or training games. The content may be categorized by the level of the action, by competition, narrative, cooperation, or solvability versus tractability. Solvability allows a player to solve the game in a reasonable amount of time; tractability keeps a player going and going, solving one problem after another, but still keeping involved in the game. A game may be designed to be process-intensive or data-intensive. Process-intensive games concentrate on the game itself, whereas data-intensive games provide a test for the player to keep piling up points and working against the game. Games may be delivered by arcade machines at the mall, home systems with a computer and a controller, television receivers and controllers, handheld units, or on a computer through the Internet.

Arcade games reflect the history of carnival games by depending on the skill of the operator to shoot birds flying by or offering an equivalent to a pinball machine. *Pac-Man* and *Asteroids* are examples of arcade games. Games involving moving a figure through a maze also fall into the arcade classification. Early games concentrated on such techniques, partially because they were easy to design codewise, and because they were simple for people to learn to play.

Strategy games depend on the operator using brains as much as thumbs. The concepts are based on solving a puzzle of some type, or else they are based on board games such as chess, blackjack, or a motion puzzle such as *Tetris Max*. The game based on the Pixar movie *Cars* gives the player a chance to win a race by outsmarting the other drivers on the race course. War games like *Ghost Recon 2* and games involving reconstructing countries also fall into the strategy category. These games cover the entire range from simple to extraordinarily complex, challenging those who play them to raise their scores or to attempt a higher level of accomplishment.

The line between adventure/fantasy games and strategy games is blurred. The basic concept behind an adventure/fantasy game is to set the game in an environment or location that is wild and dangerous, perhaps in an unrealistic past or in a science-fiction future. The plots of the adventure/fantasy games depend more on characters and story development than strategy games, but share the concept of using the operator's skill to attain a multi-level goal or to defeat an antagonist or army of antagonists. *Star Wars: Clone Wars* falls into the adventure/fantasy category.

Games designed specifically to train the player have been produced over the years for government agencies, especially the military. Health care, emergency response, religious, political, and professional organizations use games to train large groups of employees with specific tasks that may be too dangerous or too expensive to demonstrate without exposing the trainee to the dangers; the games offer trainees practical hands-on experience of performing an action expected of them. In other cases, the games give a wide range of people the opportunity to have an experience that they could or would not be able to have because of distance or lack of equipment. The military has become a leader in using games to train soldiers in the use of highly technical, expensive, or dangerous equipment. Pilots, tank drivers, and gunners all can experience the processes they need to achieve, allowing mistakes that are only recorded in a computer, not causing death or loss of expensive equipment. Games designed to teach sporting skills also fall into this category, such as *Tiger Woods: PGA Tour 2004*.

Games may be delivered by any digital system that provides some form of interactivity. The original games were simple programs on a computer, coded to react to either an external controller or to keyboard commands. Games still may be operated with such systems, but the controllers have become much more complex, allowing more than one player to play the same game simultaneously. The controls provide the player with the means to move the characters or objects in any direction (including 3-D depth of field) at various rates of speed. The game may be stored on the home computer or within the controller on disc, tape, cartridge, or hard or floppy drive. Increasingly, games may be played alone or among a group of players on the Internet.

Writing Game Scripts

As a writer of games, you may need to fulfill the functions of developer, publisher, programmer, graphic artist, sound engineer, industrialist, or architectural designer, or none of the above. Instead, you may only set down the concept in a logical and precise manner for the rest of the crew to fulfill their individual performances based on the needs of the game and the skills of the person.

But to make certain the process of writing scripts for games moves forward in a logical manner, you must begin with a study of the potential audience and the sales potential of the game. Next, develop a specific concept that defines exactly what type of game it is intended to be: adventure, strategy, or learning. Some technical decisions need to be considered early in the planning stages, especially how the game will be distributed. Some design features will vary depending on whether the game will be designed for home use, for a commercial arcade, or for Internet distribution. You need to consider the general form of the game, including the narrative type (e.g., serious, humorous, or dramatic) and the approximate character types who will provide the movement and action.

At this stage of the game's development, it may be a good idea for you to write a *log line*, meaning one sentence that completely describes the game, its action, its characters, and its reason for being. If you cannot complete a log line, you probably are not ready to start writing the script.

Step two in preproduction writing is the creation of a treatment. Generally, treatments are written, as most transcripts are, in two parts—a preliminary treatment, and then a final treatment. The difference between the two is a matter of fine-tuning the first draft, making corrections, additions, or deletions to make the game salable and workable. The treatment should be brief but comprehensive. You should write it in narrative form, not script form, with the intention to completely describe the game, including each stage, action, and variations in flowcharts. A treatment also forms part of a sales package. The treatment is used to convince a game studio or developer to provide the funds needed to complete the game. If a developer can read a treatment and see the value in the game, the possibility of receiving funding is increased. A poorly written treatment may very well sink the concept before it moves any closer to completion.

Following a clear description of the premise (the log line works for this), then you should describe each story element and stage of action, along with the plot. You may modify the story elements as the process continues, but including as many and as highly detailed elements as possible helps the reader understand what you are trying to accomplish with the game. The next step requires complete and accurate descriptions of each of the characters, starting with the main characters and working through to the secondary and then the barely visible characters. The relationships among the characters are critical, but some of their background helps the players understand how the characters may act toward or react to other characters and their environment and to their specific actions.

You must work out the overall setting of the game, along with the setting of each scene, at this point in the treatment. Without an accurate description of where the action takes place and what the scene looks like, everything that is included in the scene will determine in a major manner how the action may move forward. Keep in mind, each new scene reached by a branch on the flowchart needs to be described.

Figure 8.1. A single frame from a game requiring one line of code may show the beginning or the ending of an action sequence.

Old LM: Excuse me sir… that weapon you hold in your hands belongs to me… May I have it back?

Haxan: Huh?

Haxan is confused to see one of his enemies, a Lizard Man, ask him to return his weapon. Haxan also wonders why the old man is wounded and tired.

Player Choices:
1. Return the sword
2. Keep the sword
3. Kill the old man

1. Haxan trusts the old man and returns his sword.

Haxan: I don't know who roughed you up… but you look like you need this more than me. Here, take this sword back old man.

Haxan returns the sword to the old man.

Old LM: Thank you… this sword isn't my finest piece of work, but it's better than anything you will find out here. In case you are wondering who I am, my name is Chip, and I am a blacksmith, just like you.

Haxan: A blacksmith?

Chip: Yes, a blacksmith. Forging weapons is the only thing I know. When that Shaman showed up he gave me a job, but when I found out what he was up to I quickly planned my escape. I barely made it out alive.

Haxan: I see. Well, now that you've escaped, what do you plan to do?

Chip: I'm going back to my old hut. I don't have much to work with anymore, but I can try to forge something powerful with what I have.

Haxan: Well, good luck with that.

Chip: Here, I'll write down directions to my hut. Come by when you can and I will give you special discounts on my wares for helping me.

Haxan: Thanks. I'll be needing your help.

Chip: See you there.
Chip walks into the woods.

2. Haxan likes the sword and decides to keep it.

Haxan: Sorry old man, but I'm sure I can make better use of it than you.

Figure 8.2. Game scripts take many different forms, depending on the individual writer or the game studio's method of operation.

A summary of the game, along with a tentative flowchart and the technical specifications, completes the treatment. You may not need to be a coding specialist to write a game treatment or script, but you should be aware of the limitations of the system within which you are working. You should at least pass your treatment by a developer as a precaution to make certain your concept is producible and within the capabilities of the planned system. Keep in mind, the first treatment is a rough draft, to be revised as you consider specific details and problems presented by your concept.

In order to gain funding, you may be required to perform a *pitch* session. At that time, you will stand in front of the developer or publisher and describe the game to the point of acting out the entire game. Depending on your enthusiasm and your ability to describe your concept, you may or may not win the pitch session and walk away with the assignment and funds you need to move onward.

Script Formats

As with any new and developing media form, the scripting process for games fluctuates as new writers and developers enter the field and as new technologies and methods of producing games change approaches and the final form of the game. No universal script format exists for games, but as with visual scripts, the basic needs of the programmers are fulfilled by semi-standardized formats. All of the visuals, actions, narration or dialogue, graphics, and character descriptions must appear in a logical and, where necessary, chronological order in each branch. Branching diagrams are part of, or perhaps even the entirety of, the total script, depending on the complexity of the game. The script may be an Excel page with columns listing a file number for each line of action, scene, dialogue, sound, and choices, as well as a final column for instructions to the developer. A game may have as many as 60,000 lines. An alternate method uses a scriptwriting program that provides four columns: two storyboard columns, one column for audio, and the fourth for visual instructions.

An adaptation of the single-column format, used for theater and television drama, fulfills most of the requirements of a game script, with the possible addition of individual scripts for branching segments or cut scenes that take the control away from the player. One addition is an indication or side note within the alternating scene descriptions and indented dialogue sections, indicating by some form of code or designation that there are alternate shots in the branching sequences.

Because games depend on interactive action from the player, alternate shots or scenes must be diagramed by you for both the developer and the programmer writing the codes to keep track of how the action may or may not move forward, depending on the choices of the player. Again, an absolute uniform manner of diagramming a multi-level chart does not exist, but writers share some conventions so that all involved in a production will understand how the flow of the action is to be programmed and produced.

Often, it helps to complete the flowchart before you complete the dialogue script. Looking at a flowchart helps in visualizing which scenes follow the action and the choices the player may be given, as well as the results of those choices. This becomes complicated when dialogue between characters may vary depending on the response of one character to another's answer or action. In most dialogue scenes, there are at least two possible responses to any one query or action. From that multi-response, there may then may be a chain that returns to the original scene or that leads off to a totally different action.

Whichever symbols are used in charting the dialogue and action, consistency is important. If a rectangle indicates an action, and a circle, a verbal response, then those shapes must continue throughout the chart to avoid confusion.

Developing Plot and Action Lines

When writing a drama, whether for a motion picture, television, or a game, the story follows the same basic pattern. A story must tell of characters (real or imagined) acting and reacting with each other, against or as a result of changing natural conditions. The story must be based on some type of conflict, be it physical, emotional, or imagined. The conflict may take the form of dramatic tension, with or without a story. Puzzle games maintain tension, but without a definite story line other than in the imagination of the player. For a game story to succeed, you must create a maximum of action since the only way an operator can interact is by making changes in the movement, positioning, or action. Too often, games rely on violence to provide the action; action does not necessarily require violence. A puzzle game's only action is provided by the player making moves or sitting and thinking about the next move.

Each game is based on a series of major action events. An action event may be a meeting between characters that leads to a conflict, resolved by a series of other actions, leading to a crisis of one character defeating the second character. Game plots depend on creating a fantasy, developing a metaphor between reality and the game. This may be developed through the narrative as written by you or by a narrative that is developed by the player through the player's imagination. The interplay of the two narratives become the dynamic of the game, building interest and excitement, or else leading to boredom on the part of the player. You may write the plot so that the player may take on the personality of one of the characters (an avatar). In these games, the player operates the game to reach a point with a series of goals, overcoming a series of obstacles set by the developer, eventually ending the conflict, or else the player manipulates the character as a third person who is not personally involved in the action. The conflict may be between characters, caused by object, or even caused by nature (e.g., a tornado, a volcano eruption, or a storm at sea). Each step of the game needs to have series of goals to be reached by resolving conflicts, in the end reaching the ultimate goal or solving levels of difficulty that are awarded with scores or a new and higher level of challenge. Each goal is a crisis that must be solved before moving on to the next level of the plot.

There may be times that you will be handed an assignment to write a game that must match new technology offered by the studio's latest engine. The developer is less interested in the plot or story than in showing the maximum abilities of the new program.

In order to complete the physical action of writing the script, you may need to start with sketches, a simple storyboard, and a list of goals and planned levels. A flowchart at this point would be helpful to keep track of how you will follow the story line. As you follow the treatment in developing the script, at each stage possible play the game to determine if it works, if it can be played, if it will hold the interest of a player, and if it will accomplish the goal you set in the premise. Keep in mind that at every stage, you will need to make modifications and changes to make the game work. Of all media writing formats, game writing requires the greatest amount of adaptability and willingness to rewrite as the process moves forward.

Summary

Despite a relatively short commercial history, the studios and game concepts started over a century ago. As the technology, basic computer sciences, and game systems evolved, some were adopted and succeeded, while others failed. The field now concentrates on three game types: adventure/fantasy, strategy, and training. The most popular games concentrate on violent action in war, sports, and crime games. Controversy over excessive violence, especially against women, has led to unsuccessful attempts by states to control game content and sales. The industry countered with a rating system that has failed to solve the problem of keeping violent games from young people because of the lack of cooperation from retailers.

Writing games is more complex than the writing of any other media genre or format due to its dependence on interactivity. A quality game will offer the player a multitude of options for actions for the characters and a multitude of reactions to every action followed. Scripts may be created on an Excel sheet, with columns of each source for every line of action. Standard script formats of either single- or dual-columns, usually with the addition of at least one extra column of storyboards, also are used for games. A flowchart showing all options and paths also may be used as a script format.

The writer is a member of a collaborative group of people with interchangeable skills, working as designers, artists, developers, programmers, and a producer, under the guidance of a publisher representing the company or studio.

Be Sure To...

1. Determine your role in the development of the game (e.g., writer, designer, or programmer).
2. Decide the type of game by content.
3. Decide the type of game by delivery system.
4. Decide the levels of solvability and tractability.
5. Write an accurate and brief log line.
6. Determine the settings and environment for each scene.
7. Determine the character cast list.
8. Outline your plot and chart each line of action.

Exercises

1. Research the history of the development of a single game company.
2. Play at least one game in the following categories: arcade, strategy, adventure/fantasy, and training.
3. Storyboard a brief 3-minute puzzle game written for one player.
4. Write a script for a short 5-minute strategy game that at least two people could play simultaneously.
5. Chart the game designed for Exercise 4.
6. Watch your favorite game and try to chart at least the primary plot line.

Additional Sources

Print

Aheam, Luke. *3D Game Textures: Create Professional Game Art Using Photoshop*. Boston: Focal Press, 2006.

Bucy, Erik P. *Living in the Information Age: A New Media reader*. 2nd ed. Belmont, CA: Wadsworth Publishing, 2005.

Crawford, Chris. *Chris Crawford on Interactive Storytelling*. Berkeley, CA: New Riders Games, 2004.

DeMaria, Rusel, and Johnny L. Wilson. *High Score! The Illustrated History of Electronic Games*. New York: Osborne/McGraw-Hill, 2002.

Gauthier, Jean-Marc. *Building Interactive Worlds in 3D*. Boston: Focal Press, 2005.

Graham, Lisa. *The Principles of Interactive Design*. Albany, NY: Delmar Publishers, 1999.

Hanson, Matt. *Building Sci-Fi Moviescapes*. Boston: Focal Press, 2006.

Hofstetter, Fred T. *Multimedia Literacy*. New York: McGraw-Hill, 1995.

Kent, Steven L. *The Ultimate History of Video Games: From Pong to Pokemon— The Story Behind the Craze that Touched Our Lives and Changed the World*. New York: Three Rivers Press, 2001.

Kerlow, Isacc V. *The Art of 3D Computer Animation and Effects*. 3rd ed. Hoboken, NJ: John Wiley & Sons, Inc., 2004.

Kuperberg, Marcia. *A Guide to Computer Animation for TV, Games, Multimedia, and Web*. Boston: Focal Press, 2002.

Marx, Christy. *Writing for Animation, Comics, and Games*. Boston: Focal Press, 2006.

Masson, Terrence. *CG 101: A Computer Graphics Industry Reference*. Indianapolis, IN: New Riders Publishing, 1999.

Miller, Carolyn H. *Digital Storytelling: A Creator's Guide to Interactive Entertainment*. Boston: Focal Press, 2004.

Pfaffenberger, Bryan, and Bill Daley. *Computers in Your Future: 2004*. Upper Saddle River, NJ: Pearson/Prentice-Hall, 2004.

Reddick, Randy, and Elliot King. *The Online Student: Making the Grade on the Internet*. Fort Worth, TX: Harcourt Brace College Publishers, 1996.

Salem, Katie, and Eric Zimmerman. *Rules of Play: Game Design Fundamentals*. Cambridge, MA: MIT Press, 2004.

Scholder, Amy, and Eric Zimmerman. *Replay: Game Design and Game Culture*. New York: Peter Lang Publishing, Inc., 2003.

Stansberry, Domenic. *Labyrinths: The Art of Interactive Writing and Design, Content Development for New Media*. Belmont, CA: Wadsworth Publishing, 1998.

White, Tony. *Animation from Pencils to Pixels*. Boston: Focal Press, 2006.

Wolf, Mark J.P., and Bernard Perron, eds. *The Video Game Theory Reader*. New York: Routledge Press, 2003.

Wright, Jean. *Animation Writing & Development*. Boston: Focal Press, 2005.

Web

www.advancedgaming.biz
www.awn.com
www.breakawaygames.com
www.dodgamecommunity.com
www.educationarcade.org
www.kelloggcreek.com

www.legacygames.com
www.objection.com
www.seriousgames.com
www.vfxworld.com
www.visualpurple.com

CHAPTER 9

Drama

Your mind starts working at night a little bit and then one day you pick up your computer and you start typing.
　　　　　　　　　　　—Steve Martin, actor, writer, producer

I'm an observer, a writer –
I observe humanity and get the best of them and put them in my movies.
　　　　　　　　　　　—Mel Brooks, writer, director, producer

A drama is a story told in prose or verse written to portray life, characters, or relationships involving emotions and conflicts through action and dialogue designed for distribution on the stage, in motion pictures, on radio, television, or via any digital medium.

Introduction

As with writing scripts for other genres, the dramatic writing process passes through several distinct stages, beginning with the research phase. Before you write a script, you must understand your story. Research may provide you some insurance against presenting implausible stories or using factually incorrect information. Research also may provide a source of inspiration and new ideas.

Once you have decided on a story idea, a log line, and a premise, several story outlines may be drafted after the research phase before a treatment is prepared. The log line and premise help you narrow your focus and concentrate your idea into a usable form. A treatment is a plot description in short-story form you use primarily as part of a proposal submitted to a potential funding source. You may submit the treatment to a funding source or producer as an accompaniment to an oral presentation or pitch. The treatment provides a guide for the writing of a complete script.

The next stage in the scriptwriting process is the writing of the script itself. A script may go through several drafts and you may involve the participation of several other writers before it is completed and production can begin. The final stage is the preparation of a shooting script, which indicates all camera placements, transition devices, and various types of effects. These may be added by the director or producer with or without your participation or approval.

Background

A dramatic performance is simply storytelling in one form or another. Primitive tribes acted out stories as they developed a verbal language and drew figures representing stages of a story in pictoglyphs scratched or painted on rock surfaces. Indigenous tribes also drew the same type of figures on the cured hides of animals so they could carry them from village to village and provide a rudimentary record of that particular story. The same people acted out their stories with dancing, singing, drumming, playing simple instruments, and staging battles and other scenes of importance to their culture. Masks and costumes helped illustrate the stories as they were performed for the gathered crowds. Many, if not all, of the early performances were based on religious ceremonies or depictions of myths and fables of their beliefs.

Ancient Egyptians and tribes in Mesopotamia (now Iraq) followed the same pattern of performing religious celebrations by staging complex and formalized festivals that depicted either tragedies or comedies. The Greeks in the 5th century BC expanded the process by formalizing the plays into acts created by a writer and performed under the guidance of a director. Three hundred years later, the Romans copied many of the Greek production techniques and added a variety of other entertainment forms: short comic plays, animal acts, and through the years, sea battles, gladiators, and feeding Christians to lions. Christians originally opposed the Roman festivals because they were staged to honor the Roman gods. Later the church realized theatrical staging of biblical stories offered a method of teaching the beliefs of the church to people with little or no means of reading the written word. The staging also gave the church the opportunity to dramatize the stories in order to make a lasting impression on the audience's minds.

Theater in medieval times was performed by roving bands of acting companies performing at churches, castles, or wherever they were allowed to set up their portable stages built on wagons. The earlier productions were morality plays, but later secular dramas were performed to avoid religious controversies.

The Renaissance found theater companies sponsored by nobility who demanded more professional performances. This period saw the development of complex stages, the proscenium theater, and the use of perspective with attempts at depicting realism in settings and acting. Writing during this period in France and Italy was weak compared to England where playwrights like Shakespeare and Jonson turned out tragedies and comedies for an audience hungry for new plays that appealed to all economic levels of the population. France and Spain followed during the 16th and 17th century with artistic writers like Moliere and Lope de Vega. By this time the pattern of writing scripts was usually set at five acts. Each story was set to occur in 1 day, with the wicked always punished and the good characters rewarded in some manner.

The 18th century found few advances in the theater world except for Germany and Scandinavian countries, where they developed their own types of theater. During the early 19th century, drama changed from teaching and leading the audience in religious training to strictly entertainment. Eugene Scribe formulated the "Well-Made-Play." The script opens with long expository dialogue setting up the characters, especially the antagonist and protagonist. The play continues with alternating periods of tension with some good and some bad news for the main characters. Several minor crises lead to a major crisis followed by a climax and then the denouement that solves all the problems and leaves no concerns unanswered. The precursor of the Indiana Jones stories was the melodrama format. It used the same basic pattern as the well-made play but also required the setting to be in an exotic location (at least for unsophisticated audiences), with good triumphing over evil with a last minute rescue or series of rescues. Both the melodrama and well-made play script formats make up the bulk of most television dramas and motion pictures.

The United States entered the theatrical world late, partially because the population was spread over such a vast space with few concentrated metropolitan areas until New York, Chicago, other East Coast cities, and New Orleans in the West, grew large enough to support theater companies. The primary dramatic forms were the melodrama and the comedy. The United States did develop a unique form of theater in the "book musical." Such shows as *West Side Story, Cats,* and *The Lion King* appeared after years of Broadway musicals like the 1929 *Show Boat* became popular.

By the early 20th century, the legitimate theater had two new competitors for audiences interested in dramatic story telling. In 1903, Edwin S. Porter directed *The Great Train Robbery,* the first film that attempted to tell a specific story. By 1915, D.W. Griffith's films, including *The Birth of a Nation,* convinced the audience that motion pictures could tell stories. Within 10 years and for the next 25 years radio held audiences spellbound with radio dramas from soap operas to daily adventure serials, and full-length dramatic performances. That hold on the audience ended with the arrival of television that offered live drama delivered into the home each afternoon and evening with the same soap operas and dramatic programs originally delivered via radio.

Despite the competition of the electronic and film media, the theater continues to offer drama; in both old and new forms as the taste of the audiences change and they demand new and more intellectually invigorating stories. Radio, except for the NPR and PRI public stations, have given up on drama; possibly there will be a return to radio drama on one or both of the satellite radio operations. Television drama has had its own competition with cable, which may depict actions and dialogue forbidden by broadcast networks and stations. Writers have had to learn to write specifically for a medium because a script in one form may be acceptable in one medium, but not in another.

Digital technology has provided today's writer with unrestricted means of telling their story. Now there is no limit to what a production crew, either film or video, can produce using the latest and yet to be developed digital technology.

Stages of Scriptwriting

Research
Log line/premise
Story outline
Treatment/proposal
Rough draft
Final draft
Shooting script

Research

Research is a creative process of uncovering new sources of information as well as confirming already known information. As the project researcher or scriptwriter, you begin by acquiring a general background in the area on which the story will focus. You collect as many books and articles as possible that deal with the general topic area and read those that seem to be most helpful and pertinent to the specific issues at hand. You may even search computer files and systems such as LexisNexis, Google, Thunderstone, Infoplease, or Stats Toolbox, as well as other databases as one of the fastest and most accurate methods of acquiring the basic information needed when researching a project. These same search engines will lead you to written sources in books and periodicals. Armed with this general knowledge, you progress by focusing more narrowly on specific areas and concerns of the story. The more knowledgeable you become, the more information you will gain from additional sources. Like a good detective, you learn that one piece of evidence leads to the discovery of another.

Production research is usually either novelistic or journalistic in approach. As a fiction writer, you conduct research in order to find details that stimulate reader interest and authenticate events and settings. A feature film or television program is often researched in this manner. Strict authenticity is sometimes sacrificed for dramatic interest and action. Journalistic research, on the other hand, aims at uncovering sources of evidence that can be used to support the presentation of information and dramatic arguments (Figure 9.1).

Figure 9.1. The beginning of any media production is the research stage. Information must be gathered, facts checked, and information documented before the script is written.

Log Line, Premise, and Outline

The first item you must create is a "log line." A log line is a one sentence statement that describe the basic story line: "Tony and Maria fall in love, but because they are associated with rival gangs, the Sharks and the Jets, there are many obstacles placed in the path of their love." If you cannot describe the complete story in one line, you are not ready to write the script. The next step, which will help localize your thinking, is writing the "premise."

A premise is basically a "what if" statement, which describes the basic story idea. For example, "what if" Romeo and Juliet sang and danced and were caught between rival gangs and ethnic groups in

New York City? This is the basic premise of *West Side Story* (1961). A good treatment is always based on a simple but interesting concept. The premise can be used later as a strong opening "pitch" for a script or screenplay to a producer by providing a concise label for the project.

On the basis of the log line and premise, an outline can be written, developing the major plot lines and characters in the story. This outline also defines all major actions and character reactions. Usually several outlines are written and revised before writing the treatment. Creating a cast list is helpful in describing the characters. Name each character, and list critical characteristics and the relationships with other characters in the story. Don't forget to indicate if the character changes his or her attitude as the story develops. Primary characters need complete descriptions, and secondary and minor characters require just enough description to remind you of who they are and how they relate to other characters.

Treatments

A treatment is an important step in the development of a script. Usually written in the third person, present tense, it provides a narrative summary of the basic story lines. In the treatment you visualize the story as it will unfold on the screen, and it gives a play-by-play of all major actions and scenes in reduced form. You compose the treatment with the hope that you may receive an approval or commission to write the script.

You devote the major portion of the treatment to a highly visual, but concise narrative presentation of characters and events. You may include a few examples of dialogue spoken by characters only if critical to an understanding of the plot. The treatment adopts a short-story format adopting a lively prose style that dramatizes the basic premise and effectively communicates the tone and flavor of the story. Camera directions and shot descriptions are used very sparingly, if at all. You convey important images by using highly visual nouns or adjectives and action verbs. A treatment is not a legal document fashioned with dry regularity and precision.

It must excite and interest a producer or funding source and serve as a thorough and helpful guide for the writing of your script or screenplay. A treatment provides some protection against future writing problems by forcing you to resolve many story and character difficulties prior to actual scriptwriting.

A treatment for a feature-length film screenplay, which will run about 2 hours, usually has about twenty to seventy double-spaced, typewritten pages. The finished screenplay will be 100 to 140 pages, since each page of a screenplay usually translates into about 1 minute of actual screen time. A treatment for a work of short fiction should probably be from five to ten pages in length. It is always preferable to err on the side of brevity, since verbose, overwritten treatments are not likely to be read with interest and enthusiasm.

Proposals

When a producer initiates a project, the treatment sometimes accompanies a proposal, which is submitted to a funding source. A proposal is a shorter description of the treatment intended for a non-media person to read and understand. A proposal also includes basic budgetary figures to give the funding source some idea of the potential financial investment needed to complete your script.

Figure 9.2. The director decides the framing of the shots in a dramatic production following the writer's description written in the script.

                              SUSAN
                    Well, I guess we just won't wait until
                    after graduation.

Danny shuffles the toes of his shoes in the dirt.

                              DANNY
                    Coach thinks I have a real chance at a
                    scholarship.

She buries her head in his shoulder and begins to cry.

                              SUSAN
                    Oh, Danny.

                                              DISSOLVE TO:

5   EXT SUSAN'S FAMILY HOME IN 1982 -MORNING   5

       A telephone is ringing from inside the house.   _DISS_   _5A_
    _5A_ _1982 NEWSPAPER HEADLINES_
                                                            CUT TO:

6   INT. LIVING ROOM ADJACENT TO KITCHEN IN 1982 -MORNING   6

       The living room is adjacent to the kitchen. A bar that
       separates the two areas allows one to see from one room to
       the next. On the bar is a telephone and next to the phone is
       a calendar/picture holder. It is November 1982. The
       photograph in the picture frame shows Susan, appearing
       slightly older than when we last saw her, in a swing. In the
       swing next to her is her daughter, DANA, at age 4.

       DANA, daughter of Danny and Susan, is a slender, attractive
       woman in her early twenties. She is standing in the living
       room next to the bar separating the living room from the
       kitchen. She is talking on the telephone with her mom wearing
       only a robe. Dana looks like she just got out of bed.

                              DANA
                         (mildly impatient)
                    Nobody in particular... Just guys mom...
                    Go dancing and stuff. Let's talk about
                    something else, ok? Yes, of course I am
                    coming over for Thanksgiving.

       Picks up the photo

                              DANA (CONT'D)
                    I know it has always been just the two of
                    us... The house is great. You oughta let
                    me fix dinner here. I can't believe you
                    don't want to live here...
                              (MORE)   (CONTINUED)
       12/18/2000   © 2000 Michael Carr

Figure 9.3. The writer's responsibility in a dramatic script is to describe
the scene, write the dialogue, and leave the exact shot selection to the
director.

A timeline also may be included indicating the length of time needed to complete the shooting script, preproduction, production, and postproduction stages required until the funding agency will have a completed project in hand ready for distribution.

Scriptwriting Formats

After you have completed the preliminary stages of scriptwriting, you begin to write a full script. The script conforms to one of the following formats: split-page, full-page, or a semi-scripted format, such as a script outline. Professional scriptwriters rely on a basic set of terms as well as the following common formats in order to effectively communicate with other members of the creative staff such as the director. (See format samples later in this chapter.)

Full-Page Master Scene Script Format

A full-page master scene script format is frequently used in dramatic fiction programs, including single-camera film and video productions, such as live-action dramas and feature films, and multiple-camera live-on-tape productions, such as television situation comedies. In a full-page master scene script format, a single column, which is devoted to both visuals and audio, fills the entire page. The script is organized into scenes, which are numbered in consecutive order. The location and time of day of each scene are specified. Actions and camera movements are described in full paragraphs. Scriptwriting computer programs are available for all computer operating systems. These programs format the script in a professional layout, relieving the scriptwriter of the tedium of worrying about margins and spacing while attempting to create a workable script.

Because you organize a full-page master scene script by scenes, you can reorganized it easily so that all the scenes requiring a single set or location can be shot consecutively. Producers and production managers try to organize production so that all the scenes at a specific location can be shot at one time, because it is usually more efficient and cost-effective than recording the scenes in chronological order as they appear in the script.

The full-page master scene script describes few, if any, camera movements and shots. It is much more common for the director to select and indicate specific shots during the preparation of the final shooting script immediately prior to production. A director's shot descriptions often specify camera-to-subject distance, angle of view, and camera movement when they are incorporated into the stage directions following the scene heading. Rather than providing shot descriptions, you can artfully visualize the scene in prose following the header without specifying camera-to-subject distances, angles, and so forth. In any case, camera shots, angles, movements, transition devices, times of day, interior and exterior settings, specific character names, and sound effects are generally typed in uppercase letters, while actions, events, and specific stage directions, including sets, props, characters, and actions, as well as dialogue, are usually in lowercase letters. Dialogue to be spoken by a specific character normally follows the stage directions and has the character's name listed in the middle of the page immediately above his or her lines of dialogue, which are slightly indented from the paragraph descriptions of actions and camera movements. The end of a scene is usually indicated by a "scene close," such as CUT TO: or DISSOLVE TO:, which indicates the transition to the next scene.

Dramatic Scriptwriting

Drama and narrative are fictional art forms that have a basis in everyday life. A drama is basically a series of actions performed by actors, such as a stage play. A narrative is a chain of events, which is told or narrated, such as a novel or short story. While most dramas and narratives draw upon everyday life and experience, effective works of fiction are often shaped and refined by carefully organizing and structuring these actions and events, and removing the dull moments of life so that viewer, listener, or reader interest can be intensified. The organization of dramatic actions and narrative events is often referred to as the elements of dramatic and narrative structure. Fiction scriptwriting has the potential to combine certain elements of dramatic and narrative structure making effective use of the basic structural elements of actions and events.

MASTER SCENE SCRIPT FORMAT
(Margins and tabs set as indicated below, assuming 80 space wide paper)

5   15   20   40   45   55   60
FADE IN:

1.   INT./EXT.   BRIEF SCENE OR SHOT DESCRIPTION   DAY/NIGHT   1

In upper and lowercase, a more detailed description of the scene giving
setting, props, and CHARACTERS position if needed with margins set at
5/60.

CHARACTER
(Mode of delivery, upper and
lowercase, margins at 20/40)

The dialogue is typed in upper and lowercase
centered within 15/45 margins.

Any other descriptions of shot framing, movement of CAMERA or
CHARACTER is at margins set at 5/60.

(TRANSITION)

2.   INT   UNIVERSITY CLASSROOM   DAY   2

Classroom is full of students, some wide awake, gossiping, others sleeping
or nodding off as they wait for the professor to arrive.

JANE
(Quietly)
Are you sure there isn't going to be an exam
during tomorrow's class?

JACK
(Bravely)
Of course not, have I ever lied to you?

The professor enters the room, walks to the lectern and the room becomes quiet.

PROFESSOR
(Emphatically)
If I am forced to repeat myself again, I WILL
be forced to give you your first examination in
tomorrow's class.

(DISS.)

3.   EXT   CAMPUS   DAY   3

The clouds suddenly darken the sky as rain, thunder and lightning start
and the lights go out, plunging the room into darkness.

If the scene goes to another page, place at the right margin --   (Cont.)

Figure 9.4. A master scene script gives the screenwriter the opportunity
to notify the director of the writer's intent without limiting the director to
specific shots. But the script must include enough information so that the
director understands what the writer had in mind and wants the actors to
say and do.

Dramatic Structure

Dramatic films and television programs can be plotted into a framework that consists of a basic three-act structure and a series of rising and falling actions, which culminate in a climax and resolution. Act One of a drama usually sets up the main plot by establishing the central characters, their goals and conflicts, as well as the basic time, place, and situation of the story. Act Two and Act Three each begin with a turning point, such as a major shift in the main plot, which moves the drama in a different direction from the previous act, generating audience interest and maintaining story momentum. Secondary as well as primary characters and themes are usually more fully developed through both main plot and subplot actions in Act Two. Conflicts and problems eventually reach a climax and are resolved as the main plot and subplot are brought together near the end of Act Three.

Rising actions include build sections, where conflicts build into a series of crises, and a final climax. Falling and horizontal actions include temporary resolutions or pauses in the action following crises, which allow the audience to catch its breath before proceeding to the next crisis or climax, followed by the final resolution of the conflicting elements that led to the climax.

These classic forms of dramatic structure ensure that actions build in a logical and exciting way on the basis of major conflicts that must be resolved. A drama may have very limited or extensive expositions of characters, situations, and settings; few or many complications, reversals, and crises; but it almost always relies upon internal or external conflicts, which build toward a climax and resolution, if it is to sustain interest, arouse excitement, and evoke a sense of fulfillment. Political dramas, such as *The West Wing*, crime dramas, such as *CSI* and *CSI Miami*, and medical dramas, such as *ER*, illustrate classic dramatic structure.

Rising Action: Crises and Climax

Dramatic action that has progressed through several complications inevitably builds to a crisis. A drama may have several crises, in which the conflict that has stimulated the action intensifies to the point that something or someone is threatened. We all encounter crises in our lives, but drama removes most of the dull moments between these crises, so that characters' actions and emotions, and viewers' interest and involvement, are intensified. The major character or characters may have to make an important decision. Perhaps it is a life-and-death situation. Should a risky surgical procedure be performed? Can a murderer be identified and sacrificed? Should a character choose between a lover or a spouse? The dramatic action usually builds through several important crises that finally culminate in a major crisis or climax.

A climax is the most decisive point of confrontation in a drama. It simply demands some form of resolution. One side must win or a compromise must be reached. The climax brings the major conflicting forces together so that they may be openly confronted and resolved. The climax is usually the highest, most intense emotional peak of the drama.

Falling Action: Resolution/Dénouement

Overcoming the basic conflict or fulfilling the goals and motivations that have stimulated the dramatic action is known as a resolution. The defeat of the antagonist, the death of the hero, the marriage of the loving couple, or the attainment of the major goal may each represent the culmination of the action. A resolution is considered a falling action compared with the rising action of a crisis or climax. The resolution section of the drama considers the implications of the climactic actions and gives the audience time to contemplate what has just transpired before new actions are initiated or the drama ends. Emotionally, the audience may need sufficient time to recuperate from the experience of the climax. A drama that ends immediately after the climax might leave some of the audience's expectations unfulfilled.

The resolution of a drama can be ambiguous or unambiguous. An ending can appear to resolve all major conflicts or allow the hero to achieve his or her major goals. In a mystery story the discovery of a secret can answer all questions. But an ending can also be ambiguous. Conflicts can persist and goals remain unachieved. Some dramatic forms have virtually no resolution at all. Soap operas rarely, if ever, reach any resolution. They consist of a series of crises. Any apparent solution, such as a marriage, is usually the source of another conflict. The absence of any resolution establishes a new convention that is unique to the open-ended, serial dramatic form. A closed dramatic form uses resolution to enforce a sense of finality or closure at the end. The drama is essentially self-contained, although the dramatic action may continue in the form of a sequel.

Text and Subtext

To be a good writer, you will not only play with the surface text of the dialogue while telling a story, but also often develop a subtext through character actions and reactions. The subtext defines what the characters are really feeling, that is, the feelings that underlie their dialogue. For example, a man and a woman may be discussing something rather innocuous, such as the weather. Their dialogue defines the text. "Don't you think that it's getting warmer?" "Yes, but my hands are freezing." "There's still a touch of winter in the air, but the ice is melting." The text indicates that the characters are aware that spring is coming and the weather outside is getting warmer. But by staging the action so that the characters gradually get closer together and begin holding hands and touching one another, the subtext (and double entendre of the dialogue) is that they are gradually warming up to each other romantically.

Narrative Structure

In addition to having dramatic structure, the structure of action, scripts also have narrative structure, the structure of time and point of view. A story can follow an uninterrupted chronological structure from beginning to end, or it can have flashbacks and flash forwards, which disrupt the continuous flow of time. A great deal of screen time can be devoted to some events and very little to others. For example, a character in a soap opera can go upstairs in one scene and come down in the next, having aged several years (and sometimes having been replaced by another actor). On the other hand, it may take several episodes or even several weeks of episodes to develop all the intrigues occurring at a party that supposedly lasted for only 2 hours on 1 day. The difference between the actual screen time and the supposed story or historical time devoted to specific events is sometimes referred to as narrative duration, and the difference between the actual order of presentation and the supposed historical chronology of specific events in the story is sometimes referred to as narrative order. Scriptwriters can manipulate narrative order and duration to effectively relate one event to another, such as providing character backstory by using a flashback to break the chronological order of the narrative and to relate a character's past history to his or her present actions.

A fictional work can also be narrated by someone else. A story can be told from a specific point of view. An omniscient or hidden narrator tells the story but does not appear as a character within it, while a dramatized narrator is a specific character who also tells the story. In media production the director can use the camera to enhance the point of view of a specific character whom you use to tell the story by placing the camera in that character's approximate physical position on the set. The audience then sees and understands what that character sees and understands from the character's point of view throughout the story.

A narrative point of view is an extremely important structural component. How something is presented is just as important as what is presented. If we experience a series of events through the eyes of a character as opposed to omnisciently through an effaced narrator, our experience of these events is quite different. Adopting the point of view of a particular character makes a difference in terms of how actions, events, and their meanings are perceived. Imagine, for example, the presentation of the Battle of the Little Bighorn through the eyes of a Sioux warrior versus those of a United States cavalryman. Arthur Penn's film *Little Big Man* (1970) presents a shifting point of view on General Custer through the ambiguous cultural identity and affiliation of its main character/narrator. The adoption of a specific point of view colors and even distorts events in a particular way, and such a perspective must be carefully and thoughtfully selected.

Characterization and Theme

You have as many ways to begin the writing of an original piece of fiction as there are works of fiction. You could begin with specific characters. Once you have these characters firmly in mind, you begin to imagine specific, exciting situations within which these people find themselves. Conflicts arise from interactions among characters who have different goals and values. Certain themes begin to emerge as the characters initiate or become involved in specific actions. This "organic" approach to fiction writing tries to ensure that actions and themes flow naturally out of real characters.

Another approach to writing fiction begins with you developing a basic theme, idea, or message. In some ways it is more difficult to begin with the theme and then find three-dimensional characters who can initiate actions to reinforce the theme. There is a real danger that the theme will become overbearing. The opposite danger faced by the character-first approach is that the actions undertaken by certain characters will not be thematically significant or interesting.

A third way you may begin a dramatic script is to begin with the plot or story structure, and then work in both directions, that is, toward characters who can carry out those actions and the themes that those actions reflect or represent. In using this method, there is a danger that characters will simply become pawns to carry out actions and that themes will be tacked on from the outside.

Where you begin is probably less important than paying attention to the development of all three fictional aspects: plot, characters, and themes. Plot, that is, the telling or presentation of specific actions and events, has already been discussed in terms of dramatic and narrative structure, but characterization and theme need further consideration.

Developing strong, believable, and interesting characters is just as important as creating an exciting series of actions and events. Complex characters give a story depth and three-dimensionality. A character's values and beliefs lead to conflicts with other characters who hold opposing values. If these values are significant and strongly held, the entire fictional experience is enhanced.

Character can be revealed through two primary vehicles: actions and words. What characters do and say reveals in large part who they are. But actions and behavior are usually more important than dialogue. Characters should show us what they believe through their actions. The important thing for the writer to remember is that communication takes place through concrete sounds and images. A character is largely created through external appearances, actions, and speech. But the external surface of a character must reflect a complex internal value system and a set of abstract thoughts, beliefs, and feelings. An external surface that is not based on a solid psychological foundation lacks depth, understanding, and true artistic potential.

You can divide characters into three categories: central characters, principal characters, and secondary or incidental characters. The central character or characters figure prominently in a story. They are the primary sources of audience satisfaction, interest, and identification. The decisions they make and the actions they initiate propel the drama. Their values, beliefs, feelings, and goals determine, to a great extent, how meaningful and significant the entire drama will become. The principal characters are usually friends or foils to the central character(s). They can offer support to the actions and thoughts of the central character, or they can present significant obstacles to the attainment of his or her goals. In a longer drama there is usually enough time to give most or all of the principal characters sufficient depth so that their interactions with the central character become important and convincing.

Secondary and incidental characters may help create a situation that provokes a conflict, but they are contributors to (rather than initiators of) major actions. There is rarely time to fully develop all the minor characters in a drama into complex individuals. They have certain traits and mannerisms that distinguish them in a crowd and add spice to the drama, but these can easily deteriorate into stereotypes or clichés. Stereotyping secondary or incidental characters often runs the risk of stereotyping certain occupational or ethnic groups and minorities. Some reliance on character types (as opposed to stereotypes) ensures immediate audience recognition of the most important aspect of a character and contributes to the drama as a whole. What minor characters say about any major character helps to develop the latter's characterization. A good deal of information about the central character can be communicated to the audience through the words of secondary and incidental characters, sometimes reinforcing and sometimes contradicting the central character's own speech and actions.

A *theme* is basically a significant statement that a work of fiction asserts or an important issue that it raises. Themes generally emanate from the values, beliefs, and goals of the central characters, but a general theme may be much broader and universal than the attitudes of any single character. The film *Citizen Kane* (1941) has several broad themes, for example. The portrayal of Kane's life focuses on such issues as the absence of love in his life and his pursuit of fame, fortune, and power. Images, symbols, and motifs, such as "Rosebud," suggest, perhaps, that the absence of a happy childhood or family or parental love and guidance can lead to an inability to love and a meaningless pursuit of money and power. This film also develops other themes concerning democracy, politics, and the press, including, perhaps, a criticism of American society and capitalism in general. Of course, not all films are so heavily thematic, but the greatness of this film is that it does not sacrifice characterization and dramatic structure in order to make meaningful statements. Important themes coexist with strong characters and a complex plot. The themes are not the sole interest of the story.

Adaptation

An adaptation is a relatively faithful translation of a play, short story, a novel, or even a comic strip into a film or television program. If you attempt an adaptation, you must be very familiar with the original literary work and make every attempt to translate it into a different medium with the central characters and themes virtually intact. A television or filmscript that is less faithful to the original is frequently said to be based on that source, while a work that uses the original written piece as a springboard for essentially new ideas is said to be freely adapted or simply suggested by the original.

You begin the adaptation process with a consideration of the author's intent. What is the basic theme and point of view from which the story is told? Which characters are particularly memorable and/or attractive, disturbing and/or sympathetic? The plot must be analyzed in detail, using some of the basic elements of dramatic and narrative structure discussed earlier as a guide to good storytelling technique in media production. Does the story have a basic three-act structure? Does it build logically and dramatically toward a climax and resolution? Does the story have a plot and a subplot, and do the two coalesce at the denouement, that is, at the point of their final solution and clarification? Are there dead spots that can be eliminated or conflicts that need to be intensified? How many different scenes and settings are required? Is the story told from an omniscient or a specific character's point of view? Is there substantial dialogue and action, or will a character's interior monologue need to be dramatized and shown rather than simply told? Does the story follow a chronological structure, or does it involve flashbacks and/or flash forwards in time?

After completing a careful analysis of the basic plot, subplot, characters, and themes, of the original work, you write a treatment and then a screenplay that usually provide a number of changes from the original work. These changes may include the following: creating or eliminating subplots; eliminating, combining, adding, or altering (usually secondary or minor) characters; cutting, shortening, or expanding and enhancing specific scenes; adding, subtracting, or altering settings. You make these changes to improve a story's dramatic and narrative structure; to enhance the characterization and theme of the original novel, play, or short story; and to increase the efficiency and often decrease the cost of actual production.

If you attempt a full and complete adaptation of a lengthy novel, for example, it could substantially exceed the normal time restrictions of most media productions. You must then decide which elements are crucial to the story, which will be the most dramatic, what scenes or portions of the plot can be eliminated entirely, and how others can be shortened. Sometimes characters can be combined, so that the ideas and values they espouse are not lost but simply condensed. Dialogue or action scenes may have to be added, however, in order to dramatize information that was presented in the novel as pure description or characters' inner thoughts. The story should be shown, not just told. Literary dialogue must work well as spoken dialogue, and dialogue should not become so lengthy and informative that it substitutes for action. As an adaptation scriptwriter, you must understand the production problems and costs involved in composing a faithful adaptation of an original piece of writing. You must also understand the needs and expectations of the audience so that an effective, exciting, and interesting presentation of characters, actions, and themes will be created on the screen.

Before the adaptation process commences, the rights to a published and/or copyrighted work must be secured, of course. An original novel, short story, play, history, or biography may be protected by copyright for up to 75 years, and any television or film producer who attempts to adapt it, however freely, without paying for the right to do so can be held liable for damages to the value of that property.

Short Fiction Genre

Some short fiction forms, such as television situation comedies, may require different treatment, including the use of alternative dramatic and narrative structures and story construction, from that of longer forms, such as feature films. For example, half-hour episodes in a television situation comedy series present the same set of characters in a slightly different situation each week. The relatively short duration of an individual episode encourages a different organization and approach.

A sitcom episode is usually organized into two acts with three scenes per act and a tag or epilogue after the last commercial to keep the audience tuned in and to reinforce any message or theme. The opening of an episode must grab the attention of the audience members to prevent them from switching channels. A major conflict or problem must be presented in the first five minutes (Act One, Scene One), prior to the first commercial break. The dramatic device that grabs the audience is called a *hook*. It often takes the form of a problem or conflict that excites the viewer and foreshadows events that occur later in the story. A specific object

or idea introduced early in a drama, which becomes an important factor during the final resolution, is called a *plant*. Planting
and foreshadowing are effective devices in terms of hooking the
audience. The conflict builds through a series of complications or
misunderstandings until the end of Act One, where a new com-
plication is introduced. In Act Two things begin to get sorted out,
and the main conflict is resolved in Act Two, Scene Three. With
the opening credits, closing tag, and commercials between scenes,
you have only about 20 minutes to quickly develop the basic conflict or situation, add a few complications, and then neatly resolve
it. The structure of a situation comedy follows this basic formula,
regardless of the exact setting and characters. There is a constant
need for imagination and creativity within this tight, somewhat
restrictive format.

Other types of short fiction are not as formulaic as situation comedy, but they nonetheless demand tight dramatic structure. There
simply isn't enough time to develop many minor characters or a
complicated subplot. A short drama usually has a short exposition section. New characters and situations must be developed
very quickly and efficiently. A few lines of dialogue can establish
who new characters are and their basic motivations. The plot must
develop several complications to promote interest and variation,
but it must also build toward a climax. Loose ends are quickly tied
up and resolved.

Dramatic Script Formats

The scripts used by drama directors and actors evolved over the
years as new media surfaced. In the theater, motion pictures, and
radio the original dramas had little in the way of formal scripts. As
each of the media became more complex, written instructions and
guides to the action and dialogue needed to be formalized.

Motion Picture

The first dramatic motion pictures were shot continuously with one
roll of the camera on a fixed set not unlike the proscenium arch of

live theater. Since sound was not recorded, the director simply stood next to the camera and called out instructions as to where the actors were to move, what action to follow, and what lines to mouth. Once sound arrived and each shot was made with a different camera set-up and eventually shot out of order, a clearly defined and precise script needed to be created. Screenwriters and directors, often the same person, used a version of theatrical script format that many were accustomed to using from their previous experience in the theater. With minor adaptations, including adding scene numbers, precise dialogue, transitions, and instructions in media terms, the motion picture script format evolved.

The format defines various aspects of the scripts by varying the width of the margins and by capitalizing certain portions of the copy. The rules at first seem complex, but they can be summarized as follows:

- Each shot starts with the shot number at the extremes of the right-hand and left-hand margins. In uppercase type, either the word DAY or NIGHT indicates lighting conditions, followed by either INT or EXT, to indicate location.
- Camera directions, scene descriptions, and stage directions are typed next, within slightly narrower margins. How the line is to be delivered is typed in still narrower margins within parentheses, and dialogue is typed within even narrower margins.
- The name of the speaking character is centered above his or her line in uppercase letters.
- Single-spacing is used for dialogue, camera angles and movements, stage directions, scene descriptions, sound effects, or cues.
- Double-spacing is used to separate a camera shot or scene from the next camera shot or scene, a scene from an interceding transition (FADE IN/FADE OUT, DISSOLVE), the speech of one character from the heading of the next character, and a speech from camera or stage directions.
- Uppercase type is used for: INT or EXT, DAY or NIGHT, in heading line; indication of location; indication of day/night; name of a character when first introduced in the stage directions and to indicate their dialogue; camera angles and movements; scene transitions; and (CONTINUED), if a scene is split between pages (avoid if at all possible).

MOTION PICTURE DRAMA FORMAT

1. EXT   Surface of the planet Burmus   DAY   1

Two space ships take off from the surface of the planet
With a fleet of warrior space ships waiting

2. INT   Konscoll command ship   DAY   2

Commanding the operation is Captain Guidle, with
Assistants Blake and Brooke and an observation robot, Max

BLAKE
One minute to critical point.

GUIDLE
OK, calculate the distance.

BLAKE
Sir?? Hold on, what's that on the scope?
It looks like a ship leaving Burmus.

GUIDLE
From Burmus ??

BLAKE
Just as I thought. Your plan is a failure.

GUIDLE
Shut up, we'll keep them from escaping
Brooke—fire up all engines and fix the heading
straight for Burmus.

BROOKE
There's at least seven ships heading this way.
The setting you gave me guarantees a collision.

3. INT   Gollkirk's command ship   DAY   3

The crew frantically trying to set new headings

SMSLO
Besides the Konscoll I see another ship leaving
Burmus heading our way.

DISS

Figure 9.5. Motion picture script format evolved from live theater script
format with additions required by film and technology operations.

Radio Drama

Radio drama grew from duplicating live theater performances of the early 20th century. Since theater performances rely heavily on dialogue, the transference of scripts, production methods, and acting techniques occurred easily. The two major differences came from the audience needing to use greater powers of imagination for radio, and the actors could concentrate on their voices and not their appearances. Although theater used sound effects and music, radio developed the use of the two to a fine art later copied later by the motion picture business.

Instructions, actors' names, sound effects (SFX), and MUSIC are entered in capital letters, dialogue is entered in upper and lower-case letters, with a 2" margin on the right, 1" on left. All lines are double-spaced, descriptions of SFX and music are enclosed in parentheses. The character's name is flush left followed by a colon, several spaces, and then the dialogue.

Soap Opera

Television soap operas, the daytime serial dramas aimed at women and originally sponsored by household product manufacturers, evolved from radio dramas of the same type and sponsorship. Originally soap operas were performed live or later recorded live-to-tape in the studio usually using four cameras each feeding a separate recording medium. The output of the switcher also was recorded but on a fifth recorder. Immediately following the recording session, the files are downloaded and edited into a final form. As technology changed, much of the program could be shot in the field with the field segments combined with the studio footage either simultaneously or during postproduction. Since a new episode must be completed each day of the week, the process must move quickly and with little room for error or correction of any except horrendous mistakes. The script was in constant evolution from the first writer's meeting until the final taping and editing. Since the actors worked with limited rehearsal, much of the dialogue was ad-libbed or created spontaneously during the performance.

RADIO DRAMA FORMAT

Each line of radio copy needs to be numbered, even if the same character continues a speech.

Margins for line numbers and character names can be flush left, but the margins for copy to be read should be set at 2" from the left, and 2" from the right. Music and SFX may be underlined, but it is not necessary.

EXAMPLE

1.	SHIRLEY:	Good morning, Neville dear.
2.	NEVILLE:	Good morning.
3.	SHIRLEY:	Are you feeling well today?
4.	NEVILLE:	Yes, I think quite well. And look, it certainly is a fine
5.		day. Some alto cumulus with a few strato cumulus for
6.		accents. Very effective.
7.	SHIRLEY:	Does that mean a good day?
8.	NEVILLE:	(SLOWLY, REFLECTIVELY) Too early to tell yet.
9.		You know, after I go to work, I fix breakfast for myself,
10.		and I sit there at the table and watch the clouds.
11.		Sometimes it's hours ... and I see the wind, not just
12.		the clouds moving, but when I stare for a long time, I
13.		can actually see the wind.
14.	SHIRLEY:	Really? What does the wind look like?
15.	SFX	WIND HOWLING LOUD - RUSTLING BRANCHES
16.	SHIRLEY:	Oh !!!

Figure 9.6. Radio drama copy follows basic radio copy format. The format evolved from a combination of theatrical and motion picture scripts, but deleting any references to movement, action, or entrance/exits.

The script format of necessity remains fairly flexible due to the tight production schedule, but some traditions continue. All copy, both dialogue and instructions, are entered double-spaced. Character names and instructions are entered in capital letters, and dialogue lines are entered in uppercase and lowercase letters in a column on the left side of the page with an inch and a half margin. The video column on the right is left blank, and all framing, blocking, actor and camera movements, and shots are added by the director during rehearsal.

The show title and episode number appear on the upper left corner of the page, with the page number and number of script version (since every script passes through several rewrites before taping) placed on the upper right hand corner of the page.

Sitcom

If the situation comedy is shot using four video cameras with a live audience, the script format generally used is the same as the soap opera script format. Sitcoms are also shot with single-camera video or film, or multiple-camera film. In those cases the script format usually used is the same as the dramatic film format. Some additions to the script include episode numbers, writer's name, and script date. Act designations are placed in caps at the top of the page of the first page of that act. Scenes may be indicated with letters instead of numbers at the beginning of each scene. Action descriptions on sitcoms are shorter than dramatic programs since the cast spends several days reading scripts and script revisions until the afternoon of the first recorded rehearsal. The producer and director have by then worked out any final details of camera placement and shot framing.

Television Drama

Since most full-length television dramas are shot single-camera using film as the recording medium, the preferred script by both writers and directors is the same format that feature-length motion picture writers and directors use. There are minor deviations in script formats depending on the studio and/or the producers' method of operating and their relationship with their writer(s). The differences are not enough to try to learn all the formats used in the business; a well prepared script using the format in Figure 9.5 is acceptable to professionals.

SOAP OPERA SCRIPT FORMAT

Oltl-3352   II-30

                    JOHNNY

Why would he lie to you?

                    TINA

I don't know—but one of them

Did. And I'm going to find out why.

(CUT TO: TONY'S PLACE –

CONTINUE WITH TED & VICKY)

                    TED

And how does Karen plan to

Recognize this so-called

Murderer?

                    VICKI

She didn't say ...

                    TED

You know, it's almost funny

-- like a dime story novel

-- with Karen the private eye.

                    VICKI

She is serious about it.

                    TED

She ought to go into business.

Figure 9.7. Soap opera script format is very simple design for the director to add video notes by hand during rehearsal to the single left-hand column containing all dialogue and audio cues.

SITCOM SCRIPT FORMAT

1. INT   Four guys standing around a nearly empty shabby Philadelphia apartment. INT 1.

All four look embarrassed. Sam reaches into a bag and pulls out a bottle of wine, appearing unopened.

                              ROBIN
                   Really, Sam, its not necessary.

                               JOE
            Yeah, that's what I said. Then I got called funny names.

                              SAM:
                     (Hands Robin the bottle)
                 I think you'll like it, it's expensive.

                             ROBIN
                        (Looks at bottle)
                        It's half empty.

Sam is stunned. He grabs the bottle. He looks right at Brent.

                              SAM
            You drank it when we stopped for gas, didn't you?

                             BRENT
                         I was thirsty.

                             ROBIN
                   Hey, it doesn't matter.

                              SAM
                        (To Woody)
                 Twenty-five bucks a bottle.
                 If you were thirsty, get a Coke.

                             BRENT
            You know what its like riding with you in traffic?
                      A Coke won't do it.

                              SAM
                     You owe it to me.

                             BRENT
                        Up yours.

Figure 9.8. Sitcom script formats vary depending on the shooting method: film or video, single-camera or multiple-camera.

Internet Drama

Scripts used by producers of the mini-dramas distributed via the Internet follow whichever medium the producers used to create the original before distribution. As the popularity of Internet distribution and distribution for mini-screens on cell phones, PDAs, and iPods increases to the level of earning a profit, unique methods of creating the dramas will develop. With that development will come changes in formats paralleling the changes that occurred as film, radio, and television found their audience and market. For now, those preparing scripts for the new digital media will use the format they have used to create analog or digital productions or those they are familiar enough to use comfortably. The production unit or the funding source may determine the choice.

Summary

The dramatic form of storytelling dates back to the beginning of civilization, varying only in the medium of performance. From cave drawings to Internet blogs, people want to tell and absorb how others have faced and solved life's challenges. Today's dramatic productions require some level of preparation, planning, and recording of key documents to facilitate the production process. It begins with research and ends with completed and well-edited final shooting scripts. Statements of purpose, proposals, treatments, budgets constitute essential written elements within the preproduction process.

The dramatic structure and narrative styles have not changed much over the years. Strong recognizable characters interacting within plots that interest and excite the audience create memorable stories. Whether the stories are told in melodramatic or well-made form, the audience must find in the drama a reason to stay tuned and listen/watch to the end. A series of crises, solutions leading to a final climax, and dénouement resolve the concerns of the audience, leaving it satisfied with either a happy or unhappy ending.

The physical form of the script varies depending on the medium of production, but each owe their heritage to scripts originally written for directors and actors performing on the stage of a theater. Motion pictures, radio, television, and the Internet all borrowed from that original form and modified the form to better fulfill the needs of the production crew and cast.

Be Sure To...

1. Complete your research before you try to formulate the concept of your story
2. Fully understand what you are trying to tell your audience
3. Make certain the genre you have chosen is appropriate for your subject
4. Fully outline your story line and characters before trying to write a script
5. Write your proposal and treatments so that a non-media person will understand the story you are telling to make it worth their time and funds to support you.
6. Don't hesitate to rewrite and rewrite until your story rings true for the audience.

Exercises

1. Watch a half-hour sitcom and outline the plot, act breaks, crisis, and resolution.
2. Perform the same analysis of an hour-long TV drama.
3. Perform the same analysis of a feature-length motion picture.
4. Write a log line and premise for a short drama.
5. Write a log line and premise for your favorite feature film.
6. Write all preproduction forms for a feature-length film up to a rough draft of a shooting script.

Additional Sources

Print

Armer, Alan A. *Writing the Screenplay: TV and Film.* 2nd ed. Long Grove, IL: Waveland Press, Inc., 2002.

Brockett, Oscar G. *The Essential Theatre.* 6th ed. Fort Worth, TX: Harcourt Brace College Publishers, 1996.

Cooper, Patricia. *Writing the Short Film.* 3rd ed. Boston: Focal Press, 2004.

Friedmann, Anthony. *Writing for Visual Media.* 2nd ed. Boston: Focal Press, 2006.

Grose, D,. Donald, and O. Franklin Kenworthy. *A Mirror to Life: A History of Western Theatre*. New York: Holt, Rinehart and Winston, 1985.

Hacker, Diana. *A Pocket Style Manual*. 3rd ed. Boston: Bedford/ St. Martin's Press, 2000.

Henson, Wendy J. *Screenwriting: Step by Step*. Boston: Allyn & Bacon, 2005.

Hilliard, Robert L. *Writing for Television, Radio and New Media*. 8th ed. Belmont, CA: Wadsworth Publishing, 2004.

Hyde, Stuart. *Idea to Script: Storytelling for Today's Media*. Boston: Allyn & Bacon, 2003.

Johnson, Claudia H. *Crafting Short Screenplays that Connect*. 2nd ed. Boston: Focal Press, 2005.

Kessler, Lauren, and Duncan McDonald. *When Words Collide: A Media Writer's Guide to Grammar and Style*. 6th ed. Belmont, CA: Wadsworth Publishing, 2004.

McGrath, Declan, and Felim MacDermott. *Screenwriting*. Boston: Focal Press, 2003.

Miller, Carolyn Handler. *Digital Storytelling: A Creator's Guide to Interactive Entertainment*. Boston: Focal Press, 2004.

Rabiger, Michael. *Developing Story Ideas*. 2nd ed. Boston: Focal Press, 2005.

Vale, Eugene. *Vale's Screen and Television Writing*. Revised ed. Boston: Focal Press, 1998.

Willis, Edgar E., and Camille D'Arienzo. *Writing Scripts for Television, Radio, and Film*. 3rd ed. Fort Worth, TX: Harcourt Brace Jovanovich College Publishers, 1993.

Web

www.annenberg.nwu.edu
www.chdramaworkshop.homestead.com
www.empirecontact.com
www.igc.org
www.imdb.com
www.newmedia.com
www.powereproduction.com
www.screentalk.org
www.storyispromise.com
www.writersguild.org
www.writersstory.com
www.writerswrite.com
www.zayamsbury.net

CHAPTER 10

The Internet

If I have been able to see farther than others, it was because I stood on the shoulders of giants.

—Sir Isaac Newton

The Internet exists as a global digital network linking computers of universities, corporations, government agencies, scientific laboratories, and private citizens providing interactive communication between individuals and among members of networks.

Introduction

The Internet revolutionized the field of communication to a greater extent than any other technical or social change in the history of humankind. The Internet created a worldwide controlled broadcast system offering the means to disseminate information, provide collaboration, and allow interaction among groups and between individuals through some form of digital operating mechanism. The extent of the effect the Internet will have on society in general and all aspects of the communication world is impossible to predict. Like all new media, it will converge with some media, change others, and possibly supplant some.

Background

The relatively short history of the Internet may be traced to the activities of the military, which requested a decentralized, secure communication system in the late 1950s that could be used instantaneously around the world. The research arms of four universities in this country connected their mainframe computers to a network created by the Defense Advanced Projects Research Agency, (DARPA) funded by the military. Various other universities joined MIT, UCLA, Stanford, and the University of Utah to solve the problems with different computers communicating with each other over long distances using a standardized system called a protocol. The TCP/IP code of the protocol would tell a message where it was to be delivered and where it came from, and also how to reassemble the individual "packets" of digital information carrying the information. Originally the signals were sent using the circuit switched system used by telephone systems, but that system was inadequate to handle the amount and type of traffic intended for the Internet. Although the concept of breaking the information into packets and sending the packets along different lines at different times seemed to be inefficient and impractical, under the controlled digital systems developed by DARPA in the late 1960s and early 1970s, it worked and remains the delivery system used today on the Internet, as the DARPAnet came to be known.

Once the DARPAnet opened for use for units besides the military and researchers, demand for a practical method of addressing and managing the system become important. In 1975, 100 individual computers were communicating on the DARPAnet, 1,000 by 1984, and over 100 million by the turn of the century. The user base moved from just the original users, to vast numbers of individuals using their business and home computers especially after the development of the practical and relatively inexpensive personal computer in the 1980s. A categorizing system was developed to facilitate keeping track of the burgeoning number of users since the original address was the numerical unique TCP/IP address for each computer connected to the Internet. A typical address was a complex number (e.g., 256.2.127). Instead of the complex TCP/IP number, the domain name system was invented. Each address consisted of a hierarchical set of host names (e.g., www.rbm.org).

The military separated from the Internet into their own system as the Internet grew rapidly and began to be used for communication other than messages. By the 1980s, electronic mail, or e-mail, as it now is called, became the message system. In the 1990s, the World Wide Web developed and spread rapidly as a subcategory of the

Internet. In 1998, Internet2, better known as the Abilene Network, began operating between 220+ universities and research sites. Its purpose is to provide support for and advanced network services to members. Originally it delivered content at a rate of 2.5 gigabites (Gbps) per second, and later upgraded to 10 Gbps, with plans for a 100 Gbps by 2008. By 2002, 840 million individuals on 200 million hosts accessed the Internet. It is estimated that by 2010, 80% of the world will be using the Internet.

Today, the Internet has become a heavily commercialized commodity service in support of other commercial services. It will continue to evolve as new purposes will be invented and designed that the developers of the Internet never would have conceived of only 60 years ago.

Since 55% of American households use computers to connect to the Internet, the U.S. Census indicates that represents 62 million households. Ninety-five percent of American households with income over $100,000 own a computer, 92% are connected to the Internet, and over half are now connected through a broadband service, rather than dial-up phone service.

As a writer, this potential audience for your work should be motivation enough to learn how to use the Internet properly and efficiently. Although Americans do not spend as much time on the Internet, averaging 11.4 hours per week, as opposed to China's citizens at 17.9 and Japan's at 13.9, the 11.4 hours is half again as much time as the average viewer spends each week watching television/cable.

As an indication of the value of reaching Internet users, the *New York Times* newspaper recently combined its 40-member Web site staff with the much larger print staff. The merger took place to allow both types of reporters and editors to understand each other's method of operating, and to integrate the staff to being able to work in both media as easily as they did their original job assignments. Other major international daily papers like the *Washington Post* and *Wall Street Journal* may consider such a move in the near future.

The broadcast industry also realizes the value of distributing its product via the Internet and other new digital media. Warner Bros.

Television group in 2006 began selling some sitcoms into a combination syndication of both television and a broadband release. The Comedy Central cable channel earns over $150 million each year from the sale of download clips, advertising on its broadband service, and its comedy record label. MTV recently began releasing selected programs simultaneously on cable and on a broadband service. Comcast, the nation's largest cable provider, launched a broadband Internet channel just for children. Much of the content for the channel will be provided by the Disney company with some of the programming offered for free and others on a pay basis. Comcast's premier online service, www.comcast.net, offers news, sports, weather, stock market reports with streaming video, sound, and on-demand news stories, interviews, and animated cartoons.

Types of Internet Messages

People mainly use two types of formats to access the Internet: electronic mail (e-mail) and the World Wide Web (WWW). Both systems developed independently and both serve different unique purposes.

E-Mail

E-mail evolved from messages sent between scientists and engineers working on earlier version of the Internet, ARPAnet, during the late 1960s and early 1970s. Originally intended to be sent through closed networks, its value spread from one group to another until by the late 1970s it became obvious a formal system of sending messages between computers was a necessity. The first commercial use of the system by Compuserve in 1989 followed an experimental system used by the National Research Initiative the year before. In 1993, AOL and Delphi connected their mail systems to the Internet and widespread adoption by others quickly followed.

A text-only message is placed on the Internet from an individual computer through an Internet Service Provider (ISP). The message carries an address that the system recognizes and delivers to the receiver's ISP. The address is in two parts separated by the "at" sign "@."

The first part is the name of the receiver, and the second part is the name of the ISP plus one or more subsections assigned by the domain system or requested by the receiver: musburgermedia@comcast.net. If the sender requires graphics or a precise formatted message, then those items must be assembled on a separate file and "attached" to the e-mail. The graphics are then downloaded by the receiver if he or she has the correct application on his or her hard drive. The attachments may increase the memory required to send the message and the time it takes to download the complete attachment. People spend approximately 57% of their time on the Internet sending and receiving e-mails, in chat rooms, and instant messaging.

Chat Rooms/Lines

Chat rooms or chat lines allow the participants to send and receive messages between two or more participants at the same time. The concept was designed to give people the opportunity to carry on the equivalent of a telephone conversation by entering their conversation on the computer instead of speaking it out loud. Some chat lines are private and can be viewed only by the originators of the chat, while others are public and anyone can jump in and add their thoughts. Chat rooms do not operate on real time; there is a delay between messages. The length of the delay depends on the length of the message. The type of circuits used, and the amount of traffic on the circuits.

Instant Messaging

Instant messaging is a combination of e-mail and chat lines. Messages are passed between two or more participants without entering a chat room but the messages are passed in real time. Instant messaging requires a specific application and membership in order to communicate in real time.

Newsgroups

Another specialized form of communicating on the Internet is called newsgroups. Newsgroups evolved from Bulletin Board Systems that allowed users to post messages on a specific site where anyone could access that site to read any of the messages. If they wished, they could add their own thoughts to the topic being discussed. Within a short period of time an archive of opinions and thoughts on the topic become available for research or refreshing memories. Each newsgroup's topic is determined by the founders of the group and generally is a subject of common interest by a group of people in the same profession or hobby.

Telnet

The Telnet application allows the user to log on to a remote computer to access information on that computer or use an application on the remote computer. It is only text-based and was designed to access such mainframe computers as the Library of Congress by researchers. Find an example at telnet:/locis.loc.gov.

World Wide Web

The WWW originally was designed to provide scientists with a means of sharing information on demand without waiting to receive an e-mail. The system was text-based using Hypertext Transfer Protocol (HTTP) as the coding system. It allowed files to be edited on screen from any site accessing the file and later graphics, enhanced text, and all other multimedia were added by using Hyper Text Markup Language (HTML) codes. HTML, for some people, is a complex coding system, but the code may be created by using preset Web editors that offer the user the option of viewing the layout on screen as it is being created. This process is called What You See Is What You Get (WYSIWYG). Each location on the Web has an address called a Uniform Resource Locator (URL). The form follows the format of: service://domain name/full path name. As an example, http://www.comcast.net/explore.html. A Web editor program will create the HTML codes, but you must decide on the content and design the layout. To access a site on the web, the user must have a browser installed on his or her computer. The browser is a computer application that interprets the HTML codes so the viewer sees the frame as WYSIWYG, not computer code. To locate a specific site, the user enters the URL in the browser and the browser will find and display the site.

The Web is no longer restricted as a means for researchers to communicate among themselves. Instead the Web has become a means for the casual user as well as the confirmed Web junkie to scan and surf in order to share ideas, thoughts, creations, create new contacts for socializing, to play games, and watch the news and weather. Most importantly, the Web offers the ability to self-program and control what you want to see, how and when you want to see it, and what you want to say about what you do see. The Web now competes with traditional media: television, radio, cable, magazines, newspapers, and even books. As such, it has become an extremely powerful force in today's society that should be handled with caution and responsibility.

The very pervasiveness and popularity of the Web may undue its "net neutrality" that allows all users equal access without a system of fees for use and content control by the telecommunication industry or government.

Types of Web Sites

Surfing

One of the most popular Web activities is called surfing. As a surfer you explore search engines like Google, Yahoo, and others. By simply entering a name, a topic, or a location, the surfer will be presented with a list of possible sites to open and investigate. The process may be followed for the pure pleasure of exploring or for the goal of finding answers to specific questions. Surfing can be addicting, leading the surfer to hours spent following a series of leads to new, unexpected topics. The danger comes from the uncontrolled and unsupervised nature of the Web. Anyone may enter any information they wish, whether it is true, based on fact, a fallacy, or an intentional falsehood. As a surfer, you must guard against easily accepting everything found on the Web. Cross-checking from different sources, including print sources, may be required.

Wikis

An example of the types of information source that need cross-checking are Wikis. A Wiki is a Web site that allows users to create their own entries, edit some other person's entry, and have your own edited by someone else. New pages are created using simple text syntax and includes hyperlinks to other sites. The value of a Wiki is the accumulation of information on a single source from a wide variety of different points of view and experiences. If properly supervised, a Wiki may be very helpful as a source of information as well as a method for you to publish your definition of the term in question. See http://en.wikipedia.org/wiki/Wiki.

Really Simple Syndication (RSS)

RSS is a Web format designed to make distribution of news stories and other series of stories efficient and economical. To be distributed, the story must be defined in one of the RSS formats, each of which is a

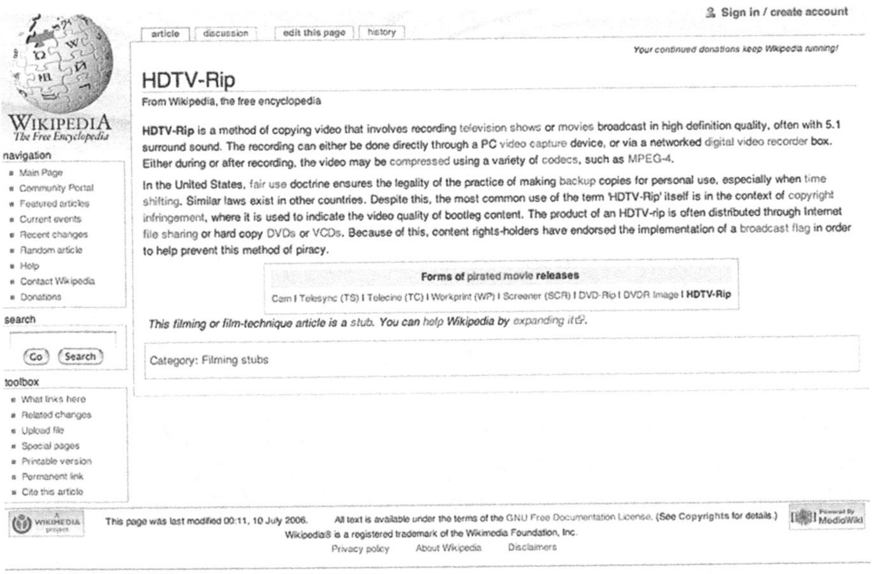
Sign in / create account

article | discussion | edit this page | history

Your continued donations keep Wikipedia running!

WIKIPEDIA
The Free Encyclopedia

navigation
- Main Page
- Community Portal
- Featured articles
- Current events
- Recent changes
- Random article
- Help
- Contact Wikipedia
- Donations

search

Go Search

toolbox
- What links here
- Related changes
- Upload file
- Special pages
- Printable version
- Permanent link
- Cite this article

HDTV-Rip

From Wikipedia, the free encyclopedia

HDTV-Rip is a method of copying video that involves recording television shows or movies broadcast in high definition quality, often with 5.1 surround sound. The recording can either be done directly through a PC video capture device, or via a networked digital video recorder box. Either during or after recording, the video may be compressed using a variety of codecs, such as MPEG-4.

In the United States, fair use doctrine ensures the legality of the practice of making backup copies for personal use, especially when time shifting. Similar laws exist in other countries. Despite this, the most common use of the term 'HDTV-Rip' itself is in the context of copyright infringement, where it is used to indicate the video quality of bootleg content. The product of an HDTV-rip is often distributed through Internet file sharing or hard copy DVDs or VCDs. Because of this, content rights-holders have endorsed the implementation of a broadcast flag in order to help prevent this method of piracy.

Forms of pirated movie releases

Cam | Telesync (TS) | Telecine (TC) | Workprint (WP) | Screener (SCR) | DVD-Rip | DVDR Image | **HDTV-Rip**

This filming or film-technique article is a stub. You can help Wikipedia by expanding it.

Category: Filming stubs

This page was last modified 00:11, 10 July 2006. All text is available under the terms of the GNU Free Documentation License. (See Copyrights for details.)
Wikipedia® is a registered trademark of the Wikimedia Foundation, Inc.
Privacy policy About Wikipedia Disclaimers

Figure 10.1. Wikis provide quick and easy definitions and a variety of sources of information, but since they are not reviewed in any systematic way, they may include misinformation.

derivative of HTML. As a writer, to distribute your stories you must be able to write in HTML or use of one several commercial applications that will convert your input to one of the two present RSS formats. Once you format your story it must be registered with aggregators. They act as syndicators, making your story available to anyone interested in the topic by its listed title. People interested in your topic can check with their RSS feed and they will receive an updated list of titles. If a title indicates the subject they are interested in they can click on the topic and read the complete file. RSS feeds also may be downloaded to cell phones, PDAs, or voice updaters.

The value of the RSS system is its ability to make a single copy of a story available to an infinite number of sites rather than having to duplicate a story and distribute each copy to as many sites as may have shown an interest. Designers are writing new applications that will increase the systems of sorting and matching topic interests with story sources.

Blogs

A blog is a diary of a person's thoughts, opinions, and activities, with Web links open to certain people chosen by the blogger. The term blog is a contraction of "Web log," but be careful not to confuse with the term Web log, which is a server's list of a log's files. As a writer, your blog will give you the opportunity to publish anything you want people to read and respond to. Some use their blog to organize their thoughts, while amateur journalists attempt to publish what they consider news as well as opinions. A blog may become a means of delivering a sermon or a soap-box speech on political or social topics.

One of the problems with blogs is their lack of rules or control. Without control, items on blogs must be considered undocumented, possibly inaccurate, intentionally libelous, or misleading from a lack of journalistic experience or effort. Interestingly, legitimate news gatherers rely on some bloggers as an indication of the attitudes of the public, and as an indication of what much of the audience feels it is not being told by the establishment. Families, organized groups, teams, or organizations may use a blog to pass information quickly between and among the group and allow immediate response to the information. Photos and audio files also may be blogged, if common applications exist on the blogger's and receiver's hard drives.

In order to create a blog, you open an account, name the blog, choose a template, and fill in the blanks. The process is much like creating any Web site, but with the specific purpose of communicating your personal thoughts to a select audience.

E-Commerce

A specialized use for the Internet was developed to serve the business world. Electronic commerce (e-commerce) consists of two types of business. For communication involving sales, marketing, and other communication between businesses, business-to-business (B2B) evolved. Separate from, but operating on the same concept of interactive communications involving some type of commercial transaction, business-to-consumer (B2C) evolved. Popular B2C sites include ebay, Hotel.com, Alaskaair.com, Travelocity.com, and Amazon.com among many others. Businesses discovered people want to shop and purchase from the comfort of their homes or offices, and if they can get equivalent service and reasonably quick delivery, they will remain loyal to that company. But for the system to work, the Web site must be consumer oriented, include all of the information needed by the customer, and provide simple and direct instructions to place an order and to make decisions concerning payment and delivery.

The same qualities also must exist for B2B, except on a more professional and comprehensive basis. Today B2B is used for a rapid, secure, and efficient method of buying and selling products and services. The electronic system works much faster and more accurately than older, physical paper-driven systems.

Streaming Media

Streaming media is a means of transporting information, not an actual media. Streaming is a method of moving audio, video, graphics, and even text, although that is a waste of energy since text may be distributed easily with other methods such as e-mail, RSS, newsgroups, and blogs. The methods of streaming are based on the large amount of data required to move video and audio on the Internet. Compression systems reduce the bandwidth required for video and audio streaming, but other factors also apply.

Streaming video or audio may be viewed/heard either on demand or live. If on demand, then the signals are stored in a server and wait until they are called upon to be delivered. If live, the signals move from the origination point to the requesting computer as the material is created and is available only once. The major problem with streaming using either method is the amount of bandwidth needed to stream video, with less for audio. Both media may be compressed to help reduce the problem, but newer equipment including fiber optic lines and other high bandwidth systems also help. Legal issues also play a part. The ease of streaming signals from one computer to another using a peer-to-peer (P2P) system tempts people to stream material that is not licensed to be streamed or may have copyright restrictions that must be cleared before sharing. Some security systems prevent streaming if the program has been encrypted to prevent sharing. The Digital Millennium Copyright Act (DCMA) also prevents sharing of some digital files.

A more direct problem with streaming is the existence of three different non-compatible download formats: Real (Real Networks), QuickTime (Apple), and Windows Media Player (Microsoft). The basic player for each is free, but for higher quality and greater download rate, each format offers upgrades for an additional fee.

Audio Streaming

Streaming radio programs and the entire schedule of a station has become the most popular form of audio streaming. The audio file may be listened to in real time or downloaded and stored on your own hard drive to listen to at your convenience. For audio fans, streaming must compete against two other new broadcast formats. Satellite radio and HD radio broadcast in a digital format and offer access to a wide range of program formats and music genres. Both

Figure 10.2. Each of the three download formats process and stream signals differently, but to the consumer, they offer approximately the same service.

require special receivers or adapters and neither is intended to be recorded for delayed listening. Both offer some of their programs on the Internet. Internet radio first offered advertising-free programming, but competition and expense of maintain an operation forced the operators to use some advertising to fill the financial gap. Internet radio is divided primarily between juke-box style continuous music operations and retransmission of terrestrial stations.

Audio podcasts also are gaining in popularity but require a special program to participate. They offer the epitome of "open mic" do-it-yourself radio with little regard for advanced planning or critical thinking. Without government rules almost anything goes, but the format allows an outlet for people who have limited access to commercial radio of their liking. It also often offers rare recordings not available in any a store, primarily of independent bands who play original music for which they hold all of the rights. The danger, of course, is that even without FCC control any broadcast of licensed or copyrighted music is a violation of the law.

Dubbing audio from CDs or tapes to a hard drive and then to an iPod is not a violation of the law as long as there is no further duplication of the music. A transfer of the audio from one format to another under the control of the original owners without any transfer of ownership is legal. This process allows an individual to create his or her own program of just the music he or she wants to listen to and in the order the person wants to hear without the interference of a mouthy DJ or commercials. IPods, satellite radio, and Internet radio all threaten standard terrestrial radio. But radio has fought back with digital HD radio, giving listeners a wide range of choices. In the history of media, as each new media emerges, old media are forced to change and often improve from their former formats and operational methods.

Video Streaming

To be able to view streaming video on the Internet requires a solution to the problem of bandwidth. Full 30-frames-per-second color video on the Internet is impractical as of 2007. Solutions have taken two forms: compress the signal to the point where it can be viewed, regardless of the loss of quality and size of the image on the screen, or develop expensive compression and restoration schemes that allow the delivery of full-screen images.

Most video streamed today is delivered using the Flash application that allows low-quality, less than full-screen images, designed to be downloaded or viewed live on a computer screen. The signal may be downloaded using a program such as iTunes or other fee-based systems. The television networks provide news clips directly to the computer. The low-definition signals are ideal for loading onto cell phones, iPods, and PSPs. The low quality is not important on those devices. But the networks also will deliver programming on advertiser-supported channels such as CBS's "Innertube" used to introduce new programs and give viewers a chance to watch older programs from the network's archives. Despite the move toward HD television and higher quality films in theaters, a movement toward the opposite end of the quality spectrum has created a demand for production for the small, low-quality screen. Student productions, small independent companies, even the broadcasters and cable channels are considering producing specific programs or program segments for the small screen.

Two competing systems to deliver Internet Protocol Television, (IPTV) will use different methods to deliver a TV signal to the home computer. The telephone companies plan on a system that is connected directly to the home via a fiber optic line. The other system is based on programming delivered through the Internet on a program-on-demand basis. Neither system is fully functional as of this writing, but major companies on both sides of the technical solution press for practical solutions to appeal to viewers as soon as possible.

A high-quality solution has been developed by a company that offers its clients the opportunity to deliver full-screen video clips with minimal download time. The concept was developed to enable clients to deliver to their customers commercials, trailers, or corporate communications at the highest possible quality. To view an example, access www.vivicas.com. If this format can be expanded to include full-length motion pictures and or television programs, then a solution to high-quality delivery of streamed video may have been reached. The problem of immediate acceptance and consumer use is the expense of the application and security issues.

Writing for the Internet

When you write for the Internet you are writing for a mass medium. Sitting at your computer you may feel as if you were writing using a personal message system, but any e-mail, live chat, Web page, blog, or video game may be viewed by over 100,000 strangers. Do not enter anything on the Internet that you would not say to your grandmother or hand to the first stranger you run into on skid row. At the same time, the Internet may be one of the few contacts outside for the disabled, retired, unemployed, or some students. The Internet may also be a major factor in the lives of part- and full-time workers who work abnormal schedules. Make certain what you enter has value and is not a waste of your time or the time of a reader. Use your skills for positive results, not just to kill time or to massage your ego.

E-Mail, Chat Lines, and Instant Messaging

Writing for the Internet is no different than writing for any other medium. The first requirement is to COMMUNICATE. Whether the message is for e-mail, instant message, or a chat line—if the message is confusing, misunderstood, inaccurate, misleading, or even incorrect, then you are not communicating. You should write as if you are speaking to a single person or group; if the message is addressed in that manner, keep your copy conversational but directly to the point. Rambling on without a goal or a reason for connecting is a waste of both your time and that of anyone who opens your message.

Be grammatically precise; sloppy wording and sentence construction is the quickest way to have your message misunderstood. Review using the suggestions in Chapter One, and if your word processing program includes a spelling and grammar checker, USE IT. But such programs are not infallible; you still need to know how to spell and construct sentences properly.

Be careful to avoid the following:

1. Abbreviations. As tempting as it may be to short-cut your message, the abbreviation may mean nothing to the message receiver.
2. Slang that makes no sense to the message receiver
3. Use of "code" of-the-moment that seem funky and cool but will mean absolutely nothing to the message receiver
4. Use of emoticons
5. Private or personal information
6. Inappropriate comments
7. Inappropriate language

8. Hate messages
9. Messages written in anger (Wait 24 hours after writing, reread, and then if you still feel the same, send it, knowing you could be committing slander.)

Remember, your audience may follow different ethnic, religious, and social values and may interpret your wording differently than you intended. Be aware that you have no control upon whose computer your message will finally end. This is especially important if you reveal personal data such as home address, phone numbers or photographs. Remember, you don't know who is watching your message without your knowing, who it may be, and why they are interested in your personal information (icluding the CIA).

To make certain the party will open your message, ensure that the subject line accurately reflects your message. This is critical if your e-mail address does not reflect who sends the message. This is especially a problem if your address is a clever phase, slogan, or code that means nothing to anyone but yourself. Your address should not be your full name, but enough of your name so a receiver will know who sent the message. With the increase in spam and virus-laden messages, many people will not open a message unless they are sure they know who sent it. Instead, they will simply label your message as spam and your messages may then be shut out of some circuits.

Newsgroups and Blogs

More sophisticated systems of Internet communication appeared in two different means of exchanging ideas, opinions and information. Newsgroups serve two basically different purposes. First, all manufacturers of modern equipment maintain one or more (Microsoft has more than two dozen) newsgroups that act as conduits of information between customers and sales and/or service branches of the company. One of the advantages is that many service questions, especially on digital equipment, may be answered with an e-mail or written inquiry. Often, common problems may be solved with a review and reading of a list of Frequently Asked

Questions (FAQ), which are listed on the newsgroup site. If those answers on the lists don't solve the problem a customer may simply explain the condition and symptoms on the newsgroup site and wait for someone who may have had the same or similar problem and may offer a solution. The collection of FAQs, questions and answers become service archives that saves the company hours of service personnel's time and energy. At the same time, the list may contain information on new updates, accessories, or items of interest to the customer.

If you supervise such a group, your title generally is Editor or Administrator, and you will be responsible for managing the site by screening messages and deleting duplicates and irrelevant submissions. As the administrator, once you have cleared a submission you then send it out to everyone on the list. The job requires knowledge of the equipment, an editor's eye for copy quality control and the ability to make quick decisions so that queries are answered as soon as possible. As a contributor, you are expected to ask concise, detailed questions directed at a single problem at a time. As a responder, the same holds true. A concise, detailed explanation that will assist the contributor solve his or her problem without adding unnecessary personal opinions.

Blogs are a much more informal and loosely organized system of passing information. Originally, a blog was intended as a personal diary of the writer. The subjects were limited to items of interest to family, friends, and a few curious souls who happened to drop in on the site. Later, much wider range of topics appeared, including politics, religion, and news items of the day. Regardless of the subject, a blog is highly personal, opinionated, and specifically from the point of view of the writer. Anyone else who reaches the site may add his or her opinions with each new comment added to the top of the page, creating an archive of the topic. The editor may delete and additions at his or her own pleasure.

To operate a blog, you sign up for a Web-based service, either for free or a fee. Once you have the account you write your copy, edit it, and make certain that is what you really want the rest of the world to locate, read, and possibly disagree with. The same rules should apply to blogging as to e-mail. A certain level of civility, consideration, and reasonableness should prevail in both the original comments and the responses.

An interesting response to blogging has occurred in the past few years. Some bloggers have decided to become journalists without a portfolio, that is, without training, professional experience or the advantage of a second person to edit and check their "facts." Blogs now exist written specifically as daily news sources on topics of the day. Professional journalists, both print and electronic, now check carefully many blog sites for leads and information on stories they may not have had access. Blogs have covered many aspects of the Middle Eastern wars well before the national newspapers and television networks were able to discover the information to build their own stories. The major problem with accepting information from blogs is the lack of certainty that their information is accurate, which questions their creditability.

Writing a blog could lead to a professional career in journalism, if the basic ethics rules of journalism overcomes the "anything goes" attitude of the blog world.

Interactive Producing

As you write interactive projects, you will be leaving the comfortable and familiar world of linear thinking and writing. Now your mind must multitask as you think through your project's reason for being. Although all formats using the Internet base their operation on some form of interactivity, the two most dependent on interactivity are Web page designs and computer game designs.

Some of the shared techniques used in writing interactive projects are:

1. Staff assignments
2. Use of many different media forms within any one project
3. A structure based on some form of potential action taken by the user
4. Nonlinear story or pattern design
5. A reward for accomplishing the goal

Topic in microsoft.public.mac.explorer

Start a new topic - Subscribe to this group - About group   (Search this group)

                                                                                             Messages 1 - 6 of 6

what version of internet explorer can I download for my mac X, hopefully FREE

All 6 messages in topic - view as tree   Fixed font - Proportional font

From: sam - view profile   Not yet rated   Sponsored Links
Date: Thurs, Jul 20 2006 5:09 am   show options   Virtual Machines
                                                          Migrate Hundreds of Physical
I need to download a version of internet explorer to access a work   Servers to Virtual Machines Fast!
website. Which version will work?   www.platespin.com

▸ Reply   Virtual Machine
                                                          Virtual infrastructure solutions
                                                          from Intel and VMware.
From: Mickey Stevens - view profile   Not yet rated   intel.com
Date: Thurs, Jul 20 2006 10:00 am   show options
                                                          Network Monitoring Tool
Consistent with the product support lifecycle for Microsoft products,   Powerful, Effective & Affordable.
Internet Explorer for Mac is no longer available on the Microsoft website. Check Out Free/Trial Versions Now.
You can still get a copy here: www.OpManager.com/SNMP-Monitoring
<http://snipurl.com/iaa>
                                                          See your message here...
Note that Internet Explorer for Mac does not support all features that may
be necessary to access sites designed for Internet Explorer for Windows.
Other options to access sites that are Internet Explorer only are to have
your browser identify itself as Internet Explorer (available in Opera &
Safari), or to use Internet Explorer for Windows on a Windows machine.

On 7/20/06 7:09 AM, in article
1153397373.924948.21...@i3g2000cwc.googlegroups.com, "sam"

<samnyg...@yahoo.com> wrote:
> I need to download a version of internet explorer to access a work
> website. Which version will work?

—
Mickey Stevens (Microsoft MVP for Office:mac)
PowerPoint FAQ featuring PowerPoint:mac: <http://www.pptfaq.com/>
Entourage Help Page: <http://www.entourage.mvps.org/>

▸ Reply

From: Hugh Watkins - view profile Not yet rated
Date: Thurs, Jul 20 2006 4:02 pm   show options

- Show quoted text -

or a windos virtual machine on mac-on-intel

Figure 10.3. Newsgroups serve the function of distributing information outside of the traditional forms of journalism and as a means of providing information quickly and efficiently.

Interactive Staff

The head of the project is called a Producer or Project Manager. Her responsibility parallels that of a producer in radio/television/film with some modifications. An interactive producer must be knowledgeable about all aspects of the field, including the ability to write, design flow charts, and know programming and coding.

The equivalent of a media director in interactivity is called the Lead Designer, Art Director, Interactive Director, Game Developer, or Graphics Designer. Depending on the organization of the staff, he or she may have greater authority over the artwork, graphic page layout, casting and character design, or interactive menu and link design.

A writer is called a writer, or head writer if there is more than one writer assigned to the production. Obviously, the writer is responsible for scripts, type to be set on the page, input on menu design, and the flowchart.

The software design and writing is the responsibility of the Head Programmer, Technical Director, Programmer, or Coder. The programmer must rely on all of the other members of the staff to prepare and organize all of the material going into the project before she can write the codes to make it all work. Additional staff may be called Puzzle Master, Researcher, or Video or Sound Engineer.

Of all electronic media production crews, interactive crews work much more collaboratively than any other. Much, if not nearly all, of the work required to assemble an interactive production may be completed by several of the crew individually or as a committee. Such collaboration requires that those who work on interactive productions must have knowledge of and some skill at accomplishing all of the functions required to complete the project.

Interactive Writing

As a writer of an interactive production, you will follow the basic pattern of most professional media projects. The first step is to create and write a concept document. It may be called a precise, a log line, a treatment, or a proposal, but the concept must be reduced to a simple comprehensive statement easily understood by everyone involved in the project from the source of funding to the Coder. This document will pass through several stages of revision and modification as the entire group working on that concept will add input and suggestions from their past experiences and responsibilities on the project.

With the Producer, you will work on a budget (primarily the Producer's responsibility) and production schedule (with the Interactive Designer's input). By then a draft script should be available for all to begin creating their individual contributions. The differences between a Web page and a game now become major as a game script now takes the form of a fully scripted drama, whereas the Web script is much simpler.

Web Scripting

The Web script concentrates on three areas: the purpose or goal, the design layout, and the technical interface. As the writer, your concern will be the content carrying out the goal. You should work with the Design Director on the layout, but that is not your primary responsibility. Other than making certain the technical interface works with your script, that aspect is the responsibility of the Coder.

With the final goal in mind, you will need to list the types of choices you expect the user to need to reach his or her goal. You may list the choices by type of objects, or by the topic and subtopics, depending on your concept. The choices must be unique, offering the user clear choices of all possibilities without any overlapping. When viewing the choices the user should be able to decide between the choices without thinking some offer the same direction, or that they can think of a direction that is not listed as a choice. Your Web program may be a simple one-page Web that the user scans down to read all of the information available on the one page. Or the page may start with a home page, which would explain the basic concept of the program with either menus for further information or links leading to other pages to complete the project. You should create a flowchart, or at least an outline of the menu or link choices so that you have clearly in your mind the relationships between each choice. A Web page flowchart is a map for you and everyone working on the project to maintain consistency of the direction that actions may take. Your description accompanying the flow chart should be written as simply and directly as possible, but at the same time it must not cause confusion with illogical directions. Others on the team rely on the outline or flowchart to indicate to them what they need to create to complete your concept.

Game Scripting

Game scripting takes the writing process a step farther than a simple Web page or series of pages. A game is a complex drama and is analyzed, researched, and written the way a drama is written, except it is non-linear in structure. Chapters 8 (Games) and 9 (Drama) fully describe the process for writing the dramatic structure for game scripts.

August 14, 2006

FCC CLARIFIES CLOSED CAPTIONING
FOR EMERGENCY ANNOUNCEMENTS

In 2005, the FCC fined three San Diego television stations for failing to make emergency information accessible to persons with hearing disabilities in a timely manner when covering the October 2003 wildfires. The sanctions were the first actions taken for violation of the FCC's rules governing the provision of emergency information. Later that year, the commission proposed fines for three Washington D.C. stations for failing to follow closed captioning rules during a major storm that hit the area in 2004. It was clear that the FCC was serious about enforcing rules relating to emergency announcements for those with hearing disabilities.

On July 20, 2006, the commission issued a Public Notice reminding video programming distributors - including broadcasters, cable operators, and satellite television services - of their obligation to make emergency information accessible to persons with hearing and vision disabilities. It includes this paragraph:

"In the case of persons who are deaf or hard of hearing, Commission rules require that emergency information provided in the audio portion of the programming must be made accessible using closed captioning or other methods of visual presentation, such as open captioning, crawls, or scrolls that appear on the screen. Emergency information provided by these means should not block any closed captioning, and, closed captioning should not block any emergency information provided by crawls, scrolls, or other visual means. This rule regarding access to emergency information for persons with hearing disabilities became effective on August 29, 2000."

Figure 10.4. Web pages vary in complexity, use of color, and graphics, but each page must have a central purpose to serve the user.

Electronic Commerce

E-commerce is divided into two uses: for business reaching customers, B2C, and for businesses to reach other businesses, B2B.

The most common B2C interactive sites are designed for online shopping. Businesses publish electronic catalogs that allow customers to browse through the offerings until they find the item they wish to purchase. It is added to a shopping cart, purchased, and shipped from a warehouse. Amazon.com, Priceline.com, and Apple.com offer both products and services to purchase, but also in some cases service suggestions for equipment already purchased along with sales announcements. Writing the sites for B2C follow the same process as writing for B2B.

The B2B site must include information of sales offers, marketing, inventory, and delivery systems. As with all writing, you must start with research of the company, all of its operations, policies, and goals for the site. A study of the customer base is the beginning point of the research leading to the design of the system for the company. If the site does not give the customer (either retail or wholesale) what they are looking for on the site, then the site is a failure. The site must be simple to read and follow, yet flexible enough for all possible customer choices. Keep in mind what you write may be viewed on the small screen of a cell phone, PDA, or miniature laptop. If you have designed the site poorly and the customers are frustrated because they can't find what they want or how to use the site efficiently, they will go elsewhere and your boss loses a client.

You must write instructions logically so the customers can follow the path from throughout the catalog to the item(s) they are looking for, then to the section that shows how to go about making the connection or purchase. This is the most difficult section to write since unless the customer uses this site regularly, he or she will need a clear path to guide him or her through the purchase process. First, item numbers and descriptions need to be as short as possible and they must clearly define the object. The form to fill out should indicate where the item is to be listed, and separate columns or places on the order form should indicate where to list such information as colors, the number of items, or other special needs. If taxes must be paid, a simple method of calculating the tax as well as simple instruction calculating shipping costs should appear next on the form. The final part of the form indicates a total to be paid and how the payment is to be made; charge account, check, or if a business, a transfer of funds account. If possible, the tax, shipping, and total should automatically calculate from within the site.

There are times, but not often, when the users can't adapt what they are trying to do to the design of the site. As the writer it is critical for you to create a well-designed site to help the customer who needs some method to reach a human to describe and solve their problem. Two choices work well. One is a semi-chat line arrangement where the customer types a question on the form and the question is sent by e-mail to the customer service desk where a service employee hopefully will be able to immediately respond with an e-mail back to the same site. An alternate is a 1-800 phone number where the problem may be solved by a voice-to-voice discussion.

Internet Problems

When you write for the Internet, you may or may not know who will be scanning your work or why this person is reading it. Because the Internet is an open network, except for some private sites and networks, anyone can access your messages. For that reason your work may be misunderstood or your carefully designed site will be hacked and destroyed or changed to say the opposite of your

Figure 10.5. Both B2B and B2C Web sites must be clear and easy to follow or their original intent is lost.

intent. At all times when working on the Internet, the realization of your vulnerability should be kept fresh in your mind. This includes the interference of spam, attachment of viruses to your work, or of someone using your work for his or her benefit without either notifying or paying you.

It is important to avoid placing any personal or revealing information of yourself on the Internet. The danger of someone stealing your identity becomes more widespread as the number of people accessing the Internet for illegal or illicit reasons increases. The danger of sexual predators has reached alarming levels and must be guarded against by not revealing any personal data about you on any open chat line or blog.

Summary

The Internet developed from a research and military need for a quick, universal, and secure communication link among several different locations. As the number of users proliferated, new systems of addressing and managing the signals evolved into the present URL addresses and TCP/IP protocols that control the flow of signals in patches. A variety of different methods of using the Internet to send messages include e-mail, chat lines, instant messaging, newsgroups, and the World Wide Web. Types of Web sites developed to fill different needs of the users from search engines, encyclopedia listings, news gathering, personal diaries, and e-commerce.

The Internet developed to a sophisticated level to enable users to stream audio and video programming. The ability to stream raised questions of illegal distribution of copyrighted material and security issues that have not yet been totally solved. The three incompatible streaming formats complicate the distribution of streamed programs.

Writing for the Internet requires the ability to think and create in a nonlinear manner. Material to be posted must offer the user choices whether it is in a game, an e-commerce purchase, or a communication link between two or more users. Security and a lack of total compatibility between systems prevents the Internet from reaching its maximum level of efficiency.

Be Sure To...

1. Carefully research any Internet project you create.
2. Be careful of what you reveal about yourself on chat lines, blogs, or other open networks.
3. Remember you are communicating; if you want to be funny, write a comedy, not an e-mail.
4. Use newsgroups, blogs, and Web sites as sources of information, but remember the information is not validated, just someone's opinion.
5. Using the Internet is a privilege, a relatively free privilege; don't misuse or abuse the privilege.
6. Writing on the Internet is not that much different than writing for any electronic medium; it's a difference in distribution and lack of control of that distribution.

Exercises

1. Find a newsgroup of a topic that interests you. Follow it for a few days and then if you have something worthwhile to add, enter it and see what the response is to your comment.
2. Monitor a chat line. See how long it takes before someone adds a stupid, irrational, even dangerous comment and note the response from others.
3. Monitor a blog of someone you know, or a famous person's blog. Perform the same analysis as #2 above.
4. Surf the Web until you find a B2C site that you didn't know existed and see how simple or complex it is written for the consumer. Draw a flowchart.
5. Open a computer game; instead of playing it, analyze how it is organized and draw a flowchart.
6. Monitor an Internet radio station, an audio podcast, and if possible a satellite radio station and an HD radio station. Compare the quality of the signal as well as the professionalism of the programming.

Additional Sources

Print

Barnes, Susan B. *Computer-Mediated Communication: Human-to-Human Communication Across the Internet*. Boston: Allyn & Bacon, 2003.

Bucy, Erik P. *Living in the Information Age: A New Media Reader*. Belmont, CA: Wadsworth Publishing, 2002.

Garrand, Timothy. *Writing for Multimedia and the Web*. Boston: Focal Press, 2000.

Gehris, Dennis O. *Using Multimedia Tools and Applications on the Internet*. Belmont, CA: Wadsworth Publishing, 1998.

Graham, Lisa. *The Principles of Interactive Design*. Albany, NY: Delmar Publishers, 1999.

Grant, August E., and Jennifer H. Meadows, eds. *Communication Technology Update*. 10th ed. Boston: Focal Press, 2007.

Kent, Steven L. *The Ultimate History of Video Games: The Story Behind the Craze that Touched Our Lives and Changed the World*. New York: Three Rivers Press, 2001.

Krol, Ed, and Bruce Klopfenstein. *The Whole Internet: User's Guide and Catalog*. Belmont, CA: Wadsworth Publishing, 1996.

Maciuba-Koppel, Darlene. *The Web Writer's Guide*. Boston: Focal Press, 2000.

Mack, Steve. *Hands-On Guide to Webcasting*. Boston: Focal Press, 2005.

Max, Christy. *Writing for Animation, Comics, and Games*. Boston: Focal Press, 2007.

Miller, Carolyn Handler. *Digital Storytelling: A Creator's Guide to Interactive Entertainment*. Boston: Focal Press, 2004.

Reddick, Randy, and Elliot King. *The Online Student: Making the Grade on the Internet*. Fort Worth, TX: Harcourt Brace College Publishers, 1996.

Shedletsky, Leonard, and Joan E. Aitken. *Human Communication on the Internet*. Boston: Allyn & Bacon, 2004.

Stansberry, Domenic. *Labyrinths: The Art of Interactive Writing and Design, Content Development for the New Media*. Belmont, CA: Wadsworth Publishing, 1998.

Wagstaff, Sean. *Animation on the Web*. Berkeley, CA: Peachpit Press, 1999.

Web

www.ask.com
www.batleby.com/62

www.bartleby.com/63
www.bartleby.com/141/index.html
www.brisney.com/internet-writing
www.groups.google.com/advanced_group_search
www.metacrawler.com/index
www.newsgroups.com
www.northernlight.com
www.tile.net/news
www.webpronews.com/ebusiness.contentandcopywriting
www.webreference.com
www.wgaeast/org/mba/internet
www.writerswrite.com/jounal

CHAPTER 11

Future

In order that people may be happy in their work, these three things are needed: They must be fit for it. They must not do too much of it. And they must have a sense of success in it.

—John Ruskin, Victorian author and scholar

Introduction

The future of electronic media, including motion pictures, is only partially dependent on the advances in the development of new equipment. Smaller, less expensive, higher-quality equipment will make a difference, but knowledge and inventive use of communication is the key—software and brain ware, not hardware, will determine the future of electronic media, especially for you as a writer. Social, civic, legal, and economic forces interact to guide changes, either to advance or to impede progress in any changing aspect of society. Each step in the move of communication to the digital world has done so only with the combined final agreement of each of the levels of society: government, corporations, the law, and finally the people determine the final outcome of the next step.

As a writer, you will need to study and follow the changes in distribution methods, since convergence has brought distribution methods into question as to which one will serve which market. Today, new technology and audience demands provide you with two extremes—high-definition widescreen, or low-definition on a miniature screen. HDTV or mobiles each demand a different type of technical production and as of now, there is no certainty as to what type of creative production will serve each better than the other. At the same time, no one knows what the newest distribution system will be. As of this writing, the decision between HD-DVD and Blu-Ray as a home distribution is undetermined, even as a newer and better system, Holographic Versatile Disc (HVD), is being developed. Technology will continue to free individual workers, such as writers, to find their most comfortable environment for working, whether it occurs with a group in an office, or in isolation for concentration in their home or hideaway.

The premium skill you depend on is your ability to use the best writing skills applied to whatever market or audience exists. The opportunity has widened with the narrowing of the audience into smaller interest groups, providing niche positions for new topics not previously acceptable for the mass media. It is more than likely that English will dominate as the world language, but at the same time an understanding of non-English cultures, customs, and languages will be needed. There always will be more writers and potential writers than positions to be filled. Despite the industry's continuous cries for new talent, the competition always will be tough; getting the first job without experience, when experience is the first requirement, will not change. Follow the suggestions in this chapter, and hopefully that break will come your way.

The Search

Although some businesses (broadcasting and companies funded by the federal government) must by law advertise publicly for any open position, other companies do not have to openly advertise. Even with advertised positions, they may be filled immediately, often from within the same company. Relying on advertising is a poor method of finding potential job openings. Some of the best methods of learning of job openings come through networking, knowing people in the industry, being related to someone in the field, or serving a semester as an intern. Joining a professional organization such as the student branches of the Radio TV News Directors Association (RTNDA), Public Relations Society of America (PRSA), or the American Association of Advertising Agencies (AAAA), or the *Gamer's Association Annual* will teach you the inside scoop about that business as well as give you access to people working and in position to know of openings. Belonging to a newsgroup, monitoring blogs, and keeping close contact with your professors who have contacts in the business provide potential career contacts.

The search for that first job, or for that matter, each job as you move through your career, consists of three basic steps; finding the opportunity, preparing the paperwork, and surviving the interview. For most media-oriented jobs, the technique known as networking serves as the most efficient way to locate a potential job. The paperwork consists of three parts; a cover letter, the resume, and your portfolio. The heart of interviewing involves preparing for the interview. More about interviewing and paperwork is detailed later in this chapter.

Networking

The first step in building a network consists of sitting down and creating a list of everyone you know, who your family knows, and who your friends know in the media business. Let them know you want to find a position in the business. The list needs to include the complete name (proper spelling), title, company, address, phone and e-mail address. This list also should include all of the contacts you have developed at your internship (more about internships later), volunteering at nonprofits, and even names of people you read about in the newspaper or professional publications. This is the first of several research phases you will go through in your job search, so approach this phase as a very important one. Take accurate notes, think in broad terms of finding contacts that might lead you to potential positions, and also people who might assist you in your search.

Each of the media fields publishes some type of listing of all of the companies in that field. In broadcasting it is an annual publication titled *Broadcasting Cablecasting Yearbook*. It is an expensive volume, but most large libraries carry the latest copy. It lists all broadcast stations, cable channels, many production companies, and companies associated in some manner with broadcasting. The list includes addresses, phone numbers, and management-level employee names and titles. Before you call or write to an individual, call the company first and make certain that person still holds that position. Managers come and go at a high rate in broadcasting, and you don't want to ask to speak to or mail a resume to the incorrect person.

Don't ignore personal contacts. Check with all of your relatives and friends, and ask if they know someone in the business or at the company you are interested in. Don't hesitate to use your family or friends' names in requesting an interview after you have gained their permission. As an absolute rule, never use another person's name without specifically asking permission to do so, and that includes using them as a reference. More about references later.

Your job search needs to include exploring market sizes and knowing the differences between a major market, a middle market, and a smaller market. Larger markets seldom hire inexperienced people unless it is at a small operation within that market. Middle markets will consider some inexperienced people for their lowest-level entry positions. Small markets often welcome people willing to start in a small operation to learn the business and get the experience needed for a major market or company. It is much easier to make mistakes to learn a business when the financial stakes are not high and forgiveness comes easier since your pay is low enough in a small operation to make up the difference. Explore industries just beginning the move to the digital or interactive world. They will be expanding and needing people with digital training, especially writers. This includes newspapers, magazines, radio stations, television stations, cable channels, film studios, and small independent production houses. If they have not yet begun using digital media including Web sites, newsgroups, and other interactive forms, they will need qualified help.

If you are working already but want to move on to another job, be aware that the person who may hire you wants to talk to your present boss. You can ask for confidential respect, up to a point. At some time you are going to have to be honest and up front with your present employer. Also make certain you give proper notice, 2 weeks minimum, but have the same consideration of your present boss as you would expect him to have of you.

Internship

One of the best network possibilities is the people you will meet during your internship. But you need to earn an internship first. Depending on the policy of your school and the companies that offer internships, there are minimum qualifications to be placed as an intern. An internship does not replace coursework. Don't expect an intern host to teach you everything you need to know to work in the field of your choice. The knowledge you acquired in school should prepare you to qualify as an entry-level employee. You should wait until near the end of your academic career before enrolling in an internship. There are two reasons for this decision. First, you need the education and background to prepare you for the internship. Second, if the internship works well and you are offered a full-time job, you need not be placed in the position of having to choose between accepting the offer requiring you to quit school before graduating, or turn the offer down because you realize you must finish your degree. Any company offering you a full-time position while serving an internship will be willing to wait if you are in your last semester of school.

Also, if you do an internship during the fall or spring semester, make certain you carry as light an academic load as possible. To take full advantage of an internship, free yourself of as many obligations as possible to concentrate your energies and time on the internship. If you apply for an internship during the summer, expect very heavy competition from many different schools that allow students to intern only during the summer. During the internship, work to prove you will make a good employee. Perform any job assigned to you, be positive about all of the activities at the host company, even if some of them are boring, repetitious, and not at all what you thought the industry was all about. Ask if you can perform work not assigned to you, but ask first and make certain you know what to do and then do the job well.

Be aware of two negative incidents that may occur during an internship. If your assignments consist only of clerical work, answering telephones, getting coffee, running errands, or sitting around just watching people work, you have the right to report this to both your school's intern supervisor, your supervisor on the job, or the human resources (HR) office of the company. Expect to be assigned to low-level jobs during an internship, but it also is an educational activity and there must be some potential for learning, or it is of limited value to you. Your school needs to be aware of your insufficient work assignment. The second is the more serious matter of sexual harassment. If you feel threatened at any time or are approached by an employee in an offensive manner, report the incident immediately to the HR department and your school's intern supervisor. At the same time, make certain you dress appropriately and act professionally toward all employees at all times.

An internship should not be designed to replace the work of a full-time employee. This may be a difficult judgment to make, depending on the type of company and the manner in which they assign work to their employees. Too often a company will attempt to avoid hiring the full-time staff they need by taking on as many interns as possible and assigning each of them a part of the job of an employee. The determination of this judgment is the responsibility of the school's intern supervisor, but it may not be obvious to him or her unless students report back such a situation in their weekly reports. An internship at a for-profit company must be performed for academic credit or some level of pay. Labor laws and legal responsibilities can only be fulfilled with credit or pay. The rule does not apply to nonprofit corporations such as public broadcasters PBS and NPR stations. You may volunteer as an intern with those organizations, but the job responsibilities are the same at a for-profit company and in some cases the opportunities for excellent work experience are better at nonprofit operations.

As part of your preparation to serve an internship, you should begin assembling your job application file, which consists of four documents: your resume, cover letter, portfolio of your work, and a package of personal information for interviewing and for filling out application forms.

Resume

Although a cover letter precedes a resume, writing your resume will organize the information you need to write cover letters that you prepare for each job application. Your cover letter describes who you are, how you got to where you are, and where you want to go. It needs to be succinct, comprehensive, accurate, and without any typos, grammatical errors, or superfluous filler. Your resume may be organized as either a list of all of your information aesthetically arranged on the page, or a narrative written as a short monologue of who you are. As a writer the last form may seem to offer an opportunity to show your creative writing ability, but be very careful of this format. A resume's basic purpose is to succinctly tell someone who you are in a form that quickly reveals the critical information the reader wants to see. The narrative form requires a thorough reading, and therefore requires more time and effort on the part of the reader.

Whichever format is used, keep in mind the KISS rule: keep it simple and succinct. Hold it to one page if possible, and no more than two unless an additional page of references is called for. Don't try to be humorous, especially in the narrative form; save showing your writing skills for your portfolio. Avoid overly unique design, layout, paper, and font styles. Make it readable but enjoyable at the same time. Keep in mind the reader may glance only at the first part of the front page, so make it stand out and stick in his mind so that he will continue reading the entire document

Begin with your full name, the one you want the interviewer to call you by—no nicknames unless you are stuck with one. Include accurate contact information: address, phone number(s) indicating whether cell or land line, and your e-mail address and Web site if you have one and you want the interviewer to see it. This is a good time to clean up your Web site and any other site with your name on it. Keep in mind your potential employer may have the research staff look for you wherever you may have left your name. Your contact information must be accurate and current. If you are about to return home or move to a new city, make certain you can be found easily. No one will want to hunt you down. If the first try to reach you fails, the interviewer will go to the next candidate and dump your resume.

The order of the next list of items depends on the job you are applying for and the strength of several of your past characteristics. For someone just graduating, you first list your schooling. List each school's

RESUME
Greg McCamasters   November 20, 2007
9160 South Breaswood
Houston, TX 77035
713-574-2323
gmcc@aol.com

OBJECTIVE: To become as versatile as possible in writing for electronic media. I have
educated myself with everything from designing my own Web page to writing series of scripts
for various media productions.

EDUCATION: Attending University of Houston's School of Communication with a
degree to be awarded December, 2007 with an overall GPA of 3.63.

EXPERIENCE: I wrote two scripts on Drug Abuse and AIDS Prevention selected to be
produced and distributed to the student body. While at the University of Houston, each of the
scripts I wrote in class were produced. A video copy is attached to this resume. I also directed
and edited each of the accepted scripts.

SKILLS: I have been trained to operate both linear and nonlinear editing programs
including Final Cut Pro. I am conversant with MS Word, Photoshop, and Excel programs.

AWARDS: Was the recipient of the Outstanding Academic Achievement-
Extraordinary Student award for 4 consistent years of high school participation.
I was awarded one of the University of Houston's Outstanding Academic Achievement
Scholarships.

WORK EXPERIENCE: One year as a YMCA lifeguard, 3 years experience as assistant
manager of an antique store, and for the past 3 years as the manager of the dairy department
at Safeway.

REFERENCES ATTACHED:
PRODUCTIONS ATTACHED:

Figure 11.1. A narrative resume appears to be a short story of who you
are, but it is more difficult for the reader to obtain the critical information
needed in a job application.

full name and location if the name does not clarify its location (no high
schools, unless you went to a specialized school that taught media
writing), the date of graduation, and your GPA if over 3.0. Indicate
your major and minor if it adds to your value (no animal husbandry
unless applying to a veterinarian publication). If you attended more

than one college, list only, the last one, unless the others included specialized media training. List honors awarded and extracurricular activities especially if they represent any form of media connection. Any publications, research, or academic media production work needs to be listed. Fraternity or sorority activities may be listed only if they involved responsible or elected positions. Other elected campus responsibilities also may be listed, but only if there is space and the activity indicates some value to your future career.

If your employment record includes items that specifically prepared you for a writing career, then list important employment next. Employment could be listed ahead of education if your job record contains media or writing experience. List jobs by the title of your job, a very brief description of your duties as they either apply to your career choice, or indicate specialized responsibility or management experience. List only those jobs that would impress a prospective employer, but be prepared to fill any gaps with a package of personal information later in your interview. If as part of your job experience you were involved in research, media production, or publications, list those items under the employment record, but indicate where and how you participated.

Specialized computer and media production skills, language proficiency, and international travel experience round out your life's history. You must make a judgment about what is most important and fit the information neatly on the page so that it reads easily and quickly.

Often your references may be on a separate last page. You may change the references depending on the company and job requirements. List at least three people who know your work habits and your writing skills. Do not list your religious contact; he or she never say bad things about anyone, and your prospective employer wants to know the truth about you. Make the reference choices based on your perceived knowledge of the personal attitude toward you and the person's willingness to spend some time responding to specific questions about you and your writing ability.

Do not list anyone unless you have contacted them first and made certain they are willing to act as a reference and that they do remember

	Sarah Jones	
816-532-2892	2835 Granite Kansas City, MO 64131	sjones@comcast.net

EDUCATION
The University of Missouri-Kansas City   June, 2007
Bachelor of Arts
Major: Communication
Minor: Computer Graphics
GPA 3.6

EXPERIENCE
May 2006-present
Brandon, Fife, and Lewis Advertising   Kansas City, MO
Receptionist
Handled telephone and guest duties
Entered data and typed letters, proposals, and scripts

May 2005-May 2006 Outback Steakhouse   Overland Park, KS
Waiter/bartender
Accurately handled cash register, tended bar, and waited tables
Trained incoming employees

HONORS and
ACTIVITES
Communication School Scholarship, 2 years
Member Omicron Delta Kappa Honorary
Writer, Producer, Director UH TV
Volunteered for various community fundraisers
Internship, WDAF-TV

ADDITIONAL
INFORMATION
Proficient with both PC and Mac operating systems, MS Word, Excel,
Power Point, FileMaker Pro, Photoshop, Illustrator.
Final Cut Pro and other editing systems.
Attended NAB conference, completed media production workshops,
and attended broadcast lectures and panels.

REFERENCES

Michael J. Brandon
Partner
Brandon, Fife, and Lewis Advertising
1235 North Loop West
Kansas City, MO 64105
816-862-1860
mjbrandon@att.net

Wendy Adair
Manager
Outback Steakhouse
2100 195th St.
Overland Park, KS, 66207
913-365-4122
wadair@outback.com

Jennifer Ayles, Ph.D.
Director, School of Communication
UMKC
Kansas City, MO 68108
713-743-2108
jayles@umkc.edu

Figure 11.2. An outline resume lists important information in a manner that is easy for the interviewer to read and pick out critical information he or she needs to know.

who you are. It is helpful to them if you would send a copy of your resume by letter or e-mail to help them remember you. Add the classes you took from that person and your grade in that class, and the date of the class. Don't lie about the grade; most professors keep grade records until they die. While asking for permission to use them as references, make certain you have the correct spelling of their names, their present titles, accurate addresses, phone numbers, and e-mail addresses. Most prospective employers want to talk directly to references but do not want to spend much time trying to track them down. If they can't find the references, they will go to the next applicant.

Cover Letter

Your cover letter will offer the first impression to a potential boss. Research and write it with the best prose you have ever created. If you have completed the research suggested above for your resume, then you have completed much of the background work for your cover letter. Each job you apply for requires a separate cover letter written specifically for that job and company. The well-written cover letter accomplishes three goals. First, it is your introduction to a complete stranger. Show your best side, personally as well as professionally. Second, show that you know what the company produces and what you offer that will benefit the company. Third, give enough of your background and experience that they will want to meet and interview you to find what else you can give to the company.

Remember, this is a business letter. Use a standard business letter format; this is not the place to show your creativity, but rather your ability to be responsible and organized. Start with a business heading: the name, title, company, and address of the person you are approaching or answering, nicely spaced on the upper left side of the page. Don't forget to date the letter just above or at the top line of the heading. Make certain you spell the person's name correctly and use his or her correct title.

The greeting should be to the specific person, never "To Whom it May Concern." The best addresses are Mr., Dr., or Ms. followed by his or her full name. Your first line may explain why you are writing but only if there is a specific reason such as answering an advertisement or responding to a letter. Don't waste your time with a lengthy explanation; get to the point. Briefly outline your quali- fications (leave the details to the resume) and why you would be a good fit for the job. Indicate if you have enclosed your resume, and if you also enclosed any writing samples. Be sure to specify which job you are applying for. Never say "any job available." If they are not hiring for the job you ask about, they may have something else, but give them the opportunity to indicate that fact. Never try to rationalize why you want a job at that location. They don't care if you want to be near a beach, if you have relatives nearby, or if you like mountains.

Your last paragraph must include a statement that you will fol- low the letter with a phone call within a week or ten days (specify which) and then be sure to call within that time block. Within that statement indicate that the reason you will call is to give him or her a chance to discuss your resume, answer any questions he or she may have, and if possible arrange for an interview. This last para- graph is as important as the first line of the letter. This indicates you are willing to take the initiative by following the letter with the call and not just sit back waiting for a response. This is a little pushy, but remember you have to find some way to stand out among the hundreds of other people applying for the same job.

Sign off the letter with a closing such as "Sincerely," a handwritten sig- nature, your full name, and a block of all of your contact information. Lay out the material in an open but compact design. Use white space to separate sections; don't cram the entire body in a clump at the top of the page, but spread it out for a pleasing visual appearance.

Portfolio

Your portfolio provides a means for you to show what you are capa- ble of doing and have accomplished in the past. As an artist, you are proud of your work and you want to show it in the best light possible. Your portfolio is the setting to do just that. The approach you use may follow two different paths. One, show samples of at least one example of each type of writing that you are capable of. The other method is to create a portfolio containing only one type

Sarah Jones
2835 Granite
Kansas City, MO
64131
816-532-2892
sjones@comcast.net

May 20, 2007

Mr. Charles Profiot
Operations Manager
KCMO-TV
P. O. Box 5555
Kansas City, MO
64555

RE: Production Associate Position

Dear Mr. Profiot:

My media production experience and academic training provides the basis for consideration as a Production Associate at KCMO-TV. I will graduate this month with honors in Communication and a minor in Computer Graphics. While at the University, I worked all positions at the student-operated television station including writing, producing, and directing a weekly public affairs program.

I spent last semester as an intern at WDAF-TV as a Production Assistant operating studio equipment and assisting the directors and producers. I suggested ideas for programs at Channel Four, where they were accepted and aired successfully. During that time I watched your operation and believe I could be of benefit to you and KCMO-TV.

I feel my broad liberal arts education including study of theatre, art, and music as well as the study of media history, communication law, and audio, video, and computer graphics production courses with a GPA of 3.6 prepares me for a career in media production.

I worked part time while attending school, paying for part of my education and gaining valuable work experience. My former employers and references will honestly evaluate my work habits and potential for a career in electronic media.

I look forward to meeting you and will call on Monday, May 25th to discuss my application and for an interview. Thank you for your consideration.

Sincerely,

Ms. Sarah Jones
816-532-2892
sjones@comcast.net

Enc: Resume, references

Figure 11.3. The cover letter is the first impression an interviewer will have of you. Make it speak well of you, make it professional and to the point, summarize, don't duplicate your resume.

of work. The latter selection is best used if you are applying for a specific job such as copywriting at an ad agency, or as a newswriter for a television station. Some jobs require a range of work, from short spot writing to lengthy documentary or dramatic writing. A portfolio for that type of job should include as wide a range of samples as possible. If you are talented in several different genres, use the best sample of each, but be sure to include only excellent samples to show your abilities.

An important consideration requires that you include only your best work. The impulse to include every piece that you like or have an emotional attachment to creates a mediocre portfolio. It is better to have one excellent example of your work rather than one good one and several mediocre. The reader will remember the mediocre samples. Choose wisely and critically as if you are looking at someone else's work, not your own. If there were production restrictions beyond your control, you may explain, but do not rationalize or excuse poor or mediocre work—just don't include it in the portfolio.

Once you have chosen your work, use only clean copies, preferably printed with a laser printer. Ink jet printers are okay, but not a dot matrix printer. Check every page for typos, grammar and punctuation errors, printer smudges, or wrinkled paper. Make certain each page is carefully written in professionally formatted styles. Each page should have your name on it. Very few examiners will look at the entire portfolio, so make certain the first few pages are the very best and will entice the reader to look farther into the samples. A separation page with a brief explanation preceding each sample will give the reader a context for the work. A table of contents with tabbed pages separating different examples will facilitate scanning through the portfolio. All of the material should be mounted in some type of loose-leaf binder so the work may be removed and viewed by more than person at a time and yet may be reassembled to its original order and form. The case should have a clean professional appearance; again save your creativity for what's inside the case, not the case itself. But it needs to be carefully labeled on both the front surface and on the spine, if the case has one. The labels need to be visible and contain your name and contact information.

Selling writing is a brutal business. Editors, news directors, film, TV, game, Web producers, and agency managers all are busy people often faced with a deluge of portfolios and submissions. If your presentation does not grab them within the first 30 seconds, your work may never receive full consideration. Every portfolio won't appeal to every interviewer; you may need to redesign the portfolio for each different type of job that you apply for. Often your portfolio will not be viewed until you have been given an interview, and as a part of that interview you will be given the opportunity to show your portfolio. If you have prepared it well, it should speak for itself, relying only on you for explanations or more detail about your experience.

If the portfolio is mailed, make certain you have copies of all of the work contained in the package. If necessary, have a professional mailing service wrap and ship the portfolio to make certain it will not be damaged in shipment and will arrive at its destination on time. A little money spent at this point will pay dividends in the long run. Also include a prepaid self-addressed return-shipping label if you expect to have the portfolio returned. An alternate to shipping the actual portfolio is to burn a CD of the portfolio contents and ship the CD with your resume and cover letter.

Interviewing

For most people, including those who have gone through the process more than once, interviewing for a job can be an uncomfortable situation. It doesn't have to be, if you prepare yourself and your materials. Remember, both you and the interviewer have a common goal: to find out if you will fit the requirements they have for a position. The session need not be a confrontational battle, but a give and take of you explaining who you are, what you are capable of doing, and how it fits with the needs of the company. If there is no fit, then don't take the rejection personally. It is better you don't accept a position that doesn't match your interests or capabilities than end up on a job that will make you unhappy and not allow your creativity to blossom.

To begin with, it is crucial for you to be yourself, your adult self, not your campus comedian and style leader. Avoid extremes of clothing, hairstyle, metal accessories, and tattoos. Many companies that specialize in artistic and creative works may not show any concern about such extremes in appearance, but it is better to appear more conservative at the first meeting and show your creativity in appearance later, once you are on the payroll. This caution is especially important if your interview is with the HR department representative and not the head of the department you expect to work for. At the same time, they do want to know who you really are and if you will fit with the rest of the employees, but they are interested in the adult you, not the immature you.

Be willing to start at or near the bottom of the rank and file. Don't stay in that position long; more than 2 years in an entry-level position means it's time to look for another company if there is no possibility moving up at your present operation. The amount of money you make should not be the major motivating factor in the choice of your first positions. Find work that gives you the opportunity to prove yourself, get experience, and develop those all-important networking contacts. Once you are working, then you will have the opportunity to submit script, game, Web designs, and story ideas with some chance they will be viewed as coming from a professional. Don't expect to follow a linear path from your first job until you reach your final goal. Often, that path will not appear because as you work toward your goal it will change and you will discover more satisfying opportunities that you didn't even know existed when you left school.

Thoroughly research the company, the job you want, and the work you may be expected to perform. Be prepared to answer questions that reveal your knowledge of all of those subjects. You may not be asked detailed questions at the first interview, but knowing what you have learned from your research will give you confidence in talking intelligently about the company, and confidence is one of the best characteristics to show during an interview. Arrive on time fully prepared for both the face-to-face part of the interview and depending on the size of the company, a stack of forms to fill out.

To prepare for the forms as part of your research—research yourself. Arrive with every possible bit of information about your past that they might be interested in. The list needs to include your last three to five residences, the addresses and who you paid your rent to, your past three to five employers, supervisors, pay, addresses, and telephone numbers. You may be asked to name someone as a contact in an emergency and their contact information, what medical insurance you have and your primary doctors. After you have been hired you may need to list family members, spouse, children, or anyone you may be responsible for. You may be asked to make decisions on what type of medical coverage and retirement programs you want to enroll in. Some of these decisions arrive fast and furious and may have important bearings on your future; think about them in advance to be able to make accurate and beneficial choices for you and your family. Depending on the company and what you position you are applying for, you may be asked to submit to an examination or test. For a writer, you may be asked to quickly write a story, commercial, or treatment with basic information provided. They may intentionally ask you to complete the test in your handwriting or they may give you access to a computer. Your portfolio should provide this type of information, but some companies will want to see if you can write with basic information against a deadline.

If your primary interview is through a telephone interview, it may be a conference call with several other people listening and possibly asking questions. At the beginning ask for each person's name and title and try to remember what their voices sound like. Don't hesitate to pause after each question is presented; think carefully of your answer, but don't wait so long that they wonder what you are doing on the other end of the line. Have a copy of your resume, cover letter, and portfolio in front of you as references. Also keep close at hand a copy of all of your personal information to provide quick answers if asked.

Negotiating pay and benefits is a difficult challenge for all new employees, but even more so for creative applicants. We all know what we think we are worth, but it is difficult to face someone across a desk in a suit and demand that figure. Again, begin this part of the process with research. Find out what such a position in that company or similar companies in the same market size pay beginning employees. Don't be afraid to ask for more if the figure they offer is less. Knowing your own value again shows confidence. Don't argue. If you are told the figure is the maximum the company is willing to pay, don't walk out the door. Explore other perquisites (perqs) such as car or clothing allowances, provided equipment, overtime pay,

moving expenses, or a signing bonus. Don't take rejection personally; try to assume a pleasant negotiating stance, not an argumenta-
tive position. If you cannot come to terms satisfactory to you, don't
hesitate to thank the interviewer for his or her time and for considering you for the position. Leave your resume and cover letter
for possible future positions or budget changes that will allow you
to reach an agreement for accepting a position later with that company. If the rejection comes from a complete lack of your fitting in
with this company, always ask if he or she knows of any other open
positions with that company or any other the interviewer might be
aware of. Always leave on a positive note, even though you may be
disappointed and hurt.

If the interview ends with a "we'll call you," be sure to ask how
soon you might expect a call. If you are told or the ad you answered
says: "don't call," then don't call. Wait a reasonable amount of time,
2–3 weeks maximum, and then send an e-mail inquiring about
your interview. Even the busiest of HR people will reply to an e-
mail. This may give you a quick rejection, but that is better than
waiting without knowing whether to pursue other possibilities and
get on with your search. Most companies will have the courtesy
to respond within a reasonable amount of time, but there may be
extenuating circumstances beyond their immediate control. They
may be waiting for budget clearance, depending on the job, or they
may be waiting on security or personal clearance information. At
this point patience is a virtue, but don't ignore other possibilities
while you wait.

Sending blind inquiries may yield a result, but be prepared to send
hundreds if not more to get one or two responses. Never send
unsolicited portfolios or scripts. They will be returned unopened
or destroyed. Submit scripts only when requested, but unsolicited
resumes and cover letters may receive some limited attention.

Freelancing

Freelancing allows you the opportunity to work for yourself or
your own company by finding an individual project and selling your
services to the client. It would be best to avoid trying freelancing

until you have had several years' experience working on staff at other companies, saving money, and building a list of clients and potential clients. You will need to sell yourself or work with a partner who enjoys the selling end of the game. When you first start you may have to accept projects that don't offer the creativity or even the pay you would prefer, but early on you can't be too choosy; you need to build a sample reel of your work. Do follow a set of ethics; never take a job that you can't philosophically accept. As a freelancer, the second major problem after getting work is getting paid for it. The standard in the industry for writers is to be paid on the one-third system. You bill and receive one third of the budgeted figure on acceptance of the idea and on a signed contract. Then you bill one third and collect on acceptance of the rough draft, and the final one third on completion and final acceptance. Finding quality clients and collecting your legitimate fees for creative personnel are onerous and annoying parts of the field.

Representation

The problems of finding jobs and clients, negotiating salary and fees, and collecting the money owed created the field of artist representation. At a certain level in your career you may feel you would prefer to leave those awkward and unpleasant activities to an agent or representative. The agent's responsibility permits him or her to sell you and your work for a 10% cut of whatever your fee is. That means unless an agent gets you work, he or she doesn't make any money. At the same time the agent becomes a liaison between producers, station managers, and company HR departments to bring to them only the best possible person to fill the job the company needs. That means an agent won't represent you unless you have had experience, can write what is needed, and make a good appearance for an interview or a pitch. You must give the agent work to sell; an agent can't wait until he or she finds a job and then have to wait for you to turn out a script. Give the agent good work and his or her job is to find a producer who needs that script. There must be a good deal of mutual trust between you and your agent, so don't sign with an agent until you are ready, have the work to sell, and you have carefully researched to make certain you have found the correct match for you in an agent.

For freelancers, an agent is almost a necessity. Producers and publishers normally will not speak directly to you as a writer. They are afraid if they look at your work they may be sued for stealing your work. If they go through an agent, a record exists of the transaction. An agent is not a union steward, he or she can negotiate for you, but you must handle grievances yourself, through a manager (another 10% off the top), a lawyer, or through the Writers Guild of America (WGA). Two Writers Guilds represent writers across the country: the WGA-W (West represents more film and West Coast writers) and WGA-E (East represents more network television and East Coast writers). WGA-W offers special contracts for freelancers: one for games and CD-ROMS, and the other for Internet scripts. Their major responsibility is to write contracts for staff and freelance writers as a group who work for the studios.

Summary

Finding work as a writer for both staff writers and freelance self-employed writers follows the same pattern. The best search philosophy requires a three-step plan. First, a detailed search based on research gathered on the companies who might be hiring, developed contacts from friends and family, and your internship. An internship is one of the most beneficial activities you as a soon-to-graduate student can engage in to prepare yourself for building contacts and learning on a practical level what a job in the field of your choice actually is like.

Once a reasonable goal has been sighted, preparation of the paperwork needed to apply for and gain worthwhile employment becomes your next job. You write a cover letter written for each individual company and position, a resume that describes you completely but succinctly, who you are and what you are capable of giving to an employer, and your portfolio. Each must be carefully and professionally prepared since they each represent who you are and what you are capable of doing. Hopefully, an interview will follow, and again you need to do background research into the company, what they produce, what their pay scales are and how your skills may be attractive to them.

WGA 2004 THEATRICAL AND TELEVISION BASIC AGREEMENT
TELEVISION COMPENSATION

PAYMENT SCHEDULE

Company will make its best efforts to pay writer within 48 hours of delivery but in no event more than seven (7) days after delivery.

Payment shall not be contingent upon the acceptance or approval by the Company of the literary material so delivered.

TELEVISION LONG-FORM REVISIONS

In certain instances on long-form television movies, the network (or other licensee) has agreed to reimburse the Company for a "producer's draft," even when such draft is not delivered to the network (or other licensee). Please call the Contracts Department for further information.

TEAMS

The minimums are generally payable to each writer. However, a bona fide team of two writers who agree, prior to employment, to be a team, may split not less than minimum.

In addition, a Company may employ a team of 3 writers for no less than 200% of minimum initial compensation (150% in the case of a television team of 3 production executives). No individual writer may receive less than 1/3 of the above increased minimums. Pension and Health ceilings and the Upset Price increase accordingly. Note: There are no teams under aggregate formulas in Appendix A.

MADE-FOR PAY TELEVISION OR VIDEOCASSETTE/VIDEODISC

The minimum initial compensation for a writer shall be the same as the applicable minimum initial compensation for a "free" television program. Where the program is of a type generally produced for network prime time, the network prime time rates are to be utilized.

MADE-FOR BASIC CABLE

For high budget dramatic programs, the provisions of the MBA apply. For all other types of programs, the Company must either use the terms of the MBA to employ writers or notify the Guild not later than 30 days prior to production so that negotiations may commence regarding the production.

MADE-FOR THE INTERNET

The Guild offers a special contract for writing for the Internet. Contact the Organizing Department at WGAw or the Signatories Department at WGAE for details.

INTERACTIVE/MULTIMEDIA PROGRAMMING (DISC, CARTRIDGE, CD-ROM, TELEVISION, THEATRICAL, ETC.)

The Guild is currently offering a modified contract for Interactive/Multimedia writing. Contact the Organizing Department at WGAw or the Signatories Department at WGAE for information on applicable provisions.

INFORMATIONAL PROGRAMMING

For informational programming the Guild offers a special contract. Contact the Signatories Department for details.

ANIMATION

The Guild negotiates terms and conditions for animated projects. Contact the Organizing Department for details.

Figure 11.4. The freelance contract is designed to protect the work and career of writers who are self employed and belong to the WGA.

Hiring an agent and/or a representative serves a useful purpose once you have reached the professional and experience level and income to support another person. Few people in creative fields follow a linear path in their careers. First, many find their original choice is not what they expected it to be like as a employee. Second, and most important, if your ideal position is not open or available to you, take whatever job you are able to perform and learn all you can from that position. You may find it provides a better view of the world than your original goal and may open entire new possibilities for your creative drive.

Be Sure To...

Now that you are working, staff or freelance, here are some helpful hints.

1. Avoid legal complications from copyright, patents, and trademarks under Intellectual Property Laws.
2. Aggressiveness and competitiveness are positive values, but they require restraint.
3. Small business anti-golden rule: What goes 'round comes 'round. Whatever dirty deed you do to someone else in the business, the chances are very good he or she will have the opportunity to pay you back plus more.
4. Get organized fast and stay organized.
5. Your first job probably won't last long. Prepare for jobs #2 and #3 right away.
6. Accept constructive criticism and reviews as a positive means of improving.
7. Be flexible, multi-skilled, and constantly learn new techniques.

Exercises

1. Assemble all of your personal data that you will need to fill out employment forms.
2. Using the *Broadcasting Yearbook*, compile a list of all of the companies (TV, radio stations, cable companies) that you are interested in working for, and call to make certain the person you need to send an application to still works there and that they still accept applications.
3. Using the *Gamer's Annual Guide*, find a game company near your location and call for an interview.

4. Google PRS and AAAA, and check their Web sites for instructions on applying for jobs in those industries.
5. Do the same for RTNDA and NAB.

Additional Sources

Print

Attkisson, Sharyl, and Don R. Vaughn. *Writing Right for Broadcast and Internet News*. Boston: Allyn & Bacon, 2003.

Bermont, Todd. *10 Insider Secrets to a Winning Job Search*, Franklin Lakes, NJ: Career Press, 2004.

Bucy, Erik P. *Living in the Information Age: A New Media Reader*. Belmont, CA: Wadsworth Publishing, 2002.

Crawford, Tad, and Kay Murray. *The Writer's Legal Guide*. 3rd ed. New York: Allworth Press, 2002.

Edwards, Christina. *Gardner's Guide to Finding New Media Jobs Online*. Herndon Lane, VA: GGC Publishing, 2003.

Kent, Simon. *Careers and Jobs in Media*. London: Kogan Page Limited, 2005.

Levy, David B. *Your Career in Animation: How to Survive and Thrive*. New York: Allworth Press, 2006.

Miller, Carolyn Handler. *Digital Storytelling: A Creator's Guide to Interactive Entertainment*. Boston: Focal Press, 2004.

Reddick, Randy, and Elliot King. *The Online Student: Making the Grade on the Internet*. Fort Worth, TX: Harcourt Brace College Publishers, 1996.

Taylor, Jeffrey, and Douglas Hardy. *Monster Careers: How to Land the Job of Your Life*. New York: Penguin Press, 2004.

Tuggle. C. A., Forrest Carr, and Suzanne Huffman. *Broadcast News Handbook: Writing, Reporting & Producing in the Converging Media World*. 2nd ed. Boston: McGraw-Hill, 2004.

Web

www.career.com
www.careermosaic.com
www.cpb.org/jobline
www.gamejobs.com/
www.inktip.com
www.iwantmedia.com/jobs/

www.jobweb.org
www.nap.org/bcc/jobbank/
www.rescomp.stanfield.edu/jobs
www.rileyguide.com/comp.html
www.wga.org
www.wm.edu/catapult/jobsall.html

APPENDIX A

The Children's Advertising Review Unit

Council of Better Business Bureaus, Inc. Self-Regulatory Guidelines for Children's Advertising

1. Advertisers should always take into account the level of knowledge, sophistication, and maturity of the audience to which their message is primarily directed. Younger children have a limited capacity for evaluating the credibility of information they receive. They also may lack the ability to understand the nature of the personal information they disclose on the Internet. Advertisers, therefore, have a special responsibility to protect children from their own susceptibilities.
2. Realizing that children are imaginative and that make-believe play constitutes an important part of the growing up process, advertisers should exercise care not to exploit unfairly the imaginative quality of children. Unreasonable expectations of product quality or performance should not be stimulated either directly or indirectly by advertising.
3. Products and content that are inappropriate for children should not be advertised or promoted directly to children.
4. Recognizing that advertising may play an important part in educating the child, advertisers should communicate information in a truthful and accurate manner and in language understandable to young children with full recognition that the child may learn practices from advertising that can affect his or her health and well-being.

5. Advertisers are urged to capitalize on the potential of adver-
    tising to influence behavior by developing advertising that,
    wherever possible, addresses itself to positive and beneficial
    social behavior, such as friendship, kindness, honesty, justice,
    generosity, and respect for others.
6. Care should be taken to incorporate minority and other groups
    in advertisements in order to present positive and pro-social
    roles and role models wherever possible. Social stereotyping
    and appeals to prejudice should be avoided.
7. Although many influences affect a child's personal and social
    development, it remains the prime responsibility of the parents
    to provide guidance for children. Advertisers should contrib-
    ute to this parent–child relationship in a constructive manner.

These Principles embody the philosophy upon which CARU's
mandate is based. The Principles, and not the Guidelines themselves, determine the scope of our review. The Guidelines effectively anticipate and address many of the areas requiring scrutiny
in child-directed advertising, but they are illustrative rather than
limiting. Where no specific guideline addresses the issues of concern to CARU, it is these broader Principles that CARU supplies in
evaluating advertising directed to the uniquely impressionable and
vulnerable child audience.

APPENDIX B

PRSA Member Code of Ethics 2000 Preamble

Public Relations Society of America Member Code of Ethics 2000

- Professional Values
- Principles of Conduct
- Commitment and Compliance

This Code applies to PRSA members.

The Code is designed to be a useful guide for PRSA members as they carry out their ethical responsibilities. This document is designed to anticipate and accommodate, by precedent, ethical challenges that may arise. The scenarios outlined in the Code provision are actual examples of misconduct. More will be added as experience with the Code occurs. The Public Relations Society of America (PRSA) is committed to ethical practices. The level of public trust PRSA members seek, as we serve the public good, means we have taken on a special obligation to operate ethically.

The value of member reputation depends upon the ethical conduct of everyone affiliated with the Public Relations Society of America. Each of us sets an example for each other—as well as other professionals— by our pursuit of excellence with powerful standards of performance, professionalism, and ethical conduct. Emphasis on enforcement of the Code has been eliminated, but the PRSA Board of Directors retains the right to bar from membership or expel from the Society any individual who has been or is sanctioned by a government agency or convicted in a court of law of an action that is in violation of this Code.

Ethical practice is the most important obligation of a PRSA member. We view the Member Code of Ethics as a model for other professions, organizations, and professionals.

PRSA Member Code of Ethics 2000
PRSA Member Statement of
Professional Values

This statement presents the core values of PRSA members and, more broadly, of the public relations profession. These values provide the foundation for the Member Code of Ethics and set the industry standard for the professional practice of public relations. These values are the fundamental beliefs that guide our behaviors and decision-making process. We believe our professional values are vital to the integrity of the profession as a whole.

Advocacy

- We serve the public interest by acting as responsible advocates for those we represent.
- We provide a voice in the marketplace of ideas, facts, and viewpoints to aid informed public debate.

Honesty

- We adhere to the highest standards of accuracy and truth in advancing the interests of those we represent and in communicating with the public.

Expertise

- We acquire and responsibly use specialized knowledge and experience.
- We advance the profession through continued professional development, research, and education.

- We build mutual understanding, credibility, and relationships among a wide array of institutions and audiences.

Independence

- We provide objective counsel to those we represent.
- We are accountable for our actions.

Loyalty

- We are faithful to those we represent, while honoring our obligation to serve the public interest.

Fairness

- We deal fairly with clients, employers, competitors, peers, vendors, the media, and the general public.
- We respect all opinions and support the right of free expression.

APPENDIX C

Code of Ethics and Professional Conduct

Radio-Television News Directors Association

The Radio-Television News Directors Association, wishing to foster the highest professional standards of electronic journalism, promote public understanding of and confidence in electronic journalism, and strengthen principles of journalistic freedom to gather and disseminate information, establishes this Code of Ethics and Professional Conduct.

Preamble

Professional electronic journalists should operate as trustees of the public, seek the truth, report it fairly and with integrity and independence, and stand accountable for their actions.

Public Trust

Professional electronic journalists should recognize that their first obligation is to the public.

Professional electronic journalists should:

Understand that any commitment other than service to the public undermines trust and credibility.

Recognize that service in the public interest creates an obligation to reflect the diversity of the community and guard against over-simplification of issues or events.

Provide a full range of information to enable the public to make enlightened decisions.

Fight to ensure that the public's business is conducted in public.

Truth

Professional electronic journalists should pursue truth aggressively and present the news accurately, in context, and as completely as possible.

Professional electronic journalists should:

Continuously seek the truth.

Resist distortions that obscure the importance of events.

Clearly disclose the origin of information and label all material provided by outsiders.

Professional electronic journalists should not:

Report anything known to be false.

Manipulate images or sounds in any way that is misleading.

Plagiarize.

Present images or sounds that are reenacted without informing the public.

Fairness

Professional electronic journalists should present the news fairly and impartially, placing primary value on significance and relevance.

Professional electronic journalists should:

Treat all subjects of news coverage with respect and dignity, showing particular compassion to victims of crime or tragedy.

Exercise special care when children are involved in a story and give children greater privacy protection than adults.

Seek to understand the diversity of their community and inform the public without bias or stereotype.

Present a diversity of expressions, opinions, and ideas in context.

Present analytical reporting based on professional perspective, not personal bias.

Respect the right to a fair trial.

Integrity

Professional electronic journalists should present the news with integrity and decency, avoiding real or perceived conflicts of interest, and respect the dignity and intelligence of the audience as well as the subjects of news.

Professional electronic journalists should:

Identify sources whenever possible. Confidential sources should be used only when it is clearly in the public interest to gather or convey important information or when a person providing information might be harmed. Journalists should keep all commitments to protect a confidential source.

Clearly label opinion and commentary.

Guard against extended coverage of events or individuals that fails to significantly advance a story, place the event in context, or add to the public knowledge.

Refrain from contacting participants in violent situations while the situation is in progress.

Use technological tools with skill and thoughtfulness, avoiding techniques that skew facts, distort reality, or sensationalize events.

Use surreptitious news-gathering techniques, including hidden cameras or microphones, only if there is no other way to obtain stories of significant public importance and only if the technique is explained to the audience.

Disseminate the private transmissions of other news organizations only with permission.

Professional electronic journalists should not:

Pay news sources who have a vested interest in a story.

Accept gifts, favors, or compensation from those who might seek to influence coverage.

Engage in activities that may compromise their integrity or independence.

Independence

Professional electronic journalists should defend the independence of all journalists from those seeking influence or control over news content.

Professional electronic journalists should:

Gather and report news without fear or favor, and vigorously resist undue influence from any outside forces, including advertisers, sources, story subjects, powerful individuals, and special interest groups.

Resist those who would seek to buy or politically influence news content or who would seek to intimidate those who gather and disseminate the news.

Determine news content solely through editorial judgment and not as the result of outside influence.

Resist any self-interest or peer pressure that might erode journalistic duty and service to the public.

Recognize that sponsorship of the news will not be used in any way to determine, restrict, or manipulate content.

Refuse to allow the interests of ownership or management to influence news judgment and content inappropriately.

Defend the rights of the free press for all journalists, recognizing that any professional or government licensing of journalists is a violation of that freedom.

Accountability

Professional electronic journalists should recognize that they are accountable for their actions to the public, the profession, and themselves.

Professional electronic journalists should:

Actively encourage adherence to these standards by all journalists and their employers.

Respond to public concerns. Investigate complaints and correct errors promptly and with as much prominence as the original report.

Explain journalistic processes to the public, especially when practices spark questions or controversy.

Recognize that professional electronic journalists are duty-bound to conduct themselves ethically.

Refrain from ordering or encouraging courses of action that would force employees to commit an unethical act.

Carefully listen to employees who raise ethical objections and create environments in which such objections and discussions are encouraged.

Seek support for and provide opportunities to train employees in ethical decision-making.

In meeting its responsibility to the profession of electronic journalism, RTNDA has created this code to identify important issues, to serve as a guide for its members, to facilitate self-scrutiny, and to shape future debate.

Adopted at RTNDA2000 in Minneapolis September 14, 2000.

Glossary

AAAA (American Association of Advertising Agencies)—A professional organization representing advertising agencies.

AAF (American Advertising Federation)—A professional organization representing advertising agencies.

Abilene Network—A second Internet designed for high-speed research and university use. Better known as Internet2.

actualities—Unstaged audio or video recordings of events as they happened.

adjacencies—Spot positions immediately before or following a radio or television program.

ADSL (Asymmetric Digital Subscriber Line)—A high-speed telephone line used for digital communication that sends signals in both directions at different speeds.

aesthetics—The study and use of beauty, art, and taste.

affiliates—Broadcast stations contracted to carry programs from a specific network.

agency—A commercial business that serves clients who need advertising or public relations materials and airtime purchases.

aggregator—A collector of diverse items or objects.

airtime—The broadcast space available for programming, spots, or both.

AM (amplitude modulation)—The original method of broadcasting radio by impressing a signal on a high-frequency carrier by varying the amplitude.

ambiance—A sense of an atmosphere or location.

anathema—To be cursed or disliked, or to take the opposite view.

antagonist—The major character who opposes the actions of the protagonist.

Arbitron—A television rating service; formerly the American Research Bureau.

arc—A camera movement combining both a dolly and a truck.

arcade—A business with video games and other game machines.

ASCAP (American Society of Composers, Authors, and Publishers)—A licensing agency that collects residuals for musicians.

aspect ratio—The relative height and width of a frame. The ratio for NTSC, 16-mm, and 35-mm film is 4×3 wide-screen television is 16×9; and wide-screen motion pictures vary from 3×2 to 2×1.

Associated Press (AP)—A nonprofit news cooperative providing state, national, and international news to newspapers and radio and television stations around the world.

audio—The sound portion of a media production.

aural—Any sound.

auteur—A director who totally controls the aesthetics of a production.

availables (avails)—Opening in a broadcast schedule for placing a spot.

avatar—A digital substitute for an object or person.

B2B (business-to-business)—A digital sales operation that serves businesses.

B2C (business-to-consumer)—A digital sales operation that serves the consumer.

background—The visual or aural space behind an object.

backstory—The part of a dramatic story that may not be shown but is referred to in a way of explaining the actions of characters.

bankroller—A person or company providing funds to produce a media project.

beats—In dramas, the spacing of accents in the performance that sets the rhythm of the scene.

bias—A tendency toward prejudice.

bible—The collection of the background information on a story and the biographies of the characters.

block booking—A system used by motion picture distributors to make certain that "B" quality films will be exhibited by combining them with "A" films in a package that the exhibitor must take as a whole.

Blog—Contraction of "Web log"; the thoughts and attitudes of the blogger.

Blu-Ray—An advanced digital disc format.

BMI (Broadcast Music, Inc.)—A licensing company that collects fees for musicians.

book musical—A popular play whose plot is based on music, dancing, and singing.

boom—(1) A long arm to which a microphone or camera may be attached to give greater reach. (2) To move a camera at the end of the boom.

branching—The ability in a program allowing the player to choose among more than one path when playing the game.

bridge—A written transition device that connects two parts of a program.

broadband—A transmission system that supports a wide frequency range or combination of several signals at a relatively high rate of speed.

"B" roll—A second recording of a scene used in editing to cover jump cuts or to add visuals to an interview.

bromide—A tiresome or commonplace person or statement.

browser—Software that allows a user to search for information on the Internet.

caricature—A distorted depiction of a person or object, generally for the sake of humor.

cartridge—A container that holds film or tape, designed for ease in cueing and operating.

CD-ROM—May refer to either the compact disc drive or to the disc designed for read-only digital signals.

cel—A shortened term for celluloid, used in animation. The clear plastic sheets on which the images are painted are called cels.

CGI (computer graphics imagery)—A digital-image-generated file.

charge-back—A budgeting system that allows a production unit within a company to charge other units within the same company for their production services.

chroma key—A video effect created by shooting the foreground image against a solid-colored background, usually blue or green, and electronically inserting that signal into another background signal.

chronological—In order by time.

cinema verité—Also know as "direct cinema"; an effort to show candid truth.

climatic action—The point in a drama that leads to the major crisis of the plot.

climax—The major confrontation of a drama.

coalesce—To bring divergent topics or groups together.

coding—Writing computer codes to carry out the design of the writer of the game.

collage—A work of art created by combining several different images.

commercial (comml)—A sales message broadcast on radio, TV, or cable.

conformed (film and digital)—Creating a finished program by editing original footage to match a trial-edited program.

console—An electronic control board designed to manipulate and combine signals into a finished product.

content expert—A person with superior knowledge of the topic of a production.

content outline—A listing of all the parts of a production in the order in which they will appear in the final edited production.

controller—An electronic device used to operate other equipment, such as recorders.

convergence—Combining of technology or technical systems.

CPB (Corporation for Public Broadcasting)—The funding source for public broadcasting.

crab—Camera movement by a camera mounted on a four-wheeled dolly that allows movement in any direction.

crane—See **boom**.

crisis—A confrontation over the problem introduced by the actions of the character in a drama.

cross fade—A production term describing one audio source slowly fading out as a second source fades in. Full volume is kept by the addition of the two sources.

CTW (Children's Television Workshop)—Producers of *Sesame Street*.

CU (close-up)—The framing of a tight shot, excluding most of the setting, concentrating on one object.

cue—(1) To signal someone to start. (2) A mark indicating the beginning of a recording.

cut—An instantaneous change in signal, either audio or video, also called a *take*.

cutaway—A shot of a part of a scene that is not visible in the master shot.

cut-in—A close-up shot revealing detail of a master shot.

DARPA-ARPA—The government agency that developed the Internet.

DARPANET—The original name of the Internet.

defamation—To expose someone to a negative or evil reputation.

demographic—Statistical analysis of population with reference to size, density, and vital statistics.

denouement—The final scenes of a drama that explain the complications and resolve the crisis of the climax.

dialog—Lines spoken by actors.

dial-up—A telephone circuit connection between computers.

dichotomy—The division of two common or divergent groups.

digital—Anything that uses discrete numerical values to represent signals or data.

disseminate—To distribute.

dissolve (diss)—A transition of one signal fading out while another fades in.

DMCA (Digital Millennium Copyright Act)—A bill passed in 1998 to clarify copyright questions brought about by the expansion of digital media.

dolly—Moving a camera on wheels straight toward or away from the object.

domain name system—Allows the numerical IP addresses to be expressed by logical names.

dope sheet—A listing, by time and exposures of each cel, in an animated production.

double entendre—Two meanings, one usually hidden or subverted.

dramatic structure—The building blocks of the plot of a drama.

DSL (digital subscriber line)—A telephone line used for high-speed computer signal communication.

DVD (digital video disc)—A 12-cm optical disc designed to record digital signals or data.

e-commerce (electronic commerce)—Using the Internet to carry on business functions.

ECU (extreme close-up)—The tightest framing of a production.

effaced—To be modest.

EFX (effects)—A short term for special effects.

electronic transcription (ET)—An acetate disc used to record radio programs and spots before magnetic tape recording became usable.

e-mail (electronic mail)—Digital messages transmitted between computers using networks, telephone lines, or cable systems.

emoticon—A face made with keyboard characters, also called a smiley.

epilogue—The concluding section of a drama, usually addressed directly to the audience.

episode—A stand-alone segment of a media series.

ESBR (Entertainment Software Rating Board)—The organization that represents game manufacturers, whose major responsibility is to set ratings determining who may purchase a game.

espouse—To support a cause.

exposition—Explaining all of the background information of a dramatic production.

facet—Any single portion of a drama or subject.

fade-in—In video, to increase a signal slowly from invisibility to full view. In audio, to increase a sound slowly from silence to full level.

fade-out—In video, to reduce a full-viewed signal slowly to an absence of signal. In audio, to reduce a full-level sound slowly to silence.

fair use—Allows a limited amount of copying and using a copyrighted work without permission and payment if the use does not harm the income of the original author.

falling action—In a drama, the plot portion that reduces the tension of the drama following a crisis.

FAQ (frequently asked questions)—A listing of questions and answers provided to interested parties to avoid having to answer the same question for each concerned individual.

FCC (Federal Communications Commission)—The government agency that oversees broadcasting and telephone communication.

fiber optics—Transmitting signals in the form of light pulses through strands of glass.

FileMaker Pro—A computer program used to file data in a logical and recoverable manner.

501(c)(3)—The federal tax status of a nonprofit organization.

flashback—A scene in a drama that shows an action in the past.

flash forward—A scene in a drama that shows an action in the future.

floppy drive—A mechanical system for recording and playing back digital information from either a 5.25-inch or 3.5-inch disc.

flowchart—An interactive map showing options for branching and decision points.

FM (frequency modulation)—An electronic system for broadcasting high-quality analog audio, developed and adopted in the late 1950s.

focus group—A gathering of objective people to judge new programs or concepts.

foreground—The space closest to the camera.

foreshadowing—A dramatic structure giving the audience a hint of an action yet to be dramatized.

format—(1) The technical specifications that differentiate different types of media equipment. (2) The space organized on paper for scripts. (3) The organization of the action in a media production.

format sheet—The chronological summary of material in a production.

formulaic—Following a recurring pattern or plotline in a drama.

Fourth Estate—In modern times, the field of journalism.

FRC (Federal Radio Commission)—The predecessor of the FCC, governing broadcasting from 1927 until 1934.

FTC (Federal Trade Commission)—The government agency overseeing business matters including truthfulness of broadcast advertising.

gag—A joke, punch line, or comic action.

GBPS (gigabits per second)—A measurement of the rate of movement of digital signals. A gigabit is one billion bits.

genre—A classification of drama's types.

Google—An Internet search engine.

gratuitously—Unnecessarily.

HD (high definition)—Any video specification beyond original NTSC.

HD-DVD (high-definition digital video disc)—One of two high-resolution video disc recording media intended to replace DVDs.

HDTV (high-definition television)—A video format of 16×9 aspect ratio with 1125 lines using AC-3 Dolby sound.

homogenization—To blend diverse topics or systems into a single form.

hook—A media slang term for setting a scene that will intrigue and keep an audience in suspense and tuned in.

HTML (hypertext markup language)—A computer language used for Web pages.

HTTP (hypertext transfer protocol)—A computer system used for exchanging documents on the Web.

humanize—Creating animals or objects that take on human forms and mannerisms.

HVD (holographic digital disc)—A possible successor to DVDs, HD-DVDs, and Blu-Ray recording systems, with higher quality and larger capacity on one disc.

hyperlink—A term indicating a link between two or more digital signals, to make them act as one.

inbetween—In animation, the cels painted between the key frames that start and end an action.

in-cue—The first few words of a recording.

indecent—Any material considered offensive as measured by local community standards.

institutional—Commercials that take a soft-sell approach, selling the company on its overall value, not specific products or services.

interactive—Media programs that allow the user to control the flow and direction of the program; may include any or all media.

interweaving—Mixing and combining together.

IPTV (internet protocol television)—Television distributed by telephone or cable companies.

ISP (Internet service provider)—A company that delivers Internet access to individuals and companies.

JAN (joint army-navy)—A 16-mm film projector invented just before WWII and used for many years by the military, corporations, and educators.

JPEG (joint photographic experts group)—Both the standard-setting organization and the standard set for digitizing still photographs and graphics.

key—(1) To insert one video signal into another. (2) The major light that represents the sun. (3) A computer code.

key frames—The beginning and ending frames in an animation sequence or action.

LAN (local area network)—A connecting link among computers and peripherals within one close area.

LexisNexis—Legal and business search engines.

libel—Defamation in any form more permanent than speech, usually referring to written or electronic statements.

lip sync—Matching the movement of the mouth of a speaker with the spoken sound.

log line—A one-line description of a media production.

LS or WS (long shot or wide shot)—Framing the entire scene to establish relationships between objects.

lyrics—The words of music.

matte—An electronic hole in a video shot through which another shot may be visible.

MCU (medium close-up)—Framing an object wider than a close-up, but closer than a medium shot. On a human, often from below the chest to the top of the head.

media—Plural; more than one means of delivering electronic or print information.

medium—Singular; one means of delivering electronic or print information.

melodrama—A dramatic formula based on a hero rescuing someone in distress in which good always wins over evil.

mentions—A means of slipping in a commercial message within a drama as part of the drama.

microwave—A high-frequency line-of-sight signal distribution system.

MIDI (musical instrument digital interface)—A digital protocol used to communicate between musical instruments and computers.

mobiles—Any of the small digital handheld devices used to communicate without wires.

model sheets—In animation, a page of designs of a character showing a variety of poses and angles to ensure that everyone working with that character will maintain consistency.

morality plays—Plays of the Middle Ages based on religious beliefs, designed to teach the audience lessons of their religion.

morgue—In news-gathering operations, a gathering of archival information, past stories, photos, films, videotapes, and digital files for future reference.

motion capture (MOCAP)—Creating a duplicate of human movement by fastening reflective or magnetic spots at key positions on the body. A computer program will convert those locations to a computer-generated figure that duplicates the captured movement.

MPEG (motion picture experts group)—Both the international standards-setting organization and the standard set for digital video, with variations from MPEG-2 up to MPEG-5.

MP3 (MPEG layer-3 audio)—An audio compression method designed specifically for HDTV.

MS (medium shot)—Framing objects close enough for detail but wide enough to see the environment. For a person, from just above the waist.

multimedia—Combining audio, video, and graphics to create a media production, now produced on a computer.

narration—Copy read by an off-camera talent.

narrative—A form of dramatic structure based on an off-camera voice describing the action or characters.

narrative duration—The difference in time between actual time and the time depicted in a drama.

narrative order—Modification of dramatic time to meet historic chronology.

narrative structure—The organization of time and point of view of a drama.

natural sound (NAT)—Also known as *wild sound*. The existing sound on a location, including background sounds and the sound of the environment.

Nazism—Political philosophy based on totalitarian government and racial superiority of the Aryan race.

nebulous—Indistinct, foggy, or cloudy.

net neutrality—The political pressure to prohibit pay for parts of the Internet as requested by the telephone and cable companies.

Nielsen—A media ratings research company that determines who is watching which station.

9/11—The date of the terrorist strikes against the World Trade Center buildings in New York City and the Pentagon near Washington, DC.

NPR (National Public Radio)—A radio network partially funded by federal funds, which operates noncommercially.

NTSC (National Television System Committee)—The committee and the system that set the original practical television system used in the United States.

obscene—A class of sexual material so offensive, because it is without any redeeming value, that it is not protected by the First Amendment.

omniscient—Extraordinarily intelligent, with great knowledge.

organic—A critical central part of the whole.

OS (over the shoulder)—The framing of two objects from behind one object and facing the other.

out-cue—The last few words of a recorded segment, used to determine when the recording had ended.

outline—A listing of topics, sequence, and scenes in a production.

outsource—To hire work completed by external companies for work originally handled within a company.

pace—The perceived speed of a production.

packets—Groups of digital signals sent on the Internet to be reassembled at the destination computer.

pan—A camera movement in a horizontal manner.

paramount—Important or key item.

PBS (Public Broadcast System)—The noncommercial television network organized in 1967 as an alternative to commercial television.

PDA (personal digital assistant)—Any battery-operated handheld digital device used to create and store information.

peer-to-peer—Communication between two of the same type of organizations or persons.

perquisites (perqs)—Special benefits such as a bonus or provided equipment.

phoneticize—Breaking a hard-to-pronounce word into easily recognizable syllables.

Photoshop—A program written for the manipulation of photographs, video, and graphics.

physiology—The study and analysis of the human body.

pitch session—A meeting for the creator of a media program to gain funding or permission to proceed with the project.

pixel picture element—The smallest reflection unit on a computer screen.

plant—To place an idea or thought in the mind of the audience without revealing the reason behind the concept.

plug—To mention a product name without paying for a commercial.

pornographic—Information that is sexually explicit and meant for sexual arousal.

portable people meter (PPM)—A handheld metering system used to determine to which station the listener is tuned.

portfolio—A collection of creative works by an artist, writer, or other creative person.

POV (point of view)—The framing showing what the talent would be seeing.

PRA (project requirement analysis)—A preproduction study of an instructional media project.

premise—A concept or idea for a media production stated in one sentence.

PRI (Public Radio International)—A listener-supported nonprofit radio network.

production manager—In a television studio, the person with overall responsibility for the operation of the studio. Also may be called the executive producer.

product placement—For a fee, a product placed on the set of a motion picture or television program, with the label visible in some shots.

promo (promotion)—In broadcasting, a spot advertising a program on the same station.

prompter—A system of mirrors mounted on the front of the camera to reflect the image from a computer monitor showing the script to be read by the talent.

propaganda—Information passed to an audience or the populace to sway the attitude of understanding of a specific topic.

proposal—A short written summary of a media production indicating the general concept, budget, and reason for being funded.

proscenium—The space separating the audience from the actors on stage in live theatre.

protagonist—The hero or major star that carries the plot of a drama.

protocol—A system for computers to communicate with each other.

PRSA (Public Relations Society of America)—The professional organization for workers in the field of public relations.

PSA (Public Service Announcement)—A broadcast spot that promotes a nonprofit organization aired without charge by the station.

pseudo—Another term for fake or not real.

PSP (PlayStation Portable)—Sony's handheld game console.

psychographics—An analytical system of categorizing an audience by their interests and background, as opposed to their income and education.

puff piece—A news story without any real depth or value that fills space or makes someone else happy to see it aired.

rate—The speed of an individual performance within a production.

ratings—A statistical analysis of the audience's viewing or listening habits.

red-baiting—During the 1950s, accusation of being communist (red) without proof or being allowed the opportunity to defend one's reputation or political attitude.

reenactments—Staging a story for the news or documentary camera, considered poor journalism for news but more acceptable, within limits, for documentaries.

render—To convert an edited signal to a final digital output.

resolution—A measurement of a visual system. For computers, the number of pixels; for video, the numbers of lines; for film, a measurement of grain.

RF (radio frequency)—The frequencies above hearing and below vision.

RFP (request for proposal)—A notice that a job or project is open for bids.

rhythm—Development from a combination of variations in pace, tempo, and rate.

rising action—The portion of a plot that precedes a crisis.

ROM (read-only memory)—A disc that is designed to play back but not record.

RSS (really simple syndication)—A system of organizing and distributing information-specific topics to a specific e-mail address.

RTNDA (Radio-Television News Directors Association)—The professional organization representing electronic media news personnel.

rundown sheet—A list of individual segments of a program, with all of the items that go into the making of the program in chronological order.

satellite feed—A system that allows a news crew to feed a signal from their truck to a satellite; the station can then download the signal live or can record it for later use in a program.

SD (standard definition)—Lower resolution and lower aspect ratio than HDTV.

secular—Public, nonreligious-oriented activities.

segue—An audio transition, with the first signal starting at full level and fading to silence as the second signal starts at silence and builds to full level.

SESAC (Society of European Stage Authors and Composers)—A licensing agency for musicians.

SFX (special effects; sound effects)—Transitions and creative shots beyond standard fades, dissolves, and cuts. In audio, created sounds.

shoveling air—Working or creating without purpose or result.

site—Location or place of production, in a studio or in the field.

site survey—Taking time to physically look, measure, and analyze a location to make certain it will work for the production.

slander—Verbal defamation.

slug—The title of a news story.

solvability—In a game, the difficulty level that allows the player to feel that the game can be won or the puzzle solved.

sound bite—An audio recording, usually of an interviewee, to be used in a news story.

spam—In computers, unwanted e-mails sent to a wide range of people.

spin—Taking a story and making it sound positive, even if the story is not positive for everyone involved (e.g., explaining a massive oil spill).

spine—The flat side of a book or portfolio opposite the opening.

sponsor—The company who pays for programs or commercials.

spot—Short broadcast announcements that may be promos, public service announcements, or commercials.

static—Unwanted audio, often heard while tuning across the radio dial.

station break—The 30- to 50-second space between network programs reserved for the placement of spots and a station identification made on the hour.

stereotype—Depicting a person on the basis of gender, religion, age, or heritage.

storyboard—A visual outline of shots or frames of a media production.

stylebook—A collection of guides to tell the user which formats to use and how to meet the standards of the organization that created the book.

subservient—Of a lower level or class.

subtext—A portion of the plot not revealed or spoken directly to the audience that requires the audience to be knowledgeable about the story and setting.

succinct—Precise and straight to the point.

super—In video, a combination of two signals, with one bleeding through the other.

superfluous—Unnecessary; without usefulness.

surf—(1) A method used to explore offerings on the Internet. (2) Changing channels on a television receiver while looking for a program.

synced-synchronization—Keeping in step between video and audio and between electronic signals.

syndication—A means of earning additional income from a program after it has run on a network. The program is sold as a package to stations or other operations to run again and again.

tag—An added line or two at the end of a commercial, usually including the name, address, URL, and phone number of the client.

take—An instantaneous change of picture in television. The same as *cut* in film.

TCP/IP (transmission control protocol/Internet protocol)—A computer system used to access the Internet.

teleconference—May be either audio only or both video and audio. Two or more locations are connected by telephone lines or cable connections for instantaneous exchanges of conversation and pictures.

teletype—An analog message system used by telephone and telegram companies to connect two or more clients for continuous sending and receiving of messages.

telop—A 4- by 5-inch card covered with type or graphics for credits and other simple visuals, used before character generators became common in television.

tempo—Perceived speed of individual scenes of sequences.

terrestrial—Signals distributed on land, as opposed to satellite, telephone, or cable; usually refers to radio and television.

theme—(1) The music introducing a program or used to set scenes or identify characters. (2) a central idea or statement that may or may not be stated overtly.

tilt—A camera movement made by moving the camera up or down on the pedestal head.

timeline—A chart showing specific target dates for completion of each step of a program from preproduction through to distribution.

track—Short for sound track or control track.

tractability—The design of a game that keeps the game player involved without becoming bored, while not easily giving the game away.

trailers—The motion picture equivalent of television promos. Short, tightly edited segments of a film used to induce the audience to return when the film opens in that theatre. Also called *previews*.

transition—Any change of video or audio between scenes.

treatment—A detailed description of a media production scene by scene without dialog or technical terms. Used as a sales vehicle to convince a source of funds to supply the finances needed for the production.

truck—A camera movement made when the camera is mounted on a wheeled base that allows the camera to move from side to side on a parallel path to the subjects.

URL (uniform resource locator)—An Internet site address.

vector graphics—Images represented by mathematically defined shapes.
veracity—Truthfulness.
verbose—Overly talkative.
video—The visual portion of television and other electronic media.
virtual—An image or file existing only as a duplicate of the original.
virtual reality—A technology that creates the illusion of the operator moving in an artificial environment, usually requiring special goggles and headphones.
virus—A self-duplicating program that infects a hard drive and may alter or destroy files on that hard drive.
visual—Any part of a media production that is viewed and seen by the eye.
VNR (video news release)—A special video story prepared by a public relations firm and delivered to a newsroom with the hope that it will be aired as a legitimate news story.
VO (voice over)—Narration or dialog delivered without showing the source of the sound.

well-made play—An 18th-century play format still in use today. Based on an expository opening segment, an introduction of characters, and alternating positive and negative actions, culminating in a climax and resolution.
Wiki—A user-created Internet encyclopedia.
wild sound—Ambient sound recorded on location, also called *nat sound*.
wipe—A visual transition showing one picture being replaced by another, with the line between the two sources moving in any of several different directions.
wire copy—A source of information from the Associate Press or other press services.
wire frames—In animation, the building blocks of developing the shape of a figure before the surface is added.
WS (wide shot)—Same as long shot (see **LS**)
WWW (World Wide Web)—An Internet hypermedia system accessed using a browser.
WYSIWYG (what you see is what you get)—A program designed to show on the monitor exactly what the computer will feed back.

XCU (extreme close-up)—The tightest shot in a production.
XLS (extreme long shot)—The widest shot in a production.

yellow journalism—News reporting based on innuendo and rumor, usually with a specific political goal.

zoom—The visual movement created within a specially design lens that allows a change of focal length while shooting. A zoom is not a camera movement.

Index